Christian Nurture

Horace Bushnell
Introduction by John M. Mulder

BAKER BOOK HOUSE
Grand Rapids, Michigan 49506

"And all thy children shall be taught of the Lord;
and great shall be the peace of thy children."
Isaiah, liv. 13

Reprinted from the 1861 edition
published by Charles Scribner
Paperback edition issued 1979 by
Baker Book House Company
ISBN: 0-8010-0765-8

Introduction by John M. Mulder
copyrighted 1979 by
Baker Book House Company

First printing, October 1979
Second printing, February 1984
Third printing, January 1989

PHOTOLITHOPRINTED BY CUSHING - MALLOY, INC.
ANN ARBOR, MICHIGAN, UNITED STATES OF AMERICA

CONTENTS

Introduction   **vii**
Preface   **xxxi**

PART I—THE DOCTRINE

I. What Christian Nurture Is, Part 1   **9**

    1. The argument from human evidence

II. What Christian Nurture Is, Part 2   **33**

    2. The argument from divine revelation
    3. Possible objections to this view of Christian
       nurture
    4. Practical conclusions

III. The Ostrich Nurture   **65**

IV. The Organic Unity of the Family   **90**

    1. What is meant by the organic unity of the family?
    2. Does any such unity exist?
    3. Practical conclusions

V. Infant Baptism, How Developed   **123**

VI. Apostolic Authority of Infant Baptism   **145**

VII. Church Membership of Children   **162**

    1. The nature and extent of the church membership
       of baptized children
    2. Reasons why this relation of infant membership
       should exist
    3. Is such infant membership a real and true fact?
    4. The church's duty toward its infant members

VIII. The Out-Populating Power of the
Christian Stock   **195**

    1. God has instituted such laws of population that
       piety itself shall finally over-populate the world
    2. Evidence for this doctrine of church population
    3. The failure of individualism

PART II—THE MODE

I. When and Where the Nurture Begins   227
1. Ante-natal nurture
2. Nurture in the age of impressions

II. Parental Qualifications   253

III. Physical Nurture to Be a Means of Grace   271
1. The relation of soul and body as a fact of adult experience
2. Evil results of the wrong feeding of children
3. Methods of judicious and more properly Christian feeding
4. The external bodily habit

IV. The Treatment That Discourages Piety   294

V. Family Government   314
1. What is the true conception of family government?
2. By what methods will it best fulfill its gracious purposes?
3. Practical cautions

VI. Plays and Pastimes, Holidays and Sundays   338
1. The Christian attitude toward the play of children
2. The necessary restriction of play
3. How to use Sunday so as best to honor the day and best secure the ends of Christian nurture

VII. The Christian Teaching of Children   366
1. General considerations involved in this exhortation
2. Things not to be taught to children
3. The method of the Christian teaching of children
4. The aim of the Christian teaching of children

VIII. Family Prayers   385
1. The manner in which prayers of all kinds get their answer from God
2. The conditions of family prayer
3. The dignity and power of a genuine family religion, thus maintained

INTRODUCTION

Horace Bushnell (1802-1876) is widely regarded as the father of the Christian education movement in the United States. More than any other single factor, his work, *Christian Nurture,* established his reputation as a pioneer in this major concern of the American churches. Controversial and hotly debated in his own day, Bushnell's views "are now considered to be the basis for the modern development of religious education."[1]

In recent years theologians and historians have gained a new appreciation of Bushnell's accomplishments as a theologian mediating between the scholastic Calvinism of the seventeenth and eighteenth centuries and the newer theological movements of the twentieth century. William A. Johnson has concluded that Bushnell, "more than any other of his time, was *the* creative force in New England theology of the nineteenth century. It is correct to say that [he] was the greatest figure in American theology in his century, as Jonathan

---

1. D. Campbell Wyckoff, *The Gospel and Christian Education: A Theory of Christian Education for Our Times* (Philadelphia: Westminster Press, 1959), p. 60.

Edwards was in the eighteenth."[2] As an individual who stood between two epochs in American theology, his ideas were not always well-formulated, and as several have noted, he had a tendency to write first and read later. Yet his continuing influence, as seen in *Christian Nurture* and his other works, lies in his ability to pose many of the central questions confronting the Christian faith in the modern world.

Crucial to understanding Bushnell's theology and his best known book, *Christian Nurture,* is the fact that he was preeminently a pastor and a preacher. He represents perhaps the last of a long line of American theologians who wrote theology from the parish rather than from an academic setting. But Bushnell's vocational decision was not an easy one, and he struggled with the nature of Christian faith throughout his life. As he observed, his spiritual life "required *many* turns of loss and recovery to ripen it."[3]

Bushnell was born in Bantam, Connecticut, on April 14, 1802, the eldest child in a family of six. His father, Ensign Bushnell, moved the family to a farm in New Preston, Connecticut, when Horace was three years old, and it was in this rural setting that the young Bushnell spent his early years. He was raised in a Christian family, marked

2. William A. Johnson, *Nature and the Supernatural in the Theology of Horace Bushnell* (Minneapolis: Lund Press, 1963), p. 10.

3. Quoted by H. Shelton Smith in the introduction to *Horace Bushnell* (New York: Oxford University Press, 1965), p. 22.

particularly by the piety of his mother, to whom he was devoted. He later described his mother as exhibiting "a kind of sublimity," and when he had doubts about entering the ministry, his agony was accentuated by what he said was "the disappointment I must bring on my noble Christian mother."[4] He delayed joining the Congregationalist church until 1821, when he was nineteen. His friend Noah Porter recalled that in his youth Bushnell had become "somewhat skeptical in his religious views and joined an infidel club in a neighboring town—at the head of which was a hard-headed Deist of the type of [Thomas] Paine."[5]

In 1823 Bushnell entered Yale and the following year joined the college church, but his religious doubts continued. After his graduation in 1827, he briefly taught school in Norwich, Connecticut; he served for ten months on the editorial staff of the New York _Journal of Commerce;_ and then he returned to Yale, where he studied law and became a

4. Cited in "Horace Bushnell," _Dictionary of American Biography,_ ed. by Allen Johnson (New York: Scribner's, 1929), III: 350; Mary Bushnell Cheney, _Life and Letters of Horace Bushnell_ (New York, 1880), p. 32. Other helpful biographical sources include Smith's introduction to _Horace Bushnell,_ pp. 3-39; Johnson, _Nature and the Supernatural;_ Theodore T. Munger, _Horace Bushnell: Preacher and Theologian_ (Boston, 1889); _Minutes of the General Association of Connecticut— Bushnell Centenary_ (Hartford, 1902); Barbara M. Cross, _Horace Bushnell: Minister to a Changing America_ (Chicago, 1958); Henry Warner Bowden, _Dictionary of American Religious Biography_ (Westport, Conn.: Greenwood Press, 1977), pp. 79-81.

5. Cited by Smith, _Horace Bushnell,_ p. 22.

tutor. He had passed his examinations and was prepared to be admitted to the bar when a religious revival swept Yale in 1831. Bushnell was initially unaffected, but his faith was eventually renewed. He said this renewal came to him as the awareness of the difference between right and wrong. Abandoning plans for becoming a lawyer, he entered Yale Divinity School in the fall of 1831. His uncertainties persisted, however, even after he left Yale to become pastor of the North Church of Hartford, his only pulpit until his retirement because of ill health in 1861.

The congregation to which Bushnell ministered was middle class and relatively affluent in the increasingly prosperous capital of Connecticut. At Yale, Bushnell had often been uncomfortable due to his rural background and his inability to move easily among the wealthier members of the student body, and these anxieties emerged again in his early ministry. He confessed his difficulty in preaching many of the harsher doctrines of the Christian faith to his people, and while he could be critical of the urban, middle-class ethos in which he believed, he attempted to make the Christian faith both meaningful and acceptable to his congregation. He preached in a time of internecine Protestant controversy, which affected his own church, but he tried to bring the various factions into understanding and agreement. On the twentieth anniversary of his ordination, he remembered that as a young pastor, "I was just then passing into a vein of comprehensiveness, questioning whether all parties were not in reality standing for some one side or article of truth . . . . Accordingly . . . my preaching . . . never was to overthrow one school and set up another, neither was it to find a position of neutrality midway between them, but as far as theology is concerned, it was to comprehend, if possible, the truth contended for in both."[6]

This irenic spirit had definite limits and sometimes disappeared in Bushnell's writings, particularly when he was responding to critics, but H. Shelton Smith identifies this "Christian comprehensiveness"—an attempt to formulate a larger vision of the Christian faith—as a major theme of Bushnell's theology.[7] In *Christian Nurture*, Bushnell questioned the prevalent notion that children were outside of God's grace until they were old enough to have a conversion experience. Instead, he argued that children should reach an awareness of God's grace at the earliest possible age, and he stressed the responsibility of parents to provide religious nurture of children and an atmosphere of Christianity in their homes. In *God in Christ* (1849), he addressed himself to the doctrines of the Trinity and the atonement by formulating a new understanding of the biblical language as evocative and poetic rather than exact

6. *Twentieth Anniversary: A Commemorative Discourse Delivered in the North Church, of Hartford, May 22, 1853* (Hartford, 1853), pp. 13, 14.

7. Smith, *Horace Bushnell*, pp. 26-27, 106-126.

and scientific, and *Christ in Theology* (1851) was his effort to answer the storm of criticism prompted by this new linguistic approach. *Nature and the Supernatural, as Together Constituting the One System of God* (1858), perhaps Bushnell's most sustained and systematic theological treatise, was a far-ranging and creative essay on the nature of revelation, seeking to reconcile faith and reason. In his retirement, he turned once again to the nature of the atonement in two works—*The Vicarious Sacrifice* (1866) and *Forgiveness and Law* (1874)—both of which argued against the idea that God sent Christ to satisfy divine anger over human sin. Instead, argued Bushnell, God acts according to the law of love, and it was out of God's love for humanity, not God's judgment, that Christ died on the cross. At his death, Bushnell was working on yet another theological work—an examination of the Holy Spirit—but it remained uncompleted.

This was not, however, the full extent of Bushnell's literary production. He wrote books of essays and sermons on various subjects, most of which were addressed to religious issues but some of which treated controversial social and political questions. He bitterly attacked the Roman Catholic Church and feared the influence of "popery" in American life, as witnessed in his tract, *Barbarism the First Danger* (1847). He strongly identified the United States with God's plan of redemption in human history. He took a cautious stand on the issue of slavery, criticizing the abolitionists but condemning the fugitive slave law and hoping that slavery itself would pass away. His oration at the close of the Civil War, "Our Obligation to the Dead" (1865), anticipated a time when the trials of war might purge the nation of its sins. He glorified the early history of New England in *The Age of Homespun* (1851), and his idealized conception of the home and family had its counterpart in his opposition to the right of women to vote *(Women's Suffrage: The Reform Against Nature* [1869]).

His literary activity is especially remarkable for a man who was afflicted throughout his adult life by frail health. As a young minister, he suffered from sore throats which eventually developed into chronic bronchitis. He had the opportunity in 1840 to become the president of Middlebury College in Vermont, but declined the offer, and in 1856 he took a leave from his church to go to California to recover his health. Fascinated by the development of the West, he studied and recommended the railroad route finally chosen as the entry to San Francisco. He was also instrumental in the founding of the college at Berkeley that later became the University of California, and he was offered but turned down the presidency. He did yearn to be named the Hollis Professor of Divinity at Harvard, but his dream was frustrated by liberal opposition to his theological views.

Bushnell formulated his theology in the cross-currents of two powerful intellectual movements of

his time—New England Calvinism and romanticism.[8] By the early nineteenth century, the Puritan theology of New England was being torn apart
over the issues of the Trinity, the person of Christ,
human depravity, and the atonement; the primary
contending groups were the Congregationalists, the
Unitarians, and to a lesser extent the Transcenden-
talists. Within the Congregationalists themselves
there were sharp differences of opinion, represented
in part by the debate between Nathaniel William
Taylor at Yale and Bennet Tyler of the Connecticut
Theological Institute (now the Hartford Seminary
Foundation). Tyler was a conservative Calvinist
who criticized Taylor's positions, particularly concerning the human role in the process of redemption
and the nature of human depravity. Taylor, who
championed the "New Divinity" school of theology,
emphasized that sin was not so much a charac-

---

8. For an analysis of the developments in New England
theology during the late eighteenth and nineteenth centuries, see
Frank Hugh Foster, *A Genetic History of the New England
Theology* (Chicago, 1907); Joseph Haroutunian, *Piety Versus
Moralism* (New York: Columbia University Press, 1932); Conrad
Wright, *The Beginnings of Unitarianism in America* (Boston:
Beacon Press, 1955); H. Shelton Smith, *Changing Conceptions of
Original Sin: A Study in American Theology Since 1750* (New
York, 1955), as well as Smith's excellent summary in the in-
troduction to *Horace Bushnell;* Sidney E. Mead, *Nathaniel
William Taylor, 1786-1858: A Connecticut Liberal* (Chicago,
1942); and Sydney E. Ahlstrom, "Theology in America: A
Historical Survey," *The Shaping of American Religion,* ed. by
J. W. Smith and A. Leland Jamison (Princeton, N.J.: Princeton
University Press, 1961), pp. 232-321, and Ahlstrom's introduc-
tion to *Theology in America* (Indianapolis: Bobbs-Merrill, 1967),
pp. 23-91.

teristic of who people were but of what they did, and he stressed the importance of free will and human decision in responding to God's grace. Yet Taylor, like Tyler and the Presbyterian theologian at Princeton, Charles Hodge, believed that theology was a science in which the language of Christian doctrine could adequately interpret the reality of God.

Bushnell studied with Taylor at Yale, and although his theology was shaped by the traditions of New England Calvinism, Bushnell reacted against many of Taylor's views. The basis for his opposition came from reading Samuel Taylor Coleridge's *Aids to Reflection,* which he first encountered as an undergraduate at Yale, and he later acknowledged that he had been influenced more by this work than any other. With Coleridge and others of the romantic movement in theology and literature, Bushnell stressed the role of human experience in the process of coming to a knowledge of God, and he pointed to the importance of nature as a source of this knowledge. He argued that Christianity is known primarily through intuition, not by reason or logic, and that its basic appeal is to the heart and the spirit. Some elements of this emphasis lay within the theology of Jonathan Edwards and New England Puritanism itself, especially the distinction between the world as it is known through unaided reason and reality as it is disclosed through the divine light of the Holy Spirit.

Bushnell fused romanticism and the New England theology, maintaining that the truth of Christianity could be known only through experience and that theological language could not penetrate the depths of divine reality. But he also anticipated a major theological debate of the twentieth century over the nature of religious language by making it central to formulating Christian doctrine, and by describing religious semantics as only approximations rather than precise replications of truth. "Words of thought or spirit are not only inexact in their significance, never measuring the truth or giving its precise equivalent," he wrote, "but they always affirm something which is false, or contrary to the truth intended. They impute *form* to that which is really out of form. They are related to the truth only as form to spirit—earthen vessels in which the truth is borne, yet always offering their mere pottery as being the truth itself."[9]

These themes can be seen in several of Bushnell's basic theological concerns. For example, he opposed the Unitarians who rejected a triune God, arguing that people encountered God through three different aspects of experience—but also claiming that human beings were incapable of knowing whether there were three distinct persons in the Godhead. Similarly, his "moral influence" theory of the atonement focused on God's redeem-

9. Smith, *Horace Bushnell,* p. 92; see also Donald A. Crosby, *Horace Bushnell's Theory of Language* (The Hague, 1975).

ing love for sinners, not a process by which God responds according to the dictates of logic or law. Like the romantics, Bushnell also sought to see greater possibilities in nature as a sphere of God's revelation and grace. Nature, both physical and human, did not stand in opposition to God's grace but was used by God as means for exercising divine sovereignty over human life. Bushnell's emphasis in *Christian Nurture* on the family as an avenue of God's grace is a corollary of this view of nature as a sphere of divine revelation and redemption.

Important as these intellectual influences were in shaping Bushnell's theology, it is necessary to see that the experiences of his own life left an indelible imprint as well. His conversion during the Yale revival of 1831 gave him a perception of God as moral and prompted him to enter the ministry. However, this event was surpassed in 1848 by what his wife described as the "central event" of his life—a profound experience of God's love which resolved many of his earlier religious doubts. Bushnell, she said, had been afflicted "through mental struggles, trials, and practical endeavors"; among them undoubtedly was the acrimonious reception given to his first book, *Discourses on Christian Nurture*, published in 1847. In addition, she said, "five years before, God had spoken personally to him in the death of his beloved little boy, drawing his thoughts and affections to the spiritual and unseen." One morning she saw his spirits lifted and asked, "What have you seen?" Bushnell replied, "The gospel." He later said, "I seemed to pass a boundary. I had never been very legal in my Christian life, but I passed from those partial seeings, glimpses and doubts, into a clearer knowledge of God and into his inspirations, which I have never wholly lost. The change was into faith—a sense of the freeness of God and the ease of approach to him."[10]

A man's theology is never divorced from his biography, and certainly many of the themes of Bushnell's theology can be traced in part to this event. The experience itself warrants some special emphasis here, for it is possible that *Christian Nurture* could be misread as an anti-conversionist treatise. It should be clear that when the work is interpreted in the context of Bushnell's life and theology, it emerges as a protest against a misunderstanding of the nature of conversion and the Christian life.

The immediate context for *Christian Nurture* was Bushnell's pastoral ministry in Hartford and the prevailing practice of revivalism in nineteenth-century American Protestantism. Bushnell's congregation, the North Church, was formed by a group which split from the First Congregationalist Church, whose pastor, Joel Hawes, resented the new church. Hawes was also notoriously successful in winning converts, especially in contrast to his col-

10. Cheney, *Life and Letters of Horace Bushnell*, pp. 191-92.

league Bushnell, who saw few conversions and new members. Years later, Bushnell's recollections of his early ministry suggest both his sense of pique at being measured by the number of souls won to Christ and his objections to the entire revivalist system:

> The only difficulty I have ever encountered in my ministry, that cost me a real and deep trial of feeling, related to the matter of evangelist preachers, and what may be called the machinery system of revivals. Things had come to such a pitch in the churches, by the intensity of the revival system, that the permanent was sacrificed to the casual, the ordinary swallowed up and lost in the extraordinary, and Christian piety itself reduced to a kind of campaigning or stage-effect exercise. The spirit of the pastor was broken, and his powers crippled by a lack of expectation; for it was becoming a fixed impression that effect is to be looked for only under instrumentalities that are extraordinary. He was coming to be scarcely more than a church clock for beating time and marking the years, while the effective ministry of the word was to be dispensed by a class of professed revivalists. It was even difficult for the pastor, saying nothing of conversions, to keep alive in Christians themselves any hope or expectations of holy living, as an abiding state, in the intervals of public movement and excitement left to his care; because everything was brought to the test of the revival state as a standard, and it could not be conceived how any one might be in the Spirit, and maintain a constancy of growth, in the calmer and more private methods of duty, patience, and fidelity, on the level of ordinary life.

Bushnell concluded, "My sole object was to raise a distinction between the reviving of religion when it wants reviving, and a religion which places everything in scenes or spiritual campaigns, and tests all Christian exercise by the standards of the extraordinary."[11]

Bushnell's initial criticism of revivalism, which was part of a growing reaction in the 1830s, 1840s, and 1850s, came in an essay, "The Spiritual Economy of Revivals of Religion," delivered to a group of ministers and published in 1838. It was generally well received and was followed in 1844 by another article, "Growth, Not Conquest, the True Method of Christian Progress." In 1847, the Massachusetts Sabbath School Society issued his *Discourses on Christian Nurture,* and Tyler, Hodge, and others unleashed a barrage of criticism. The Massachusetts Sabbath School Society promptly withdrew the book, and Bushnell rushed the *Discourses,* plus his two previous articles, a response to his critics, and two relevant sermons into print the same year under the title *Views of Christian Nurture.* This volume met with even greater attacks, and one historian concludes that it "stirred theological interest like none had done for a century!"[12] Various attempts were made to bring Bushnell to trial for heresy, but he continued to have the support of his congregation, and finally he even achieved a truce with his Hartford enemy Hawes. In 1861, as he was retiring from his parish, he published a revised and ex-

11. *Twentieth Anniversary,* pp. 19-20.

12. Johnson, *Nature and the Supernatural,* p. 27.

panded version, *Christian Nurture,* and this fuller explication of his thought is reprinted in this volume.

The problem that Bushnell addressed was not simply the phenomenon of revivalism but was a problem endemic to the heritage of New England Puritanism which was preoccupied with the status of children. On the one hand, Puritans held that children participated in the covenant of redemption, and thus could be baptized; on the other hand, they insisted on a conversion experience as a requirement for church membership. The compromise they fashioned was known as "the Halfway Covenant," in which children of members and the children of baptized members could be baptized, but full membership—admission to the Lord's Supper—was restricted to those who had "owned the covenant" and experienced conversion. The First Great Awakening, led by Jonathan Edwards, George Whitefield, and others, as well as the Second Great Awakening, made conversions more common and accessible to people, but the system of church membership remained cumbersome. It left children in an ambiguous position, and for the revivalists it meant that young people were "children of wrath" until they experienced conversion.

As Bushnell saw, particularly when he looked out over his congregation on a Sunday morning, such an approach was a severe liability to a pastor working with families. His response was to emphasize the crucial role of the family and the formative period of childhood in the Christian life. "The child is to grow up a Christian, and never know himself as being otherwise" (p. 10). There is, he insisted, "some kind of nurture which is of the Lord, deriving a quality and a power from Him, and communicating the same" (p. 9). Thus, "the aim, effort, and expectation should be, not as is commonly assumed, that the child is to grow up in sin, to be converted after he comes to a mature age; but that he is open on the world as one spiritually renewed, not remembering the time when he went through a technical experience, but seeming rather to have loved what is good from his earliest years" (p. 10).

Bushnell's argument rests on three basic propositions. The first is the organic character of family life, and he insisted that the family, like other units that comprise human society, is more than simply the total of the individuals within it. Rather, their relationships mold and shape individual thought and behavior, and to ignore this dynamic, he said, is to succumb to "a merely fictitious and mischievous individualism" (p. 31). Although he described the newborn child as "a mere passive lump in the arms" (p. 28), Bushnell did not argue for the innate goodness of human nature, insisting that natural depravity was not only taught in the Bible but also exhibited in human behavior (pp. 22-23). Nevertheless, to treat children as if they were exempt from God's grace un-

til maturity or to assume that they are sinners until they are converted is "the ostrich nurture" or
"nurture of despair." Parents have the responsibility not only to recognize the way in which they
influence their children but also to insure that
those influences are Christian.

Closely related to this assertion is Bushnell's attempt to see nature—in this case the family—as
an avenue of God's grace. He developed his position
more fully in *Nature and the Supernatural,* but in
Christian Nurture he argued that the individual
must not be left to rely on merely supernatural
agencies of salvation. Rather, nature itself can be
and is a means of bringing redemption to people,
and the family is the most immediate and formative place where this should occur. At times,
Bushnell's language suggests that the family has
taken over functions previously assigned to the
church and the sacraments, for he described the
home as "the church of childhood" (p. 20) and
"the house itself" as "a converting ordinance" (p.
77). Part of this terminology can be ascribed to
rhetorical excess and the polemical situation in
which Bushnell wrote, but it also demonstrates his
consuming desire to break down the sharp dichot-
omy between nature and grace which he saw in
the theology of his day.

The third basis on which Bushnell developed his
position was his theology of baptism. Like his Puritan forebears, he maintained that God had established a covenant relationship with families, the

sign of which was baptism. In opposition to the Baptists, he cited Scripture and the practice of the early church to support the practice of infant baptism, and in contrast to the Roman Catholic position, he described the effect of baptism as presumptive rather than actual regeneration. For Bushnell, the logical consequence of this understanding of the sacrament was to see the child as existing in a relationship of grace with God, a relationship which must be nurtured and sustained by the parents.

There are aspects of Bushnell's argument which are problematic, both theologically and theoretically, but it should be recalled that he wrote at a time when the excesses of revivalism had shaped an understanding of Christianity which was obsessively individualistic and had made an emotional, datable conversion experience virtually the essence of the Christian life. Furthermore, when he wrote *Christian Nurture,* the formal discipline of psychology did not exist, and only in the twentieth century would his views about childhood receive some confirmation. Long before Freud, Piaget, and others described the formative period of infancy, Bushnell wrote, "Let every Christian father and mother understand, when their child is three years old, that they have done more than half of all they will ever do for his character" (pp. 248-249). Similarly, anticipating the work of child psychologists, Bushnell urged "a kind of teaching suited to the age of the child." Parents "should

rather seek to teach a feeling than a doctrine; ... then as the understanding advances, to
give it food suited to its capacity, opening upon it
gradually the more difficult views of Christian
doctrine and experience" (p. 51).

In addition to the theological currents of his
day, his immediate pastoral situation, and his reaction to revivalism, Bushnell's *Christian Nurture*
must also be seen in the context of other developments in nineteenth-century America. As the
American churches emerged from the American
Revolution, they found themselves disestablished
through the separation of church and state. The
ideal of Christendom—a Christian society created
by the union of temporal and spiritual power—had
been challenged, but nineteenth-century American
Protestants attempted to refashion a new Christendom through voluntary rather than legal
means. The result is what Robert T. Handy has
described as "the quest for a Christian America"
or what Martin Marty calls the pursuit of a
"righteous empire"—a nation suffused with the
ideals of evangelical Protestantism and shaped by
its morals and its politics.[13] In this respect, Bushnell and the revivalists had more in common than
they realized, for they both were committed to
"Christianizing" the nation if not the world. Their

13. Robert T. Handy, *A Christian America: Protestant Hopes
and Historical Realities* (New York: Oxford University Press,
1971) and Martin E. Marty, *Righteous Empire: The Protestant
Experience in America* (New York: Dial Press, 1970).

differences revolved around questions of methods, not goals. Where a revivalist would see God's kingdom coming through the conversion of sinners one by one, Bushnell saw it spreading through the nurture of Christian families, with the nation and the world being the Christian family writ in larger and larger letters.

Despite some notable contributions to American life, this Protestant search for a Christian society had limitations. It contradicted Paul's injunction that in Christ there was neither Jew nor Greek, slave nor free, male nor female, as well as the ideals of American politics which it tried to uphold. In Bushnell, it was colored by the influences of class, race, and religious sectarianism, as evidenced in his faith that Anglo-Saxon peoples would dominate the world and in his anti-Catholic and anti-Semitic views. The Yale University Press edition of *Christian Nurture,* first published in 1916 and the only version in print during most of the twentieth century, excised some but not all of these controversial passages at the request of the Bushnell family. Luther A. Weigle noted in the introduction, "They were stricken out because lines of division are no longer drawn as they once were, nor do those who might dissent from Bushnell's argument bear the same party names."[14] The present volume reproduces the 1861 text as a whole,

14. Luther A. Weigle, in the introduction to *Christian Nurture* (New Haven, Conn.: Yale University Press, 1916, 1947, 1966), p. xxxix.

not to exacerbate tensions but to reproduce faithfully the historical record and to place Bushnell as a man in the context of his time.

Bushnell's emphasis on the nurture of children also coincided with the development of two major institutions in American society—the Sunday school and the common public school. The Sunday school movement originated first in England in the 1780s under the leadership of Robert Raikes and others, but Americans imported the ideas and the methods to this country during the early nineteenth century. In addition, as Bushnell was bringing out his first version of *Views of Christian Nurture* in 1847, Horace Mann in Massachusetts was championing the cause of universal public education, separate from sectarian education. Bushnell's theories of religious nurture reflect the growing concern in nineteenth-century American society about the education and treatment of children.

Most of *Christian Nurture* was addressed to the issue of Christian development within the home, and its implications for religious education within the churches were initially rejected by leaders of the Sunday school movement. In the early twentieth century, Christian educators recovered some of Bushnell's main propositions. They increasingly stressed that the Christian life should be one of growth and maturation in faith, rather than radical disjunctions, and they saw that education was not the antithesis of evangelism but an important part of spreading the gospel. Perhaps most importantly, the philosophy of Christian education in the twentieth century echoes Bushnell's concern that children come to know God, rather than merely acquire an acquaintance with biblical content and Christian doctrine. Bushnell had very little to say about teaching methods or the design of curricula, but his concentration on the importance of experience in education underlies most of the work in church schools today.

Implicit in Bushnell's argument is also a major element of Western culture in the nineteenth century—the changing attitude toward children themselves.[15] Before the seventeenth century, children could be ignored, if not despised, by their parents and by the society, but particularly after 1700 these attitudes began to shift as the modern, nuclear, affective family began to develop. Partially under the influence of romanticism in the nineteenth century, children and childhood were seen in increasingly idealized terms. Wordsworth could

15. See, for example, Phillipe Aries, *Centuries of Childhood* (New York: Alfred A. Knopf, 1962); Robert H. Bremner, et al., eds., *Children and Youth in America*, 3 vols. (Cambridge, Mass.: Harvard University Press, 1970-1971); Philip Greven, *The Protestant Temperament* (New York: Alfred A. Knopf, 1977); Theodore K. Rabb and Robert I. Rotberg, eds., *The Family in History: Interdisciplinary Essays* (New York: Harper & Row, 1973); Lawrence Stone, *The Family, Sex, and Marriage in England, 1500-1800* (New York: Harper & Row, 1977); Anita Schorsch, *Images of Childhood* (New York, 1979); Bernard Wishy, *The Child and the Republic: The Dawn of Modern American Child Nurture* (Philadelphia: University of Pennsylvania Press, 1968).

declare that the child is father to the man; painters could portray children as the embodiment of purity and innocence; and Bushnell could regard children as little Christians instead of little devils. Bushnell's *Christian Nurture* is thus only part of an enormous literature by ministers and others who sought to transform the ways in which parents saw and treated their children.

Another alteration which provides part of the background for *Christian Nurture* is the changing status of women in American society and their relationship to religion and the churches in the nineteenth century. In American colonial society, women were more fully integrated into social and economic life, but in the late eighteenth and nineteenth centuries a burgeoning industrial society gradually shut middle and upper-class women out of economic roles, making them increasingly consumers rather than producers. Ministers and others preached sermons and wrote tracts hailing woman's new role as mother and guardian of virtue and religion; her "place" was in the home and in the church. Women seem to have made up the majority of church membership in American Protestantism since the late seventeenth century, but only in the nineteenth century did this "cult of true womanhood" emerge fully developed. Although Bushnell is remarkably evenhanded in his discussion of the religious duties of both fathers and mothers in *Christian Nurture,* the special role of mothers in shaping the spiritual lives of their children forms an important theme of his book and evangelical Protestantism during the nineteenth century. [16]

In sum, Bushnell's treatise is both an historical artifact and a contemporary call to responsible Christian education and nurture. It shows us the world which we have inherited to a considerable degree even in the late twentieth century. Although Bushnell's argument might be flawed in many respects, his challenge to parents and to the churches to enliven the Christian faith of families remains compelling and urgent today.

JOHN M. MULDER
Assistant Professor of American Church History
Princeton Theological Seminary

16. Barbara Welter, "The Cult of True Womanhood: 1800-1860" and "The Feminization of American Religion: 1800-1860," in *Dimity Convictions: The American Woman in the Nineteenth Century* (Athens, Ohio: Ohio University Press, 1976), pp. 21-41, 83-102; Ann Douglas, *The Feminization of American Culture* (New York: Alfred A. Knopf, 1977); Nancy F. Cott, *The Bonds of Womanhood: "Woman's Sphere" in New England, 1780-1835* (New Haven, Conn.: Yale University Press, 1977).

PREFACE

THE subject of this volume is one of the highest, in the order of consequence, both as respects the welfare of religion and of human society. No apology therefore is needed, for the giving to the public of any thing concerning it, which is honestly meant, and thoughtfully prepared.

I should have preferred, on some accounts, to write a proper treatise on the subject—which this volume is not. The shape it has taken will be sufficiently explained, by the facts and considerations, that have been determining causes, in the process of its construction. Thirteen years ago I was drawn, by solicitation from others, into the publication of two discourses, the first two of this volume, under the title CHRISTIAN NURTURE. Afterwards, these were republished with another, the fourth of the present volume, and with other articles variously related, under the same title. These publications have been out of print for some years; for I have preferred the discontinuance of publication, till I might be able to present the subject in a more adequate and complete manner. The present volume is the result.

In preparing it, I could not easily consent to lay

aside, or pass into oblivion, the two discourses above referred to; for, under the fortune that befell them, they had become a little historical. In this fuller treatment of the subject therefore, I have allowed them to stand, requiring the additions made, to take their shape or type. Thirteen new essays, in the form of discourses, though never used as such, but written simply for the discussion's sake, are thus added; and the volume, which virtually covers the ground of a treatise, takes the form of successive topical discussions, or essays, on so many themes included in the general subject.

As was natural, in this kind of treatment, I have not been careful, always, to remember in one precisely what I have said in another, and so it happens that they sometimes overlap a little; the same kind of liberty being taken that is commonly had in sermons, where there is no delicacy felt, under any particular theme, in saying what may be necessary to the fullest impression of it, even if something like it has been necessary to the impression of some other. But this, which, taking the volume as a treatise, might be a just subject of criticism, may even be an advantage, as respects the convenience of use, and the popular and practical impressions to be made by it.

I need offer no apology for retaining the old title, in a volume that is virtually new; or for reasserting, with more emphasis and deliberation, after an interval of years, what the years have only established and made firm in my Christian convictions.

H. B.

PART I—THE DOCTRINE

I

WHAT CHRISTIAN NURTURE IS

"Bring them up in the nurture and admonition of the Lord."—*Ephesians*, vi. 4.

THERE is then some kind of nurture which is of the Lord, deriving a quality and a power from Him, and communicating the same. Being instituted by Him, it will of necessity have a method and a character peculiar to itself, or rather to Him. It will be the Lord's way of education, having aims appropriate to Him, and, if realized in its full intent, terminating in results impossible to be reached by any merely human method.

What then is the true idea of Christian or divine nurture, as distinguished from that which is not Christian? What is its aim? What its method of working? What its powers and instruments? What its contemplated results? Few questions have greater moment; and it is one of the pleasant signs of the times, that the subject involved is beginning to attract new interest, and excite a spirit of inquiry which heretofore has not prevailed in our churches.

In ordinary cases, the better and more instructive way of handling this subject, would be to go directly into the practical methods of parental discipline, and show by what modes of government and instruction we may hope to realize the best results.   But unhappily the public mind is preoccupied extensively by a view of the whole subject, which I must regard as a theoretical mistake, and one which will involve, as long as it continues, practical results systematically injurious. This mistaken view it is necessary, if possible, to remove.   And accordingly what I have to say will take the form of an argument on the question thus put in issue; though I design to gather round the subject, as I proceed, as much of practical instruction as the mode of the argument will suffer.   Assuming then the question above stated, What is the true idea of Christian education?—I answer in the following proposition, which it will be the aim of my argument to establish, viz :

That the child is to grow up a Christian, and never know himself as being otherwise.

In other words, the aim, effort, and expectation should be, not, as is commonly assumed, that the child is to grow up in sin, to be converted after he comes to a mature age ; but that he is to open on the world as one that is spiritually renewed, not remembering the time when he went through a technical experience, but seeming rather to have loved what is good from his earliest years.   I do not affirm that every child may, in fact and without exception, be so trained that he certainly will grow up a Christian.   The qualifications it may be necessary to add will be given in another place, where they can be stated more intelligibly.

This doctrine is not a novelty, now rashly and for the first time propounded, as some of you may be tempted to suppose. I shall show you, before I have done with the argument, that it is as old as the Christian church, and prevails extensively at the present day in other parts of the world. Neither let your own experience raise a prejudice against it. If you have endeavored to realize the very truth I here affirm, but find that your children do not exhibit the character you have looked for; if they seem to be intractable to religious influences, and sometimes to display an apparent aversion to the very subject of religion itself, you are not of course to conclude that the doctrine I here maintain is untrue or impracticable. You may be unreasonable in your expectations of your children.

Possibly, there may be seeds of holy principle in them, which you do not discover. A child acts out his present feelings, the feelings of the moment, without qualification or disguise. And how, many times, would all you appear, if you were to do the same? Will you expect of them to be better, and more constant and consistent, than yourselves; or will you rather expect them to be children, human children still, living a mixed life, trying out the good and evil of the world, and preparing, as older Christians do, when they have taken a lesson of sorrow and emptiness, to turn again to the true good?

Perhaps they will go through a rough mental struggle, at some future day, and seem, to others and to themselves, there to have entered on a Christian life.

And yet it may be true that there was still some root of right principle established in their childhood, which is here only quickened and developed, as when Christians of a mature age are revived in their piety, after a period of spiritual lethargy; for it is conceivable that regenerate character may exist, long before it is fully and formally developed.

But suppose there is really no trace or seed of holy principle in your children, has there been no fault of piety and constancy in your church? no want of Christian sensibility and love to God? no carnal spirit visible to them and to all, and imparting its noxious and poisonous quality to the Christian atmosphere in which they have had their nurture? For it is not for you alone to realize all that is included in the idea of Christian education. It belongs to the church of God, according to the degree of its social power over you and in you and around your children, to bear a part of the responsibility with you.

Then, again, have you nothing to blame in yourselves? no lack of faithfulness? no indiscretion of manner or of temper? no mistake of duty, which, with a better and more cultivated piety, you would have been able to avoid? Have you been so nearly even with your privilege and duty, that you can find no relief but to lay some charge upon God, or comfort yourselves in the conviction that he has appointed the failure you deplore? When God marks out a plan of education, or sets up an aim to direct its efforts, you will see, at once, that he could not base it on a want of piety in you, or on any imperfections that flow from a want of piety. It must be a plan measured by Himself and the fullness of his own gracious intentions.

Besides, you must not assume that we, in this age, are the best Christians that have ever lived, or most likely to produce all the fruits of piety. An assumption so pleasing to our vanity is more easily made than verified, but vanity is the weakest as it is the cheapest of all arguments. We have some good points, in which we compare favorably with other Christians, and Christians of other times, but our style of piety is sadly deficient, in many respects, and that to such a degree that we have little cause for self-congratulation. With all our activity and boldness of movement, there is a certain hardness and rudeness, a want of sensibility to things that do not lie in action, which can not be too much deplored, or too soon rectified. We hold a piety of conquest rather than of love. A kind of public piety, that is strenuous and fiery on great occasions, but wants the beauty of holiness, wants constancy, singleness of aim, loveliness, purity, richness, blamelessness, and—if I may add another term not so immediately religious, but one that carries, by association, a thousand religious qualities—wants domesticity of character; wants them, I mean, not as compared with the perfect standard of Christ, but as compared with other examples of piety that have been given in former times, and others that are given now.

For some reason, we do not make a Christian atmosphere about us—do not produce the conviction that we

are living unto God. There is a marvelous want of
savor in our piety. It is a flower of autumn, colored
as highly as it need be to the eye, but destitute of fra-
grance. It is too much to hope that, with such an instrument, we can fulfill the true idea of Christian
education. Any such hope were even presumptuous.
At the same time, there is no so ready way of removing
the deficiencies just described, as to recall our churches
to their duties in domestic life; those humble, daily,
hourly duties, where the spirit we breathe shall be a
perpetual element of power and love, bathing the life
of childhood.

Thus much it was necessary to say, for the removal
of prejudices that are likely to rise up in your minds,
and make you inaccessible to the arguments I may
offer. Let all such prejudices be removed, or, if this be
too much, let them, at least, be suspended till you have
heard what I have to advance; for it can not be desired
of you to believe any thing more than what is shown
you by adequate proofs. Which also it is right to ask
that you will receive, in a spirit of conviction, such as
becomes our wretched and low attainments, and with a
willingness to let God be exalted, though at the expense
of some abasement in ourselves. In pursuing the argument, I shall—

I. Collect some considerations which occur to
us, viewing the subject on the human side, and
then—

II. Show how far and by what methods God has justified, on his part, the doctrine we maintain.

There is then, as the subject appears to us—

1. No absurdity in supposing that children are to grow up in Christ. On the other hand, if there is no absurdity, there is a very clear moral incongruity in setting up a contrary supposition, to be the aim of a system of Christian education. There could not be a worse or more baleful implication given to a child, than that he is to reject God and all holy principle, till he has come to a mature age. What authority have you from the Scriptures to tell your child, or, by any sign, to show him that you do not expect him truly to love and obey God, till after he has spent whole years in hatred and wrong? What authority to make him feel that he is the most unprivileged of all human beings, capable of sin, but incapable of repentance; old enough to resist all good, but too young to receive any good whatever? It is reasonable to suppose that you have some express authority for a lesson so manifestly cruel and hurtful, else you would shudder to give it. I ask you for the chapter and verse, out of which it is derived. Meantime, wherein would it be less incongruous for you to teach your child that he is to lie and steal, and go the whole round of the vices, and then, after he comes to mature age, reform his conduct by the rules of virtue? Perhaps you do not give your child to expect that he is to grow up in sin; you only expect that he will yourself. That is scarcely better: for that which is your expectation, will assuredly be his; and what is more, any attempt to maintain a discipline at war with your own secret expectations, will only make a hollow and

worthless figment of that which should be an open, earnest reality. You will never practically aim at what you practically despair of, and if you do not practically aim to unite your child to God, you will aim at something less; that is, something unchristian, wrong, sinful.

But my child is a sinner, you will say; and how can I expect him to begin a right life, until God gives him a new heart? This is the common way of speaking, and I state the objection in its own phraseology, that it may recognize itself. Who then has told you that a child can not have the new heart of which you speak? Whence do you learn that if you live the life of Christ, before him and with him, the law of the Spirit of Life may not be such as to include and quicken him also? And why should it be thought incredible that there should be some really good principle awakened in the mind of a child? For this is all that is implied in a Christian state. The Christian is one who has simply *begun* to love what is good for its own sake, and why should it be thought impossible for a child to have this love begotten in him? Take any scheme of depravity you please, there is yet nothing in it to forbid the possibility that a child should be led, in his first moral act, to cleave unto what is good and right, any more than in the first of his twentieth year. He is, in that case, only a child converted to good, leading a mixed life as all Christians do. The good in him goes into combat with the evil, and holds a qualified sovereignty. And why may not this internal conflict of goodness cover the whole life from its dawn, as well as any part of it?

And what more appropriate to the doctrine of spiritual influence itself, than to believe that as the Spirit of Jehovah fills all the worlds of matter, and holds a presence of power and government in all objects, so all human souls, the infantile as well as the adult, have a nurture of the Spirit appropriate to their age and their wants? What opinion is more essentially monstrous, in fact, than that which regards the Holy Spirit as having no agency in the immature souls of children who are growing up, helpless and unconscious, into the perils of time?

2. It is to be expected that Christian education will radically differ from that which is not Christian. Now, it is the very character and mark of all unchristian education, that it brings up the child for future conversion. No effort is made, save to form a habit of outward virtue, and, if God please to convert the family to something higher and better, after they come to the age of maturity, it is well. Is then Christian education, or the nurture of the Lord, no way different from this? Or is it rather to be supposed that it will have a higher aim and a more sacred character?

And, since it is the distinction of Christian parents, that they are themselves in the nurture of the Lord, since Christ and the Divine Love, communicated through him, are become the food of their life, what, will they so naturally seek as to have their children partakers with them, heirs together with them, in the grace of life? I am well aware of the common impression that Christian education is sufficiently distinguished by the endeavor

of Christian parents to teach their children the lessons
of Scripture history, and the doctrines or dogmas of
Scripture theology. But if they are given to understand, at the same time, that these lessons can be
expected to produce no fruit till they are come to a mature age—that they are to grow up still in the same
character as other children do, who have no such instruction—what is this but to enforce the practical
rejection of all the lessons taught them? And which,
in truth, is better for them, to grow up in sin under
Scripture light, with a heart hardened by so many religious lessons; or to grow up in sin, unvexed and
unannoyed by the wearisome drill of lectures that only
discourage all practical benefit? Which is better, to be
piously brought up in sin, or to be allowed quietly to
vegetate in it?

These are questions that I know not how to decide;
but the doubt in which they leave us will at least suffice
to show that Christian education has, in this view, no
such eminent advantages over that which is unchristian,
as to raise any broad and dignified distinction between
them. We certainly know that much of what is called
Christian nurture, only serves to make the subject of
religion odious, and that, as nearly as we can discover,
in exact proportion to the amount of religious teaching
received. And no small share of the difficulty to be
overcome afterwards, in the struggle of conversion, is
created in just this way.

On the other hand, you will hear, for example, of
cases like the following: A young man, correctly but

not religiously brought up, light and gay in his manners, and thoughtless hitherto in regard to any thing of a serious nature, happens accidentally one Sunday, while his friends are gone to ride, to take down a book on the evidences of Christianity. His eye, floating over one of the pages, becomes fixed, and he is surprised to find his feelings flowing out strangely into its holy truths. He is conscious of no struggle of hostility, but a new joy dawns in his being. Henceforth, to the end of a long and useful life, he is a Christian man. The love into which he was surprised continues to flow, and he is remarkable, in the churches, all his life long, as one of the most beautiful, healthful, and dignified examples of Christian piety. Now, a very little miseducation, called Christian, discouraging the piety it teaches, and making enmity itself a necessary ingredient in the struggle of conversion, conversion no reality without a struggle, might have sufficed to close the mind of this man against every thought of religion to the end of life.

Such facts (for the case above given is a fact and not a fancy) compel us to suspect the value of much that is called Christian education. They suggest the possibility also that Christian piety should begin in other and milder forms of exercise, than those which commonly distinguish the conversion of adults; that Christ himself, by that renewing Spirit who can sanctify from the womb, should be practically infused into the childish mind; in other words, that the house, having a domestic Spirit of grace dwelling in it, should become

the church of childhood, the table and hearth a holy
rite, and life an element of saving power.   Something
is wanted that is better than teaching, something that
transcends mere effort and will-work—the loveliness of
a good life, the repose of faith, the confidence of righteous expectation, the sacred and cheerful liberty of the
Spirit—all glowing about the young soul, as a warm
and genial nurture, and forming in it, by methods that
are silent and imperceptible, a spirit of duty and religious obedience to God.   This only is Christian nurture,
the nurture of the Lord.

3. It is a fact that all Christian parents would like to
see their children grow up in piety ; and the better
Christians they are, the more earnestly they desire it;
and, the more lovely and constant the Christian spirit
they manifest, the more likely it is, in general, that their
children will early display the Christian character.
This is current opinion.   But why should a Christian
parent, the deeper his piety and the more closely he is
drawn to God, be led to desire, the more earnestly,
what, in God's view, is even absurd or impossible ?
And, if it be generally seen that the children of such
are more likely to become Christians early, what forbids
the hope that, if they were riper still in their piety, living
a more single and Christ-like life, and more cultivated
in their views of family nurture, they might see their
children grow up always in piety towards God ?   Or, if
they may not always see it as clearly as they desire,
might they not still be able to implant some holy principle, which shall be the seed of a Christian character

in their children, though not developed fully and visibly till a later period in life?

4. Assuming the corruption of human nature, when should we think it wisest to undertake or expect a remedy? When evil is young and pliant to good, or when it is confirmed by years of sinful habit? And when, in fact, is the human heart found to be so ductile to the motives of religion, as in the simple, ingenuous age of childhood? How easy is it then, as compared with the stubbornness of adult years, to make all wrong seem odious, all good lovely and desirable. If not discouraged by some ill-temper which bruises all the gentle sensibilities, or repelled by some technical view of religious character which puts it beyond his age, how ready is the child to be taken by good, as it were beforehand, and yield his ductile nature to the truth and Spirit of God, and to a fixed prejudice against all that God forbids.

He can not understand, of course, in the earliest stage of childhood, the philosophy of religion as a renovated experience, and that is not the form of the first lessons he is to receive. He is not to be told that he must have a new heart and exercise faith in Christ's atonement. We are to understand, that a right spirit may be virtually exercised in children, when, as yet, it is not intellectually received, or as a form of doctrine. Thus, if they are put upon an effort to be good, connecting the fact that God desires it and will help them in the endeavor, that is all which, in a very early age, they can receive, and that includes every thing—repentance, love, duty, dependence, faith. Nay, the operative truth necessary to a new life, may possibly be communicated through and from the parent, being revealed in his looks, manners, and ways of life, before they are of an age to understand the teaching of words; for the Christian scheme, the gospel, is really wrapped up in the life of every Christian parent, and beams out from him as a living epistle, before it escapes from the lips, or is taught in words. And the Spirit of truth may as well make this living truth effectual, as the preaching of the gospel itself.

Never is it too early for good to be communicated. Infancy and childhood are the ages most pliant to good. And who can think it necessary that the plastic nature of childhood must first be hardened into stone, and stiffened into enmity towards God and all duty, before it can become a candidate for Christian character! There could not be a more unnecessary mistake, and it is as unnatural and pernicious, I fear, as it is unnecessary.

There are many who assume the radical goodness of human nature, and the work of Christian education is, in their view, only to educate or educe the good that is in us. Let no one be disturbed by the suspicion of a coincidence between what I have here said and such a theory. The natural pravity of man is plainly asserted in the Scriptures, and, if it were not, the familiar laws of physiology would require us to believe, what amounts to the same thing. And if neither Scripture nor physiology taught us the doctrine, if the child was born as clear of natural prejudice or damage, as Adam before his sin, spiritual education, or, what is the same, probation, that which trains a being for a stable, intelligent virtue hereafter, would still involve an experiment of evil, therefore a fall and a bondage under the laws of evil; so that, view the matter as we will, there is no so unreasonable assumption, none so wide of all just philosophy, as that which proposes to form a child to virtue, by simply educing or drawing out what is in him.

The growth of Christian virtue is no vegetable process, no mere onward development. It involves a struggle with evil, a fall and a rescue. The soul becomes established in holy virtue, as a free exercise, only as it is passed round the corner of fall and redemption, ascending thus unto God through a double experience, in which it learns the bitterness of evil and the worth of good, fighting its way out of one, and achieving the other as a victory. The child, therefore, may as well begin life under a law of hereditary damage, as to plunge himself into evil by his own experiment, which he will as naturally do from the simple impulse of curiosity, or the instinct of knowledge, as from any noxious quality in his mold derived by descent. For it is not sin which he derives from his parents; at least, not sin in any sense which imports blame, but only some prejudice to the perfect harmony of this mold, some kind of pravity or obliquity which inclines him to evil. These suggestions are offered, not as necessary to be received in every particular, but simply to show that the scheme of education proposed, is not to be identified with another, which assumes the radical goodness of human nature, and according to which, if it be true, Christian education is insignificant.

5. It is implied in all our religious philosophy, that if a child ever does any thing in a right spirit, ever loves any thing because it is good and right, it involves the dawn of a new life. This we can not deny or doubt, without bringing in question our whole scheme of doctrine. Is it then incredible that some really good feeling should be called into exercise in a child? In all the discipline of the house, quickened as it should be by the Spirit of God, is it true that he can never once be brought to submit to parental authority lovingly and because it is right? Must we even hold the absurdity of the scripture council—"Children obey your parents in the Lord, for this is right?" When we speak thus of a love for what is right and good, we must of course discriminate between the mere excitement of a natural sensibility to pleasure in the contemplation of what is good (of which the worst minds are more or less capable,) and a practicable subordination of the soul to its power, a practicable embrace of its law. The child must not only be touched with some gentle emotions toward what is right, but he must love it with a fixed love, love it for the sake of its principle, receive it it as a vital and formative power.

Nor is there any age, which offers itself to God's truth and love, and to that Quickening Spirit whence all good proceeds, with so much of ductile feeling and susceptibilities so tender. The child is under parental authority too for the very purpose, it would seem, of hav-

ing the otherwise abstract principle of all duty imper-
sonated in his parents, and thus brought home to his
practical embrace; so that, learning to obey his parents
in the Lord, because it is right, he may thus receive,
before he can receive it intellectually, the principle of
all piety and holy obedience. And when he is brought
to exercise a spirit of true and loving submission to the
good law of his parents, what will you see, many times,
but a look of childish joy, and a happy sweetness of
manner, and a ready delight in authority, as like to all
the demonstrations of Christian experience, as any thing
childish can be to what is mature?

6. Children have been so trained as never to remember the time when they began to be religious. Baxter
was, at one time, greatly troubled concerning himself,
because he could recollect no time when there was a
gracious change in his character. But he discovered,
at length, that "education is as properly a means
of grace as preaching," and thus found the sweeter
comfort in his love to God, that he learned to love him
so early. The European churches, generally, regard
Christian piety more as a habit of life, formed under
the training of childhood, and less as a marked spiritual
change in experience. In Germany, for example, the
church includes all the people, and it is remarkable
that, under a scheme so loose, and with so much of pernicious error taught in the pulpit, there is yet so much
of deep religious feeling, so much of lovely and simple
character, and a savor of Christian piety so generally
prevalent in the community. So true is this, that the

German people are every day spoken of as a people religious by nature; no other way being observed of accounting for the strong religious bent they manifest. Whereas it is due, beyond any reasonable question, to the fact that children are placed under a form of treatment which expects them to be religious, and are not discouraged by the demand of an experience above their years.

Again, the Moravian Brethren, it is agreed by all, give as ripe and graceful an exhibition of piety, as any body of Christians living on the earth, and it is the radical distinction of their system that it rests its power on Christian education. They make their churches schools of holy nurture to childhood, and expect their children to grow up there, as plants in the house of the Lord. Accordingly it is affirmed that not one in ten of the members of that church, recollects any time when he began to be religious. Is it then incredible that what has been can be? Would it not be wiser and more modest, when facts are against us, to admit that there is certainly some bad error, either in our life, or in our doctrine, or in both, which it becomes us to amend?

Once more, if we narrowly examine the relation of parent and child, we shall not fail to discover something like a law of organic connection, as regards character, subsisting between them. Such a connection as makes it easy to believe, and natural to expect, that the faith of the one will be propagated in the other. Perhaps I should rather say, such a connection as induces the conviction that the character of one is actually included in that of the other, as a seed is formed in the capsule; and being there matured, by a nutriment derived from the stem, is gradually separated from it. It is a singular fact, that many believe substantially the same thing, in regard to evil character, but have no thought of any such possibility in regard to good. There has been much speculation, of late, as to whether a child is born in depravity, or whether the depraved character is superinduced afterwards. But, like many other great questions, it determines much less than is commonly supposed; for, according to the most proper view of the subject, a child is really not born till he emerges from the infantile state, and never before that time can he be said to receive a separate and properly individual nature.

The declarations of Scripture, and the laws of physiology, I have already intimated, compel the belief that a child's nature is somehow depravated by descent from parents, who are under the corrupting effects of sin. But this, taken as a question relating to the mere *punctum temporis*, or precise point of birth, is not a question of any so grave import as is generally supposed; for the child, after birth, is still within the matrix of the parental life, and will be, more or less, for many years. And the parental life will be flowing into him all that time, just as naturally, and by a law as truly organic, as when the sap of the trunk flows into a limb. We must not govern our thoughts, in such a matter, by our eyes; and because the physical separation has taken place, conclude that no organic relation remains. Even the physical being of the child is dependent still for many months, in the matter of nutrition, on organic processes not in itself. Meantime, the mental being and character have scarcely begun to have a proper individual life. Will, in connection with conscience, is the basis of personality, or individuality, and these exist as yet only in their rudimental type, as when the form of a seed is beginning to be unfolded at the root of a flower.

At first, the child is held as a mere passive lump in the arms, and he opens into conscious life under the soul of the parent, streaming into his eyes and ears, through the manners and tones of the nursery. The kind and degree of passivity are gradually changed as life advances. A little farther on it is observed that a smile wakens a smile; any kind of sentiment or passion, playing in the face of the parent, wakens a responsive sentiment or passion. Irritation irritates, a frown withers, love expands a look congenial to itself, and why not holy love? Next the ear is opened to the understanding of words, but what words the child shall hear, he can not choose, and has as little capacity to select the sentiments that are poured into his soul. Farther on, the parents begin to govern him by appeals to will, expressed in commands, and whatever their requirement may be, he can as little withstand it, as the violet can cool the scorching sun, or the tattered leaf can tame the hurricane. Next they appoint his school, choose his books, regulate his company, decide what form of religion, and what religious opinions he shall be taught, by taking him to a church of their own selection. In all this, they infringe upon no right of the child, they only fulfill an office which belongs to them. Their will and character are designed to be the matrix of the child's will and character. Meantime, he approaches more and more closely, and by a gradual process, to the proper rank and responsibility of an individual creature, during all which process of separation, he is having their exercises and ways translated into him. Then, at last, he comes forth to act his part in such color of evil, and why not of good, as he has derived from them.

The tendency of all our modern speculations is to an extreme individualism, and we carry our doctrines of free will so far as to make little or nothing of organic laws; not observing that character may be, to a great extent, only the free development of exercises previously wrought in us, or extended to us, when other wills had us within their sphere. All the Baptist theories of religion are based in this error. They assume, as a first truth, that no such thing is possible as an organic connection of character, an assumption which is plainly refuted by what we see with our eyes, and, as I shall by and by show, by the declarations of Scripture. We have much to say also, in common with the Baptists, about the beginning of moral agency, and we seem to fancy that there is some definite moment when a child becomes a moral agent, passing out of a condition where he is a moral nullity, and where no moral agency touches his being. Whereas he is rather to be regarded, at the first, as lying within the moral agency of the parent, and passing out, by degrees, through a course of mixed agency, to a proper independency and self-possession. The supposition that he becomes, at some certain moment, a complete moral agent, which a moment before he was not, is clumsy, and has no agreement with observation. The separation is gradual. He is never, at any moment after birth, to be regarded as perfectly beyond the sphere of good and bad exercises; for the parent exercises himself in the child, playing his emotions and sentiments, and working a character in him, by virtue of an organic power.

And this is the very idea of Christian education, that it begins with nurture or cultivation. And the intention is that the Christian life and spirit of the parents, which are in and by the Spirit of God, shall flow into the mind of the child, to blend with his incipient and half-formed exercises; that they shall thus beget their own good within him—their thoughts, opinions, faith, and love, which are to become a little more, and yet a little more, his own separate exercise, but still the same in character. The contrary assumption, that virtue must be the product of separate and absolutely independent choice, is pure assumption. As regards the measure of personal merit and demerit, it is doubtless true that every subject of God is to be responsible only for what is his own. But virtue still is rather a *state* of being than an act or series of acts; and, if we look at the causes which induce or prepare such a state, the will of the person himself may have a part among these causes more or less important, and it works no absurdity to suppose that one may be even prepared to such a state, by causes prior to his own will; so that, when he sets off to act for himself, his struggle and duty may be rather to sustain and perfect the state begun, than to produce a new one. Certain it is that we are never, at any age, so independent as to be wholly out of the reach of organic laws which affect our character.

All society is organic—the church, the state, the school, the family; and there is a spirit in each of these organisms, peculiar to itself, and more or less hostile, more or less favorable to religious character, and to some extent, at least, sovereign over the individual man. A very great share of the power in what is called a revival of religion, is organic power; nor is it any the less divine on that account. The child is only more within the power of organic laws than we all are. We possess only a mixed individuality all our life long. A pure, separate, individual man, living *wholly* within, and from himself, is a mere fiction. No such person ever existed, or ever can. I need not say that this view of an organic connection of character subsisting between parent and child, lays a basis for notions of Christian education, far different from those which now prevail, under the cover of a merely fictitious and mischievous individualism.

Perhaps it may be necessary to add, that, in the strong language I have used concerning the organic connection of character between the parent and the child, it is not designed to assert a power in the parent to renew the child, or that the child can be renewed by any agency of the Spirit less immediate, than that which renews the parent himself. When a germ is formed on the stem of any plant, the formative instinct of the plant may be said in one view to produce it ; but the same solar heat which quickens the plant, must quicken also the germ, and sustain the internal action of growth, by a common presence in both. So, if there be an organic power of character in the parent, such as that of which I have spoken, it is not a complete power in itself, but only such a power as demands the realizing presence of the Spirit of God, both in the parent and the child, to give it effect. As Paul said, "I have begotten you through the gospel," so may we say of the parent, who, having a living gospel enveloped in his life, brings it into organic connection with the soul of childhood. But the declaration excludes the necessity of a divine influence, not more in one case than in the other.

Such are some of the considerations that offer themselves, viewing our subject on the human side, or as it appears in the light of human evidence—all concurring to produce the conviction, that it is the only true idea of Christian education, that the child is to grow up in the life of the parent, and be a Christian in principle, from his earliest years.

II

WHAT CHRISTIAN NURTURE IS

"Bring them up in the nurture and admonition of the Lord."—*Ephesians*, vi. 4.

WE proceed now to inquire—

II. How far God, in the revelation made of his character and will, favors the view of Christian nurture vindicated, in a former discourse, by arguments and evidences of an inferior nature? And—

1. According to all that God has taught us concerning his own dispositions, he desires on his part, that children should grow up in piety, as earnestly as the parent can desire it; nay, as much more earnestly, as he hates sin more intensely, and desires good with less mixture of qualification. Goodness, or the production of goodness, is the supreme end of God, and therefore, we know, on first principles, that he desires to bestow whatsoever spiritual grace is necessary to the moral renovation of childhood, and will do it, unless some collateral reasons in his plan, involving the extension of holy virtue, require him to withhold.

Thus, if nothing were hung upon parental faithfulness and example, if the child were not used, in some degree or way, as an argument, to hold the parent to a life of Christian diligence, then the good principle in the parent might lack the necessary stimulus to bring it to maturity. Or, if all children alike, in spite of the evil and unchristian example of the house, were to be started into life as spiritually renewed, one of the strongest motives to holy living would be taken away from parents, in the fact that their children are safe as regards a good beginning, without any carefulness in them, or prayerfulness in their life; and their own virtue might so overgrow itself with weeds, as never to attain to a sound maturity. Let it be enough to know, on first principles in the character of God, that he will so dispense his spiritual agency to you and to your children, as to produce, considering the freedom of you both, the best measure and the ripest state of holy virtue. And how far short is this of the conclusion, that if you live as you ought and may yourselves, God will so dispense his Spirit that you may see your children grow up in piety?

Observe, too, that he expressly pledges his Holy Spirit to you, as one of his first gifts, and, what is more, even commands you to be filled with the Spirit; and considering the organic relation that subsists, by his own appointment, between you and your children, how far off is he, in this, from pledging you a mercy that accrues to their benefit? He appoints you also to be a light to the world, and, by the grace he pours into your being, prepares you to be; how much more a light to minds that are fed by simple nurture from your own? And when you consider how fond he is, if I may so speak, in the blessings he pours on the good, of gathering their children with them in the same circle of favor, how many of his promises, in all ages, run—"to you and to your children," what better assurance can you reasonably ask, to fortify your confidence in whatever spiritual grace may be necssary to your utmost success?

2. If there be any such thing as Christian nurture, distinguished from that which is not Christian, which is generally admitted, and, by the Scriptures clearly asserted, then is it some kind of nurture which God appoints. Does it then accord with the known character of God, to appoint a scheme of education, the only proper result of which shall be that children are trained up under it in sin? It would not be more absurd to suppose that God has appointed church education, to produce a first crop of sin, and then a crop of holiness. God appoints nothing of which sin, and only sin, is to be the proper and legitimate result, whether for a longer or a shorter time; least of all, a mode of training which is to produce sin. Holy virtue is the aim of every plan God adopts, every means he prescribes, and we ha·, e no right to look only for sin, in that which he has appointed as a means of virtue. We can not do it understandingly· without great impiety.

3. God does expressly lay it upon us to expect that our children will grow up in piety, under the parental nurture, and assumes the possibility that such a result may ordinarily be realized. "Train up a child"—how? for future conversion?—No, "but in the way he should go, that when he is old he may not depart from it." If it be said that this relates only to outward habits of vir-

tue and vice, not to spiritual life, the Old Testament, I reply, does not raise that distinction, as it is raised in the New. It puts all good together, all evil together, and regards a child trained up in the way he should go, as going in all the ways, and fulfilling all the ideas of virtue. The phraseology of the New Testament carries the same import. "Bring them up in the nurture and admonition of the Lord," a form of expression, which indicates the existence of a Divine nurture, that is to encompass the child and mold him unto God; so that he shall be brought up, as it were, in Him.

4. A time is foretold, as our churches generally believe, when all shall know God, even from the least to the greatest; that is, shall spiritually know him, or so that there shall be no need of exhorting one another to know him; for intellectual knowledge is not carried by exhortation. If such a time is ever to come, then, at least, children are to grow up in Christ. Can it come too soon? And, if we have the opinion that any such thing is impossible, either we, or those who come after us, must get rid of it. A principal reason why the great expectations of the future, that we, in this age, are giving out so confidently, seem only visionary and idle dreams to many, is that we are perpetually assuming their impossibility ourselves. Our very theory of religion is, that men are to grow up in evil, and be dragged into the church of God by conquest. The world is to lie in halves, and the kingdom of God is to stretch itself side by side with the kingdom of darkness, making sallies into it, and taking captive those who are

sufficiently hardened and bronzed in guiltiness to be converted!

Thus we assume even the absurdity of all our expectations in regard to the possible advancement of human society and the universal prevalence of Christian virtue. And thus we throw an air of extravagance and unreason over all we do. Whereas there is a sober and rational possibility, that human society should be universally pervaded by Christian virtue. The Christian scheme has a scope of intention, and instruments and powers adequate to this: it descends upon the world to claim all souls for its dominion—all men of all climes, all ages from childhood to the grave. It is, indeed, a plan which supposes the existence of sin, and sin will be in the world, and in all hearts in it, as long as the world or human society continues; but the scheme has a breadth of conception, and has powers and provisions embodied in it, which, apart from all promises and predictions, certify us of a day when it will reign in all human hearts, and all that live shall live in Christ. Let us either renounce any such confidence, or show, by a thorough consistency in our religious doctrines, that we hold it deliberately and manfully.

5. We discover in the Scriptures that the organic law, of which I have spoken, is distinctly recognized, and that character in children is often regarded as, in some very important sense, derivative from their parents. It is thus that " sin has passed upon all men." " By the offense of one, judgment came upon all." Christian faith is also spoken of in a similar way—" The un-

feigned faith, which dwelt first, in thy grandmother Lois, and thy mother Eunice, and, I am persuaded, that in thee also." Not that, in the bald and naked sense, it had descended thus through three generations. But the apostle conceives a power, in the good life of these mothers, that must needs transmit some flavor of piety. In like manner, God is represented as " keeping covenant and mercy with them that love him and keep his commandments, to a thousand generations ;" which, if it signifies any thing, amounts to a declaration that he will spiritually own and bless every succeeding generation, to the end of the world, if only the preceding will live so as to be fit vehicles of his blessing ; for it is not any covenant, as a form of mutual contract, which carries the divine favor, but it is the loving Him rather, and keeping His commandments, by an upright, godly life, which sets the parents on terms of friendship with God, and secures the inhabitation of his power.

Declarations like those in the eighteenth chapter of Ezekiel, " the son shall not bear the iniquity of the father,"—" the soul that sinneth, it shall die,"—are hastily applied by many, not to show that the child is to be punished only for his own sin, which is their true import, but, as if it were the same thing, to disprove the fact of an organic connection, by which children receive a character from their parents. Whereas this latter is a truth which we see with our eyes, and one that is constantly affirmed in the Scriptures, both in respect to bad character and to good. " God layeth up the iniquity of the wicked for his children,"—" Visiting the iniquities of the fathers upon the children to the third and fourth generation." By which we are to understand, what is every day exhibited in actual historic proof, that the wickedness of parents propagates itself in the character and condition of their children, and that it ordinarily requires three or four generations to ripen the sad harvest of misery and debasement. Again, on the other side, " he hath blessed thy children with thee,"—" For the good of them and their children after them,"—" For the promise is to you and to your children." The Scriptures have a perpetual habit, if I may so speak, of associating children with the character and destiny of their parents. In this respect, they maintain a marked contrast with the extreme individualism of our modern philosophy. They do not always regard the individual as an isolated unit, but they often look upon men as they exist, in families and races, and under organic laws.

Something has undoubtedly been gained to modern theology, as a human science, by fixing the attention strongly upon the individual man, as a moral agent, immediately related to God, and responsible only for his own actions; at the same time there was a truth, an important truth, underlying the old doctrine of federal headship and original or imputed sin, though strangely misconceived, which we seem, in our one-sided speculations, to have quite lost sight of. And how can we ever attain to any right conception of organic duties, until we discover the reality of organic powers and relations? And how can we hope to set ourselves in harmony with the Scriptures, in regard to family nurture, or household baptism, or any other kindred subject, while our theories include, or overlook precisely that which is the base of their teachings, and appointments? This brings me to my—

Last argument, which is drawn from infant or household baptism—a rite which supposes the fact of an organic connection of character between the parent and the child; a seal of faith in the parent, applied over to the child, on the ground of a presumption that his faith is wrapped up in the parent's faith; so that he is accounted a believer from the beginning. We must distinguish here between a fact and a presumption of fact. If you look upon a seed of wheat, it contains, in itself, presumptively, a thousand generations of wheat, though by reason of some fault in the cultivation, or some speck of diseased matter in itself, it may, in fact, never reproduce at all. So the Christian parent has, in his character, a germ, which has power, presumptively, to produce its like in his children, though by reason of some bad fault in itself, or possibly some outward hindrance in the Church, or some providence of death, it may fail to do so. Thus it is that infant baptism becomes an appropriate rite. It sees the child in the parent, counts him presumptively a believer and a Christian, and, with the parent, baptizes him also. Furthermore, you will perceive that it must be presumed, either that the child will grow up a believer, or that he will not. The Baptist presumes that he will not, and therefore declares the rite to be inappropriate. God presumes that he will, and therefore appoints it. The Baptist tells the child that nothing but sin can be expected of him; God tells him that for his parents' sakes, whose faith he is to follow, he has written his own name upon him, and expects him to grow up in all duty and piety.

I have no desire to press the passages in which mention is made of household baptism beyond their true import. When Paul is said to have "baptized the household of Stephanas," our Baptist friends reply that the text proves nothing, in respect to infant baptism, because it can not be shown that there were any children in the household; and some, who practice infant baptism, have conceded the sufficiency of the objection. But the power of this proof-text does not depend, in the least, on the fact that there were children in the household of Stephanas, but simply on the form of the language.   Indeed, it has always seemed to me that the argument for infant baptism is rather strengthened than weakened, by the supposition that there were, in fact, no infants or children in this household; for a household generally contains children, and a term so inclusive in its import, could never come into use, unless it was the practice for baptism to go by households. Under a practice like that of our Baptist brethren, what preacher would ever be heard to speak, in this general inclusive way, of having baptized a household?   In the case of the jailor, too, the same reasoning holds. Here, however, our Baptist brethren go farther, endeavoring to show positively, from the language used, that there were no infants or children in the household; for

when it is said that the jailor "rejoiced, believing in
God with all his house," it is argued that, inasmuch as
infant children are incapable of believing, there could
have been no infants in the family.   Admitting the correctness of the translation, which some have questioned,
the argument seems rather plausible as a turn of logic,
than just and convincing; for, if we consider the more
decisive position held in that age by the heads of families, and how, in common speech, they were supposed
to carry the religion of the family with them, we shall
be convinced that nothing was more natural than the
very language here used.   It was taken for granted, as
a matter of common understanding, that, in a change
of religion, the children went with the parents: if they
became Jews, that their children would be Jews; if
Christian believers, that their children would be Chris
tians.   Hence all the terms used, in reference to their
religion, took the most inclusive form.   If one believed
in God, he believed with all his house: the change he
suffered, in the common understanding of the age, carried the house with him; and it occurred to no one to
question the literal exactness of such like inclusive terms.

It has been a fashion, with many modern critics, to
surrender both these passages as proofs of infant baptism, and they certainly do not prove it, in just the way
in which many have used them as proof-texts.   But if
any one will seek a point of view, whence he may be
able to give a natural and easy interpretation to the language used, or if he will ask, on the simple doctrine of
chances, what chance there was that these two house-

holds should include no children, and moreover what chance that, in the only two cases of household baptism mentioned in the Scripture, the households should have been distinguished by this singularity, he will be as little likely as possible, to concede the fact that infant baptism is not adequately proved by these passages.

But the true idea of these passages, and also of the rite itself, is seen most evidently in the history of its establishment by Christ, in the third chapter of John. The Jewish nation regarded other nations as unclean. Hence, when a Gentile family wished to become Jewish citizens, they were baptized in token of cleansing. Then they were said to be re-born, or regenerated, so as to be accounted true descendants of Abraham. We use the term *naturalize*, that is, to *make natural born*, in the same sense. But Christ had come to set up a spiritual kingdom, the kingdom of heaven; and finding all men aliens, and spiritually unclean, he applies over the rite of baptism, which was familiar to the Jews, ("art thou a Master in Israel, and knowest not these things?") giving it a higher sense. "Except a man be born of water *and of the Spirit*, he can not enter the kingdom of heaven." But the Gentile proselyte, according to the custom here described—here is the point of the argument—came with his family. They were all baptized together, young and old, all regenerated or naturalized together; and therefore, in the new application made of the rite to signify spiritual cleansing and regeneration, it is understood, of course, that children are to come with their parents. To have excluded them would have been, to every Jewish mind, the height of absurdity. They could not have been excluded, without express exception, and no exception was made.

Some have questioned whether proselyte baptism existed at this early age; but of this the third chapter of John is itself conclusive proof; for how else was baptism familiarly known to the Jews as connected with regeneration; that is, civil regeneration? There is always a historic reason for religious rites and for usages of language; and you will find it impossible to suppose that Christ appointed baptism, and set the rite in connection with spiritual regeneration, by any mere accident, or without some historic basis, answering to that which I have just described. In this manner, all his language, in the interview with Nicodemus, becomes natural and easy.

It follows that the children of Christian disciples, being baptized with their parents, as the children of Gentile proselytes were baptized with theirs, would be taken or presumed by the church to be spiritually cleansed, in the same manner. Accordingly, just as the children of Jews were accounted Jews, and not as unclean, when one of the parents was a Jew, so Paul tells us, that in the church of God, the believing party sanctifies the unbelieving, " else were your children unclean, but now are they holy ; " showing that the Jewish analogies, in regard to children, were in fact translated, or passed over to the church, and adopted there—a translation that naturally followed. from the reapplication of proselyte baptism.

Then passing into the early history of the church, we hear Justin Martyr saying: "There are some of us, eighty years old, who were made disciples to Christ in their childhood;" that is, in the age of the apostles, and while they were yet living; for it was now less than eighty years since their death. And in the expression "*made disciples*," taken in connection with the baptismal formula, "Go disciple all nations, baptizing," &c., we see that he alludes to baptism; for baptism was the rite that introduced the subject into the Christian school as a disciple; and what so natural as that the children of disciples should be disciples with them?

Then again, Ireneus, who lived within one generation of the apostles, gives us the second mention of this rite which appears in history, when he says: "Christ came to save all persons through himself; all, I say, who through him are regenerated unto God : infants and little ones, and children and youth, and the aged." Which phrase, "*regenerated unto God*," applied to parents and little ones, alludes to baptism : showing that a notion of baptism, as connected with regeneration, coincident with that which we found in the third chapter of John, was then current in the church.

I have been thus full upon the rite of baptism, not because that is my subject, but because the rite involves, in all its grounds and reasons, the same view of Christian education which I am seeking to establish. One can not be thoroughly understood and received without the other. And it is precisely on this account that we have so great difficulty in sustaining the rite of infant

baptism. It ought to be difficult to sustain any rite,
after the sense of it is wholly gone from us. You perceive, too, in this exposition, that the view of Christian
nurture I am endeavoring to vindicate, is not new, but
is older, by far, than the one now prevalent—as old as
the Christian church. It is radically one with the ancient doctrine of baptism and regeneration, advanced
by Christ, and accepted by the first fathers.

We have much to say of baptismal regeneration as a
great error, which undoubtedly it is, in the form in
which it is held; but it is only a less hurtful error than
some of us hold in denying it. The distinction between
our doctrine of baptismal regeneration, and the ancient
Scripture view, is too broad and palpable to be mistaken. According to the modern church dogma, no
faith, in the parents, is necessary to the effect of the rite.
Sponsors, too, are brought in between all parents and
their duty, to assume the very office which belongs only
to them. And, what is worse, the child is said to be
actually regenerated by the act of the priest. According to the more ancient view, or that of the Scriptures,
nothing depends upon the priest or minister, save that
he execute the rite in due form. The regeneration is
not actual, but only presumptive, and every thing depends upon the organic law of character pertaining between the parent and the child, the church and the child,
thus upon duty and holy living and gracious example. The child is too young to choose the rite for himself, but the parent, having him as it were in his own
life, is allowed the confidence that his own faith and

character will be reproduced in the child, and grow up in his growth, and that thus the propriety of the rite as a seal of faith will not be violated. In giving us this rite, on the grounds stated, God promises, in fact, on his part, to dispense that spiritual grace which is necessary to the fulfillment of its import. In this way too is it seen that the Christian economy has a place for persons of all ages; for it would be singular if, after all we say of the universality of God's mercy as a gift to the human race, it could yet not limber itself to man, so as to adapt a place for the age of childhood, but must leave a full fourth part of the race, the part least hardened in evil and tenderest to good, unrecognized and unprovided for—gathering a flock without lambs, or, I should rather say, gathering a flock away from the lambs. Such is not the spirit of Him who said, "forbid them not, for of such is the kingdom of heaven." Therefore we bring them into the school of Christ and the pale of his mercy with us, there to be trained up in the holy nurture of the Lord. And then the result is to be tested afterwards, or at an advanced period of life, by trying their character in the same way as the character of all Christians is tried ; for many are baptized in adult age, who truly do not believe, as is afterwards discovered. And yet our Baptist brethren never rebaptize them, notwithstanding all they say of faith as the necessary condition of baptism.

But there are two objections to this view of Christian nurture, which, if they are not removed, may even suffice to break the force of my argument.

1. A theoretical objection, that it leaves no room for
the sovereignty of God, in appointing the moral character of men and families.   Thus it is declared that "all
are not Israel who are of Israel," and that God, before
the children Jacob and Esau had done either good or
evil, professed his love to one, and his rejection of the
other.   But the wonder is, in this case of Rebecca and
her children, that such a mother did not ruin them both.
A partial mother, scorning one child, teaching the other
to lie and trick his blind father, and extort from a starving brother his birthright honor, can not be said to furnish a very good test of the power of Christian education.   But show me the case, where the whole conduct
of the parents has been such as it should be to produce
the best effects, and where the sovereignty of God has
appointed the ruin of the children, whether all, or any
one of them.   The sovereignty of God has always a
relation to means, and we are not authorized to think
of it, in any case, as separated from means.

2. An objection from observation—asking why it is,
if our doctrine be true, that many persons, remarkable
for their piety, have yet been so unfortunate in their
children?   Because, I answer, many persons, remarkable for their piety, are yet very disagreeable persons,
and that too, by reason of some very marked defect in
their religious character.   They display just that spirit,
and act in just that manner, which is likely to make
religion odious—the more odious, the more urgently
they commend it.   Sometimes they appear well to the
world one remove distant from them, they shine well in

their written biography, but one living in their family
will know what others do not; and if their children
turn out badly, will never be at a loss for the reason.
Many persons, too, have such defective views of the
manner of teaching appropriate to early childhood, that
they really discourage their children. "Fathers provoke not your children to anger," says one, "lest they
be discouraged;" implying that there is such a thing as
encouraging, and such a thing as discouraging good
principle and piety in a child. And there are other
ways of discouraging children besides provoking them
to an angry and wounded feeling by harsh treatment.

I once took up a book, from a Sabbath-school library,
one problem of which was to teach a child that he wants
a new heart. A lovely boy (for it was a narrative) was
called every day to resolve that he would do no wrong
that day, a task which he undertook most cheerfully,
at first, and even with a show of delight. But, before
the sun went down, he was sure to fall into some ill-
temper or be overtaken by some infirmity. Whereupon, the conclusion was immediately sprung upon
him that he "wanted a new heart." We are even
amazed that any teacher of ordinary intelligence should
not once have imagined how she herself, or how the
holiest Christian living, would fare under such kind of
regimen; how she would discover every day, and probably some hours before sunset, that she too wanted a
new heart? And the practical cruelty of the experiment is yet more to be deplored, than its want of consideration. Had the problem been how to discourage

most effectually every ingenuous struggle of childhood, no readier or surer method could have been devised.

Simply to tell a child, as he just begins to make acquaintance with words, that he "must have a new heart before he can be good," is to inflict a double discouragement. First, he can not guess what this technical phraseology means, and thus he takes up the impression that he can do or think nothing right, till he is able to comprehend what is above his age—why then should he make the endeavor? Secondly, he is told that he must have a new heart *before* he can be good, not that he may hope to exercise a renewed spirit, *in* the endeavor to be good—why then attempt what must be worthless, till something *previous* befalls him? Discouraged thus on every side, his tender soul turns hither and thither, in hopeless despair, and finally he consents to be what he must—a sinner against God, and that only. Well is it, under such a process, wearing down his childish soul into soreness and despair of good, sealing up his nature in silence and cessation as regards all right endeavors, and compelling him to turn his feelings into other channels, where he shall find his good in evil—well is it, I say, if he has not contracted a dislike to the very subject of religion, as inveterate as the subject is impossible.

Many teach in this way, no doubt, with the best intentions imaginable; their design is only to be faithful, and sometimes they appear even to think that the more they discourage their children, the better and more faithful they are. But the mistake, if not cruelly meant, is certainly most cruel in the experience; and it is just this mistake, I am confident, which accounts for a large share of the unhappy failures made by Christian parents, in the training of their children. Rather should they begin with a kind of teaching suited to the age of the child. First of all, they should rather seek to teach a feeling than a doctrine; to bathe the child in their own feeling of love to God, and dependence on him, and contrition for wrong before him, bearing up their child's heart in their own, not fearing to encourage every good motion they can call into exercise; to make what is good, happy and attractive, what is wrong, odious and hateful; then as the understanding advances, to give it food suited to its capacity, opening upon it, gradually the more difficult views of Christian doctrine and experience.

Sometimes Christian parents fail of success in the religious training of their children, because the church counteracts their effort and example. The church makes a bad atmosphere about the house, and the poison comes in at the doors and windows. It is rent by divisions, burnt up by fanaticism, frozen by the chill of a worldly spirit, petrified in a rigid and dead orthodoxy. It makes no element of genial warmth and love about the child, according to the intention of Christ in its appointment, but gives to religion, rather, a forbidding aspect, and thus, instead of assisting the parent, becomes one of the worst impediments to his success. What kind of element the world makes about the child is of little consequence; for here there is no pretence

of piety. But when the school of Christ makes itself
an element of sin and death, the child's baptism becomes as great a fiction as the church itself, and the
arrangements of divine mercy fail of their intended
power. There are, in short, too many ways of accounting for the failure of success, in the family training of
those who are remarkable for their piety, without being
led to doubt the correctness of my argument in these
discourses.

To sum up all, we conclude, not that every child can
certainly be made to grow up in Christian piety—nothing is gained by asserting so much, and perhaps I could
not prove it to be true, neither can any one prove the
contrary—I merely show that this is the true idea and
aim of Christian nurture as a nurture of the Lord. It
is presumptively true that such a result can be realized,
just as it is presumptively true that a school will forward the pupils in knowledge, though possibly sometimes it may fail to do it. And, without such a presumption, no parent can do his duty and fill his office
well, any more than it is possible to make a good school,
in the expectation that the scholars will learn something
five or ten years hence, and not before.

To give this subject its practical effect, let me
urge it—

1. Upon the careful attention of those who neglect,
or decline, offering their children in baptism. Some of
you are simply indifferent to this duty, not seeing what
good it can do to baptize a child ; others have positive
theological objections to it. With the former class I

certainly agree, so far as to admit that baptism, as an operation, can do no good to your child; but, if it has no importance in what it operates, it has the greatest importance in what it signifies; and, what is more to be deplored by you, the withholding it signifies as much, viz: that you yourselves have no sense of the relation that subsists between your character and that of your child, and as little of the mercy that Christ intends for your child, by including him with you in his fold, to grow up there by your side in the same common hopes. Had you any just sense of these things, you would look upon the baptism of your child as a rite of as great importance and spiritual propriety as your own; for, in neither case, has the form any value beyond what it signifies. The other class among you suffer the same defect; for it is my settled conviction that no man ever objected to infant baptism, who had not at the bottom of his objections, false views of Christian education—who did not hold a notion of individualism, in regard to Christian character in childhood, which is justified, neither by observation nor by Scripture.

It is the prevalence of false views, on this subject, which creates so great difficulty in sustaining infant baptism in our churches. If children are to grow up in sin, to be converted when they come to the age of maturity, if this is the only aim and expectation of family nurture, there really is no meaning or dignity whatever in the rite. They are even baptized into sin, and every propriety of the rite as a seal of faith is violated. And it is the feeling of this impropriety which

lies at the basis of all your objections. Returning to
the old Scripture doctrine of an organic law, connecting
the child morally with the parents, so that he is, as it
were, included in them, to grow up in their life; perceiving then that he is a kind of rudimental being,
coming up gradually into a separate and complete individuality, having the parental life extended to him, first,
with an almost absolutely controlling power, then less
and less, till he takes, at length, the helm of his own
spirit—every difficulty that you now feel vanishes, and
the rite of infant baptism becomes one of the greatest
beauty, and perfectly coincident with the spirit and the
rules of adult baptism. The very command, " believe
and be baptized," of which so much is made, is exactly
met, and with no modifications, save what are necessary
to suit the peculiar state and age of childhood : for the
child, being included as it were in the parental life, is
accounted presumptively one with the parents, and
sealed with the seal of their faith.

And it would certainly be very singular if Christ
Jesus, in a scheme of mercy for the world, had found
no place for infants and little children : more singular
still, if he had given them the place of adults ; and
worse than singular, if he had appointed them to years
of sin as the necessary preparation for his mercy. But
if you see him counting them one with you, bringing
them tenderly into his fold with you, there to grow up
in him, you will not doubt that he has given them a
place exactly and beautifully suited to them. And is
it for you to withhold them from that place ? Is it

worthy of your tenderness, as a Christian parent, to
leave them outside of the fold, when the gate is open,
only taking care to go in yourself?   I will not accuse
you of intended wrong, but I am quite sure your
thoughts are not as God's thoughts, and I ask you to
study this question again, and more deeply.   You are
giving your children, as they grow up, impressions that
will assuredly be very injurious to them, and robbing
them of impressions that would have great power and
value to their minds.   What can be worse, what can
make them aliens, more sensibly, from Christ's sympathies, what can more effectually discourage and chill
them to all thoughts of a good life, than to make them
feel that Christ has no place for them till their sins are
ripe, and they are capable of a grace that is now above
their years?   What more persuasive, than to know that
he has taken them into his school already, to grow up
round him as disciples?   And if God should call you to
himself, what will draw upon their hearts more tenderly
than to remember that the father and mother whose
name they revere, brought them believingly in with
themselves, to be owned in that general assembly of the
just which occupies both worlds, and become partakers
with them there, in the grace which is now their song?

You rob yourselves too of an influence which is necessary to a right fulfillment of your duty.   Their character, you say, is their own; let them believe for themselves and be baptized when they will.   You have
never the same genial feeling that you would, if you
regarded them as morally linked to your character and

drawing from you the mold of their being.   You are not
kept in the same state of carefulness and spiritual tenderness.   No matter if you are cold to them, at times,
and do not always live Christ in the house, they are
growing up to be converted, and almost any thing is
good enough for conversion!   Christ himself, too, has no
such relation to you, in your family, as to make your
piety a domestic spirit.   He has not gathered your children round you, as a flock of young disciples, pouring
all his tenderness into your family ties, to make them vehicles of mercy and blessing.   Once more I ask you to
consider whether God is not better to you than you yourselves have thought, and whether, in withholding your
children from God, you are not like to fall as far short
of your duty, as you do of the privilege offered you.

2. What motives are laid upon all Christian parents,
by the doctrine I have established, to make the first
article of family discipline a constant and careful discipline of themselves.   I would not undervalue a strong
and decided government in families.   No family can be
rightly trained without it.   But there is a kind of virtue, my brethren, which is not in the rod—the virtue, I
mean, of a truly good and sanctified life.   And a reign
of brute force is much more easily maintained, than a
reign whose power is righteousness and love.   There
are, too, I must warn you, many who talk much of the
rod as the orthodox symbol of parental duty, but who
might really as well be heathens as Christians; who
only storm about their house with heathenish ferocity,
who lecture, and threaten, and castigate, and bruise,

and call this family government. They even dare to speak of this as the nurture of the Lord. So much easier is it to be violent than to be holy, that they substitute force for goodness and grace, and are wholly unconscious of the imposture. It is frightful to think how they batter and bruise the delicate, tender souls of their children, extinguishing in them what they ought to cultivate, crushing that sensibility which is the hope of their being, and all in the sacred name of Christ Jesus. By no such summary process can you dispatch your duties to your children. You are not to be a savage to them, but a father and a Christian. Your real aim and study must be to infuse into them a new life, and, to this end, the Life of God must perpetually reign in you. Gathered round you as a family, they are all to be so many motives, strong as the love you bear them, to make you Christ-like in your spirit. It must be seen and felt with them that religion is a first thing with you. And it must be first, not in words and talk, but visibly first in your love—that which fixes your aims, feeds your enjoyments, sanctifies your pleasures, supports your trials, satisfies your wants, contents your ambition, beautifies and blesses your character. No mock piety, no sanctimony of phrase, or longitude of face on Sundays will suffice. You must live in the light of God, and hold such a spirit in exercise as you wish to see translated into your children. You must take them into your feeling, as a loving and joyous element, and beget, if by the grace of God you may, the spirit of your own heart in theirs.

This is Christian education, the nurture of the Lord. Ah, how dismal is the contrast of a half-worldly, carnal piety; proposing money as the good thing of life; stimulating ambition for place and show; provoking ill-nature by petulance and falsehood; praying, to save the rule of family worship; having now and then a religious fit, and, when it is on, weeping and exhorting the family to undo all that the life has taught them to do; and then, when the passions have burnt out their fire, dropping down again to sleep in the embers, only hoping still that the family will sometime be converted! When shall we discover that families ought to be ruined by such training as this? When shall we turn ourselves wholly to God, and looking on our children as one with us and drawing their character from us, make them arguments to duty and constancy—duty and constancy not as a burden, but, since they are enforced by motives so dear, our pleasure and delight. For these ties and duties exist not for the religious good of our children only, but quite as much for our own. And God, who understands us well, has appointed them to keep us in a perpetual frame of love; for so ready is our bad nature to kindle with our good, and burn with it, that what we call our piety, is, otherwise, in constant danger of degenerating into a fiery, censorious, unmerciful and intolerant spirit.

Hence it is that monks have been so prone to persecution. Not dwelling with children as the objects of affection, having their hearts softened by no family love, their life identified with no objects that excite gentleness, their nature hardens into a Christian abstraction, and blood and doctrine go together. Therefore God hath set Israel in families, that the argument to duty may come upon the gentle side of your nature, and fall, as a baptism, on the head of your natural affections. Your character is to be a parent character, infolding lovingly the spirits of your children, as birds are gathered in the nest, there to be sheltered and fed, and got ready for the flight. Every hour is to be an hour of duty, every look and smile, every reproof and care, an effusion of Christian love. For it is the very beauty of the work you have to do that you are to cherish and encourage good, and live a better life into the spirits of your children.

3. It is to be deeply considered, in connection with this view of family nurture, whether it does not meet many of the deficiencies we deplore in the Christian character of our times, and the present state of our churches. We have been expecting to thrive too much by conquest, and too little by growth. I desire to speak with all caution of what are very unfortunately called revivals of religion; for, apart from the name, which is modern, and from certain crudities and excesses that go with it—which name, crudities, and excesses are wholly adventitious as regards the substantial merits of such scenes—apart from these, I say, there is abundant reason to believe that God's spiritual economy includes varieties of exercise, answering, in all important respects, to these visitations of mercy, so much coveted in our churches. They are needed. A perfectly uni-

form demonstration in religion is not possible or desirable. Nothing is thus uniform but death. Our exercise varies every year and day from childhood onward. Society is going through new modes of exercise in the same manner, excited by new subjects, running into new types of feeling, and struggling with new combinations of thought. Quite as necessary is it that all holy principle should have a varied exercise—now in one duty, now in another; now in public aims and efforts, now in bosom struggles; now in social methods, now in those which are solitary and private; now in high emotion, now in deliberative thought and study. Accordingly the Christian church began with a scene of extraordinary social demonstration, and the like, in one form or another, may be traced in every period of its history since that day.

But the difficulty is with us that we idolize such scenes, and make them the whole of our religion. We assume that nothing good is doing, or can be done at any other time. And what is even worse, we often look upon these scenes, and desire them, rather as scenes of victory, than of piety. They are the harvest-times of conversion, and conversion is too nearly every thing with us. In particular we see no way to gather in disciples, save by means of certain marked experiences, developed in such scenes, in adult years. Our very children can possibly come to no good, save in this way. Instrumentalities are invented to compass our object, that are only mechanical, and the hope of mere present effect is supposed to justify them. Present effect, in the view of many, justifies any thing and every thing. We strain every nerve of motion, exhaust every capacity of endurance, and push on till nature sinks in exhaustion. We preach too much, and live Christ too little. We do many things which, in a cooler mood, are seen to hurt the dignity of religion, and which somewhat shame and sicken ourselves. Hence the present state of religion in our country. We have worked a vein till it has run out. The churches are exhausted.* There is little to attract them, when they look upon the renewal of scenes through which many of them have passed. They look about them, with a sigh, to ask if possibly there is no better way, and some are ready to find that better way, in a change of their religion. Nothing different from this ought to have been expected. No nation can long thrive by a spirit of conquest; no more can a church. There must be an internal growth, that is made by holy industry, in the common walks of life and duty.

Let us turn now, not away from revivals of religion, certainly not away from the conviction that God will bring upon the churches tides of spiritual exercise, and vary his divine culture by times and seasons suited to their advancement; but let us turn to inquire whether there is not a fund of increase in the very bosom of the church itself. Let us try if we may not train up our children in the way that they should go. Simply this, if we can do it, will make the church multiply her numbers

---

* This was written, I believe, in the year, A. D., 1846.

many fold more rapidly than now, with the advantage
that many more will be gained from without than now.
For she will cease to hold a mere piety of occasions, a
piety whose chief use is to get up occasions; she will
follow a gentler and more constant method, as her duty
is more constant, and blends with the very life of her
natural affections. Her piety will be of a more even
and genial quality, and will be more respected. She
will not strive and cry, but she will live. The school
of John the Baptist will be succeeded by the school of
Christ, as a dew comes after a fire. Families will not
be a temptation to you, half the time hurrying you on
to get money, and prepare a show, and the other half, a
motive to repentance and shame, and profitless exhortation; but all the time, an argument for Christian love
and holy living.

Then also the piety of the coming age will be deeper,
and more akin to habit than ours, because it begun
earlier. It will have more of an air of naturalness, and
will be less a work of will. A generation will come
forward, who will have been educated to all good undertakings and enterprises—ardent without fanaticism,
powerful without machinery. Not born, so generally,
in a storm, and brought to Christ by an abrupt transition, the latter portion of life will not have an unequal
war to maintain with the beginning, but life will be
more nearly one, and in harmony with itself. Is not
this a result to be desired? Could we tell our American churches, at this moment, what they want, should
we not tell them this? Neither, if God, as many fear,

is about to bring upon his church a day of wrath and stormy conflict, let any one suspect that such a kind of piety will want vigor and nerve to withstand the fiery assaults anticipated. See what turn the mind of our apostle took when he was arming his disciples for the great conflict of their age. Children, obey your parents —Fathers, provoke not your children—Servants, be obedient to your masters—Masters, forbear threatening—Finally, to include all, put on the whole armor of God. As if the first thought, in arming the church for great trials and stout victories, was to fill common life and the relations of the house with a Christian spirit. There is no truer truth, or more sublime. Religion never thoroughly penetrates life, till it becomes domestic. Like that patriotic fire which makes a nation invincible, it never burns with inextinguishable devotion till it burns at the hearth.

4. Parents who are not religious in their character, have reason, in our subject, seriously to consider what effect they are producing, and likely to produce, in their children. Probably you do not wish them to be irreligious ; few parents have the hardihood or indiscretion to desire that the fear of God, the salutary restraints of religion, should be removed from their children. Possibly you exert yourselves, in a degree to give them religious council and instruction. But, alas! how difficult is it for you to convince them, by words, of the value of what you practically reject yourselves. Have I not shown you that they are set in organic connection with you, to draw their spirit, and principles,

and character from yours? What then are they daily deriving from you, but that which you yourselves reveal, in your prayerless house, and at your thankless table? Is it a spirit of duty and Christian love, a faith that has its home and rest in other worlds, or is it the carnal spirit of gain, indifference to God, deadness to Christ, love of the world, pride, ambition, all that is earthly, nothing that is heavenly?

Do not imagine that you have done corrupting them when they are born. Their character is yet to be born, and, in you, is to have its parentage. Your spirit is to pass into them, by a law of transition that is natural, and well nigh irresistible. And then you are to meet them in a future life, and see how much of blessing or of sorrow they will impute to you—to share their unknown future, and look upon yourselves as father and mother to their destiny. Such thoughts, I know, are difficult for you to meet; difficult because they open real scenes, which you are, one day, to look upon. Loving these your children, as most assuredly you do, can you think that you are fulfilling the office that your love requires? Go home to your Christless house, look upon them all as they gather round you, and ask it of your love faithfully to say, whether it is well between you? And if no other argument can draw you to God, let these dear living arguments come into your soul, and prevail there.

III

THE OSTRICH NURTURE

"The daughter of my people is become cruel, like the ostriches in the wilderness."—*Lamentations* iv. 3.

I CITE this comparison for the sake of the comparison itself, and not to make an example of the mothers of Israel represented in it. They are not to be blamed, if, in the terrors of the siege and the wild feverings of starvation, the voice of nature has been stifled in their bosom. Indeed, it is the wonder of the prophet himself that, while the coarse sea-monsters draw out the breast and faithfully nurse their young, the human mother, so much tenderer and more loving, can be so maddened by distress as to become like the ostrich, and forget the cries of her children.

The ostrich, it will be observed, is nature's type of all unmotherhood. She hatches her young without incubation, depositing her eggs in the sand to be quickened by the solar heat. Her office as a mother-bird is there ended. When the young are hatched, they are to go forth untended, or unmothered, save by the general motherhood of nature itself. Hence the ostrich is called sometimes the "wicked," and sometimes the "stupid" bird. Job describes her with a feeling of natural dislike—"Which leaveth her eggs in the earth, and warmeth them in the dust, and forgetteth that the foot may crush them, or that the wild beast may break them. She is hardened against her young ones, as though they were not hers, her labor is in vain without care, [in our version, "without fear."] Because God hath deprived her of wisdom, neither hath he imparted unto her understanding." In other words, she is both heartless and senseless; too heartless to care for her young, and too senseless to maintain a motherhood as genial even as that of the sand.

Now there is no human mother, unless it be in some terrible stress of siege and starvation, when the mind itself is unsettled by the wild instigation of suffering, who will cease from the bodily care and feeding of her children. And yet there are many forms of nurture for the mind and character of children, that are so far resembled to the ostrich nurture, as to be fitly represented under that type. Practices are adopted, opinions accepted, theories of church life and conversion taught, that make a true Christian parentage virtually impossible, and leave the child, in fact, to a kind of nurture in the sands.

What I propose, accordingly, at the present time, is to characterize these modes of ostrich nurture, miscalled Christian, showing what they are, and the real, though doubtless undesigned, cruelty of them.

As a curious illustration of the looseness and the unsettled feeling of the times, in regard to this great subject, it is just now beginning to be asserted by some, that the true principle of training for children is exactly that of the ostrich, viz: no training at all; the best government, no government. All endeavors to fashion them by the parental standards, or to induct them into the belief of their parents, is alleged to be a real oppression put upon their natural liberty. It is nothing less, it is said, than an effort to fill them with prejudices, and put them under the sway of prejudices, all their lives long. Why not let the child have his own way, think his own thoughts, generate his own principles, and so be developed in the freedom and beauty of the flowers? Or, if he should sometimes fall into bad tempers and disgraceful or uncomely practices, as flowers do not, let him learn how to correct *himself*, and be righted by his own discoveries. Having thus no artificial conscience formed to hamper his natural freedom, no religious scruples and superstitions inculcated to be a detention, or limitation, upon his impulses, he will grow up as a genuine character, stunted by no cant or affectation; a large-minded, liberal, original, and beautiful soul.

This kind of nurture supposes, evidently, a faith in human nature that is total and complete. As the mother ostrich might be supposed to reason, that her eggs are ostrich's eggs, and must therefore produce genuine ostriches and nothing else, so it assumes that human children will grow up, left to themselves, into the most genuine, highest style of human character. Whereas, it is the misery of human children that, as free beings, answerable for their choices and their character, and already touched with evil, they require some training, over and above the mere indulgence of their natural instincts. They can not be left to merely blossom into character; or, if they are, it will most assuredly be any sort of character but that which parental love would desire. What they most especially want is, what no ostrich or mere animal nurture can give; to be preoccupied with holy principles and laws; to have prejudices instilled that are holy prejudices; and so to be tempered beforehand by moderating and guiding influences, such as their perilous freedom and hereditary damage require.

The question here at issue does not really need to be discussed, but it will greatly instruct and impress those parents who allow their minds to fluctuate in such looseness as quite unsettles the feeling of their obligation, just to notice the immense distinction between the relationship of human parents to their offspring, and that of the animals to theirs. It is not given to the animals, they will perceive, as to men, to pass any results matured by their own experience, to their posterity. They prepare no inventions, create no institutions for their offspring; produce no sciences, write no histories, preserve no records, accumulate no property or wealth that is to be transmitted; even their thoughts they can perpetuate in no literary treasures. Hence, there is no progress among them, over and above that small physiological improvement that may pass by the laws of natural propagation. So far they are all ostriches. All they can do is to follow their instincts,

and leave their posterity to follow them over again, in
the same manner, beginning at the same point. But
with men, as creatures of reason, it is far otherwise.
They are creators, all, for them that are to come after.
What they can discover, build, produce, acquire, learn,
think, enjoy, they are to transmit; giving it to them
that come after to begin at the point where they cease,
and have the full advantage of their opinions, works,
and character. One of their first duties, therefore, is
to educate and train their offspring, transmitting to
them what they have known, believed, and proved by
their experience. If they sometimes transmit their low
thoughts, and narrow opinions, and mistaken principles,
and so far give their children a great disadvantage, that
is but a necessary evil which is incidental manifestly to
a system otherwise beneficent, and for that they are of
course responsible. If nothing were to pass but mere
instincts, the disadvantage would be far greater, and the
whole scale of existence lower. How unnatural and
monstrous, therefore, is that scheme of nurture which
requires it of parents to pass nothing, or as little as possible, to their children. If they have learned wisdom,
they are not to inculcate that wisdom, lest it should
create a prejudice! If they have found their conscience
and the principles of virtue, to be their truest friends
and the best guardians of their life, they are not to hamper their children by subjecting them to the same! If
they have found the principal joys that freshen life in
God and the faith of his Son, they are still to let their
children find their own sources of strength and joy for

themselves, and not to train them, or indoctrinate them
in such ways of blessing, lest perchance they be not
sufficiently original and free in their development!
Why, if they were to discover mines and hide the
discovery forever, or acquire immense treasures of
property appointing them by their will to be sunk
in the sea, leaving their children in utter destitution,
they would not be as false to their office of parentage! God has given it to them, as rational creatures,
to transmit all possible benefits to their offspring. And
what shall they more carefully transmit than what is
valuable above every thing else, their principles and
their piety?

We find, then, a most solid ground for the obligations
of Christian nurture. It is one of the grand distinctions of humanity that it has such a power to pass, and
is set in such a duty of passing, its gifts, principles, and
virtues, on to the ages that come after. Happily, few
will need to be convinced of this; and yet there are a
great many, we shall find, who manage, even under
what they regard as truly Christian pretexts, to maintain schemes of nurture so nearly unparental and unnatural, as to have a much closer affinity with the
ostrich nurture than they suspect themselves.

We have many, for example, who have taken up
notions of liberty, or free moral agency, in religion,
that separate them effectually from the true sense of
their power and privilege in regard to their children.
Assuming the unquestionable first truth that religious

virtue, or piety, is a matter strictly personal, the free-will offering of obedience and duty to God, they subside into the impression that they are of course absolved from any close responsibility for that which lies so entirely in the choices of their children themselves. They may not take their absolution by any formal inference, and may not even be aware that they have taken it at all; but the distinction between manhood and childhood is so far hidden, or slurred over, under their supposed principle of responsibility grounded in free agency, that their self-indulgence is accommodated, by the pretext, more easily than they know. Sometimes the inference will be half uttered in their feeling; as when they ask, only not aloud—"after all, must not our children answer for themselves?" So they submit resignedly, to the supposed necessity, and do it with so much less of compunction, because they consciously have so tender a feeling for their children, and are so much pained by the sense of their religious perils. But the submission they fall into, in this pious way, amounts, in fact, to a real absolution, not seldom, from all the finest, tenderest, most faithful, most unworldly cares of their parental office. They subside thus into a habit of remissness and religious negligence; and their way of nurture becomes unparental even as that of the ostriches.

Their blame in such defections from duty is greater than they know. For God has probably instituted the reproductive order of existence, including the parental and filial relation, with a special design to mitigate the perils of free agency. One generation is to be ripe in

knowledge and character, and the next is to be put in
charge of the former, in the tenderest, most flexible,
most dependent state possible, to be by them inducted
into the choices where their safety lies.   Furthermore,
they are bound to fidelity in their charge, by the fact,
that, as they have given existence to the subjects of it,
so they have also communicated the poison of their
own fallen state, to increase the perils of existence.   In
this manner, God has put it upon them to be the more
strenuous in their charge, because of these perils, and
expects, by means of their fidelity, to reduce the otherwise disastrous results of free agency to the smallest
possible measure.   Their responsibility in the parental
office is not diminished, but increased even a hundred
fold, by the personal liberty and strict individuality of
their children.   It would be far less cruel to be negli-
gent of their bodily wants; for the body will maintain
its growth, and will even manage to increase in robustness, when it is poorly clad and fed upon the coarsest
fare.   But the mind, or soul, born to greater perils than
want or the weather, even the tremendous perils of un-
taught liberty, and principles unfixed, waits, at the
point of its magnificent infancy, to be led into the
choices, tastes, affinities, and habits, that are to be the
character of its eternity.   Tenderness every where else,
and remissness here, is only the mockery of kindness.
Let the first want be first, and the highest nature have
the promptest care; and if any thing is left to the nurture of the sands, let it be the body, where the crime of
the desertion will be less and will certainly not be hid.

Many true Christians, again, fall off, unwittingly, from the humanly parental modes of nurture, in taking up notions of conversion that are mechanical, and proper only to the adult age. They make a merit of great persistency and firmness, in asserting the universal necessity of a new spiritual birth; not perceiving under what varieties of form that change may be wrought. The soul must be exercised, they think, in one given way, viz: by a struggle with sin, a conscious self-renunciation, and a true turning to Christ for mercy, followed by the joy and peace of a new life in the Spirit. A child, in other words, can be born of God only in the same way as an adult can be. There is no quickening grace, or new creation of the Spirit, proper to him as a child. If he dies in infancy, God may, it is true, find some way, possibly, to save him, but if he stays among the living, he can not be a Christian till he is older. He is therefore left, in this most tender and beautiful and pliant age, in a condition most of all unprivileged, and most sadly unhopeful. The necessity of a great spiritual change is upon him, and yet he is wholly incapable of the change! What other being has the good Lord and Father of the world left in a condition as pitiful as this of a human child? Even the most wicked and hardened of men has, at least, the gate of conversion left open. And yet there are many Christian parents, living an outwardly decent and fair life, who consent, without difficulty, and with a kind of consciously orthodox merit, to this very unnatural and truly hard lot of childhood, and fall into easy conformity with it. Their practically accepted notion of Christian nurture, in which they mean to be piously faithful is, that they are to bring up their children outside of all possible acceptance with God, till such time as their conversion may be looked for in a church-wise form. And their whole scheme of treatment corresponds. They indoctrinate them soundly in respect to their need of a new heart; tell them what conversion is, and how it comes to pass with grown people; pray that God will arrest them when they are old enough to be converted according to the manner; drill them, meantime, into all the constraints, separated from all the hopes and liberties of religion; turning all their little misdoings and bad tempers into evidences of their need of regeneration, and assuring them that all such signs must be upon them till after they have passed the change. Their nurture is a nurture, thus, of despair; and the bread of life itself, held before them as a fruit to be looked upon, but not tasted, till they are old enough to have it as grown people do, finally becomes repulsive, just because they have been so long repelled and fenced away from it. And so religion itself, pressed down upon them till they are fatally sored by its impossible claims, becomes their fixed aversion. How plain is it that such kind of nurture is unnatural and, though it be not so intended, unchristian. It makes even the loving gospel of Jesus a most galling chain upon the neck of childhood!—this and nothing more. For so long a time, and that the most ductile and hopeful, as regards all new implantings of

good, it really proposes nothing but to have the depravated nature grow, and the plague of sin deepen its bad
infection.

Meantime, it will be strange, if the parents themselves do not fall away from all that is necessary to
their Christian power, when the conversion of their
children is postponed, in this manner, by the merely
adult possibilities of their gospel. Why should they
live so as to gain their children, when their children
are not to be gained? Were they really to live so as
to make their house an element of grace, the atmosphere of their life an element, to all that breathe it, of
unworldly feeling and all godly aspiration, their mechanical doctrine of conversion would scarcely suffice to
keep away the saving mercies of God from their children. Their children would still be converted even
before the permissible time, and burst up through the
poor detentions of their bad doctrine, to cover it with
blessed confusion. But alas! it requires but a very
little of genuine, living godliness in the house, to bring
up children for a future conversion! This kind of ostrich nurture can be cheaply maintained, and with a
very small expenditure of piety. To keep the drill on
foot, as a mere legal indoctrination; to phrase a hope
or desire of conversion, in the family prayers; to be
exact, stern, stiff in all church practices, requires no
faith; or living by faith, no sanctification of the life.
A busy, worldly, hard-natured father, a vain, irritable,
captious, fashion-loving mother, a house orthodoxly
bad and earthly in all the reigning practices, is yet a

good enough school to prepare the necessity of a future conversion for the children! How different the kind of life that is necessary to bring them up *in* conversion and beget them anew in the spirit of a loving obedience to God, at a point even prior to all definite recollection. This is Christian nurture, because it nurtures Christians, and because it makes an element of Christian grace in the house. It invites, it nourishes hope, it breathes in love, it forms the new life as a holy, though beautiful prejudice in the soul, before its opening and full flowering of intelligence arrives. "Suffer little children to come unto me and forbid them not" translates the very economy of the house, and has, in that economy, its living verification. And the promise, "for of such is the kingdom of heaven," wears no look of violence; for the kingdom of heaven is there. The children grow up in it, as being configured to it. The family prayers have a sound of gladness, and they sing the family hymn with glad voices. The worldliness of the glittering bad world without is set off and made fascinating by no doom of repression within. A firm administration is loved because, like God's, it is felt to be the defense of liberty. Truth, purity, firmness, love to Jesus, all that belongs to a formal conversion and more, is centralized thus in the soul, as a kind of ingrown habit. The children are all converted by the converting element of grace they live in. And so it is proved that there is a conversion for children, proper and possible to their age. They are not excluded, walled away from Christ by a mechanical enforcement of modes proper only and possible to adults. The house itself is a converting ordinance.

Again there is another and different way in which parents, meaning to be Christian, fall into the ostrich nurture without being at all aware of it. They believe in what are called revivals of religion, and have a great opinion of them as being, in a very special sense, the converting times of the gospel. They bring up their children, therefore, not for conversion exactly, but, what is less dogmatic and formal, for the converting times. And this they think is even more evangelical and spiritual because it is more practical; though, in fact, much looser and connected, commonly, with even greater defections from parental duty and fidelity. To bring up a family for revivals of religion requires, alas! about the smallest possible amount of consistency and Christian assiduity. No matter what opinion may be held of such times, or of their inherent value and propriety as pertaining to the genuine economy of the gospel, any one can see that Christian parents may very easily roll off a great part of their responsibilities, and comfort themselves in utter vanity and worldliness of life, by just holding it as a principal hope for their children, that they are to be finally taken up and rescued from sin, by revivals of religion. As it costs much to be steadily and uniformly spiritual, how agreeable the hope that gales of the Spirit will come to make amends for their conscious defections. If they do not maintain the unworldly and heavenly spirit, so as to make it the

element of life in their house, God will some time have
his day of power in the community, and they piously
hope that their children will then be converted to
Christ. So they fall into a key of expectation that per-
mits, for the present, modes of life and conduct, which
they can not quite approve. They go after the world
with an eagerness which they expect by and by to
check, or possibly, for the time, to repent of. The
family prayers grow cold and formal, and are often in-
termitted. The tempers are earthly, coarse, violent.
Discipline is ministered in anger, not in love. The
children are lectured, scolded, scorched by fiery words.
The plans are all for money, show, position, not for the
more sacred and higher interests of character. The
conversation is uncharitable, harsh, malignant, an effusion of spleen, a tirade, a taking down of supposed
worth and character by low imputations and carping
criticisms. In this kind of element the children are to
have their growth and nurture, but the parents piously
hope that there will some time be a revival of religion,
and that so God will mercifully make up what they
conceive to be only the natural infirmity of their lives.
Finally the hoped for day arrives, and there begins to
be a remarkable and strange piety in the house.
The father choakes almost in his prayer, showing that
he really prays with a meaning! The mother, conscious that things have not been going rightly with the
children, and seeing many frightful signs of their certain ruin at hand, warns them, even weeping, of the
impending dangers by which she is so greatly distressed

on their account; adding also bitter confessions of fault in herself. The children stare of course, not knowing what strange thing has come! They can not be unaffected; perhaps they seem to be converted, perhaps not. In many cases it makes little difference which; for if all this new piety in the house is to burn out in a few days, and the old regimen of worldliness and sin to return, it will be wonderful if they are not converted back again to be only just as neglectful, in the matter of Christian living, as they were brought up to be. Any scheme of nurture that brings up children thus for revivals of religion, is a virtual abuse and cruelty. And it is none the less cruel that some pious-looking pretexts are cunningly blended with it. Instead of that steady, formative, new-creating power that ought to be exerted by holiness in the house, it looks to campaigns of force that really dispense with holiness, and it results that all the best ends of Christian nurture are practically lost.

Again, there is another form of the unchristian nurture, over opposite to these just named, which is quite as wide of the true character. I speak of that lower and merely ethical nurture, which undertakes, with great assiduity it may be, to form and whittle the age of childhood into character, by a merely pruning and humanly culturing process. It is a kind of nurture that stops short of religion, and atones for the conscious defect, by a drill more or less careful in the moralities. The reason of this defect commonly is that the parents are too far decayed in piety and too much under the world, to put forth any really religious endeavor; but it is to their children as if no such interest of religion had existence. They are corrected on this side and on that, by human standards and methods, taught to consider what is respectable, or what people will think of them, how to win the honors of character among men, lectured on the wisdom of conduct, and the resulting happiness of a right behavior, but the fact of their relation to God, and the standards and motives furnished by religion are wholly passed by, or omitted. The cruelty of this sort of nurture is that, however delicate and careful it may be of that which lies in mere social character and standing, it exactly copies the ostrich nurture in all that relates to the higher and properly religious life. The world-ward nature is cared for, but the religious, that which opens God-ward, that which aspires after God, and, occupied by his inspiring impulse, mounts into all good character; as being even liberty itself; that which consummates and crowns the real greatness and future eternity of souls, is virtually ignored, left to the wild, dry, motherhood of the sands.

Children trained in this mere ethical nurture, are inducted into no way of faith or dependence on God. They are taught to look for no spiritual transformation. The virtue they practice is to be prayerless virtue. They grow up thus on the roots of their natural pride and selfishness, bred into the habit of testing their goodness by their appearances, and their merit by their works. That they should be molded in this manner to

a Christian life would be wonderful. Their parents
may be nominally Christian, but they have, in fact,
agreed to omit religion in the training of their children;
and it would be strange if they should compliment their
only nominally Christian parentage, by unfolding a
really Christian life. It will be well if they have any
genuine respect for religion, or even sense of what it is.
Trained to have no religious conscience, and to practice a virtue unblessed by the nobler impulsions of religious inspiration, it will be strange if they maintain
even correctness of life; and more so if their heart, undeveloped by religion, does not canker itself away in
the sordid vices of meanness, or burn itself out, as regards all worthy and great feelings, in the general hatred
of God and his truth. There may be many decencies, or
even delicacies, in this kind of nurture; and yet, in the
complete oversight or neglect of the religious nature, it
becomes profoundly and even cruelly unnatural.

There is yet another and widely prevalent misconception of childhood which, to a certain extent, involves
Christianity itself in the same unnatural methods that
are adopted by men. I speak here more especially of
the assumed fact that Christ allows no place in the church
for such as are only children. Is not the church to be
composed of such as really believe? And what kind
of faith can children have who are not yet arrived at
the age of intelligence? Hence there is supposed to
be a kind of necessity that children, up to that period
of advancement and personal maturity when they are

able to choose and believe for themselves, and become
the subjects of a genuine Christian experience, should
be excluded from the Christian church. It signifies
nothing that the seal of faith was anciently applied to
children only eight days old, as being presumptively in
the faith of their parents, and included with them in
the bonds of their covenant. As little does it signify
that Christ says "let them come, forbid them not; for
of such is the kingdom of heaven." Still they can not
believe—are not old enough to believe—how then can
they come into the church, or in any conceivable way
be included in it? Is not the church of God assumed
to be made up of them that believe? What then is
left for children but to stay without till they are old
enough to be intelligently converted, and entered into a
new life by their own deliberate choice? Hence the
Baptist brethren conceive it to be a matter perfectly
final, as regards the question of baptism, that infants
can not believe, and can not therefore have any fit place
among believers in the church. Does not the Scripture
say—"Believe and be baptized?" And how is confession to be made with the mouth, except when the heart
believeth unto righteousness?

The result of such arguments and inferences is, that
children have no place given them in the church, however modified, to suit the conditions of their age. Their
parents are called by Christ to live within and they
themselves are left without. There is no church nurture for them proper to their tender years; they can not
be in the church till they are sufficiently grown to be-

lieve. And so it is settled that there is no church mercy
for them. The church turns her back and leaves them,
separated even from their parents, to try their fortunes,
like the wild ostriches, in the desert sands without.

It would seem that the hardness and the monstrous
unnaturalness of such conceptions must revolt the mind
of almost any thoughtful person. If the grace of our
salvation took the ingenuous children away from their
sinning, unbelieving parents, and gathered them into
the heavenly fold by themselves, we should have less
reason to be shocked by the severity. But instead of
this, calling home the penitent fathers and mothers and
carefully folding them in the church of God's protection, Jesus their shepherd shuts away the lambs, we
are told, and forbids them to come in! The cruelty of
such an opinion, or doctrine, is evident, and the cruel
effects it must have, in making even childhood feel
itself to be an alien from God's mercies, are even more
so. It has no conception that there can be a Saviour
and salvation for all ages and stages of life; Christ is
the Saviour of adults only! No! Christ is a Saviour
bounded by no such narrow and meager theories—a
Saviour for infants, and children, and youth, as truly as
for the adult age; gathering them all into his fold
together, there to be kept and nourished together, by
gifts appropriate to their years; even as he himself has
shown us so convincingly, by passing through all ages
and stages of life himself, and giving us, in that manner,
to see that he partakes the want and joins himself to
the fallen state of each. Having been a child himself,

who can imagine, even for one moment, that he has no place in his fold for the fit reception of childhood? Dreadful insult, both to him and to childhood, and the greater insult, that the gospel even of heaven's love is narrowed to this, by a supposed necessity of evangelism! What a position is given thus to children, growing up to look on an adult church, instructed into the opinion that what they look upon—Christ, ordinances, covenant vows—is only for adult people!

I ought perhaps to add, in bringing this argument to a close, that the harsh imputations I may seem to some of you to have indulged, must not be hastily disallowed. Almost all parents are tender, consciously tender of their children. What will not most of you do, to clothe and feed, and educate, and, in all respects, make due provision for your children? Sacrifices here are nothing. Health, rest, ease, comfort, you gladly renounce for their sake, and some of you would not spare the sacrifice even of your soul to serve them. Are you then to be justly charged with a mode of nurture so unnatural as to be fitly resembled to that of the ostriches? Of what are you more deeply conscious than of your willingness even to die for your children. All your tenderest movings are toward them; all that you plan, or think, or do, is for them. Yes, doubtless, it is even so, as regards their nurture and comfort in this world—all your tenderest cares and studies center here. Of this there is no question, and far be it from me to suggest a doubt of you here.

No, this defection from nature, of which I have been
speaking, relates to a different matter—in quite another
field. Doing your full honor as a careful provider, a
most faithful and loving guardian, a disinterested, self-
sacrificing contriver and laborer for your children's
good, the question is whether you do not after all put
them off with a mere ostrich nurture in the matter of
the soul? whether you do not let in some one or
more of these very misconceptions I have named, to
control all your modes of conduct and discipline toward them? Do you never throw off your own Christian responsibilities for them by allowing, as a pretext,
the fact of their liberty and personal responsibility for
themselves? Are you never let down in the sense of
your most sacred obligations, by simply allowing yourself to think it enough, that your children are brought
up for conversion? Do none of you subside even to a
lower point, and bring up your children only for revivals of religion? Are there none of you that make it
your whole care to form your children by the mere
ethical standards, and finish them in the graces of a
mere human culture? Have none of you theories of
salvation and of Christ's way respecting it, such as leave
no place for children in the church, however qualified
to meet their age? Little now does it signify that you
love your children, or do even slave both body and
mind to get a footing of society and comfort for them
in this life—even beavers and bears will do as much as
that. In giving existence to your child you have set
him forth into perils that include his immortality, and

you have therefore no right to handle him neglectfully in this great concern. On the contrary, you are to accept his immortality, and in a seriously Christian sense, take it on yourself, as being in Christ's name responsible for it; responsible, that is, for making your house itself such an element of piety, love, faith, unworldly and beautiful living, that your children shall grow up in it, as in the nurture of the Lord. Take no credit to yourselves for any thing which falls short of this. You may be very tender in what falls short, but it is no Christian tenderness. You can not live in a worldly house, you can not make yourself a family drudge to serve a mere family ambition, can not piously hope that God will somehow convert your children after they have got by you and become adults, without being justly chargeable with giving their souls a mere nurture of the sands, in which the genuine Christian grace has no part whatever. And be not surprised if these children when they meet you before the Judge of your and their life, have a more severe witness to give against you than if you had merely neglected their bodies.

Probably enough there may be some of you that, without being Christians yourselves, are yet careful to teach your children all the saving truths of religion, and who thus may take it as undue severity to be charged with only giving your children this unnatural, ostrich nurture of which I have spoken. But how poor a teacher of Christ is any one who is not in the light of Christ, and does not know the inward power of his truth, as a gospel of life to the soul. You

press your child, in this manner, with duties you
do not practice, and promises you do not embrace;
and if you do not succeed, it only means that you can
not impose on him to that high extent. A mother
teach by words only? No! but more, a great deal
more by the atmosphere of love and patience she
breathes. Besides, how easy is it for her to make every
thing she teaches legal and repulsive, just because
she has no liberty or joy in it herself. What is wanted
therefore is not merely to give a child the law, telling
him this is duty, this is right, this God requires, this he
will punish, but a much greater want is to have the
spirit of all duty lived and breathed around him; to
see, and feel, and breathe, himself, the living atmosphere of grace. Therefore it is vain, let all parents so
understand, to imagine that you can really fulfill the
true fatherhood and motherhood, unless you are true
Christians yourselves. I am sorry to discourage you
in any good attempts. Rightly taken, what I say will
not discourage you, but will only prompt you by all
that is dearest to you on earth, to become truly qualified for your office. By these dear pledges God has
given you, to call you to himself, I beseech you turn
yourselves to the true life of religion. Have it first in
yourselves, then teach it as you live it; teach it by
living it; for you can do it in no other manner. Be
Christians yourselves, and then it will not be difficult
for you to do your true duties to your children. Until
then it is really impossible.

I have only to add in the conclusion of this subject—
just what is made plain by it—that there is really no
great wonder, in the fact often spoken of as a subject
of wonder, that Christian parents are so frequently
disappointed in their children. Why is it that such
correct and apparently Christian people see their children grow up unaffected by religion, or even hostile to
its sacred claims, falling possibly into a character of
vice and complete moral abandonment? The answer
is, alas! too easy. I will not say that, in every case,
the result accuses them of crime; it may be the effect
sometimes of their mistaken, or faulty conceptions of
parental duty. But no one, it seems to me, can once
distinguish these bad faults of nurture, and note the
very wide prevalence they have in the Christian homes,
without even expecting worse and more fatal results
of mischief than actually appear. Sometimes it seems
to be imagined that nothing but some dark hindrance
of divine sovereignty can account for such results.
The less we have to say in that strain the wiser we
shall be, and as much less irreverent to God. No,
there is reason enough for all such miscarriages without
charging them to God. I could not express myself as
the truth requires, my brethren, if I did not say, that
when I observe the wide-spread delusions of nominally Christian parents, their false aims, their worldly
pretexts, their habitual separation from any living faith
in God, in the ends, plans, practices, and spirit of their
administration, I rather wonder that results a great
deal worse do not appear. It would even be a fit

subject of wonder, if children trained in this manner, should not turn out badly. If indeed they are so much as converted afterwards, saying nothing of their growing up in a sanctified character, it is well—more than could be rightly expected.

No, my friends, these mistaken modes of nurture ought not to make Christians; they must even falsify their own nature to do it. Let us be just to God, and lay our griefs no longer to his charge. If we can not come into his way in the training of our families, let us not complain that we do not succeed in ways of our own. After all, there is no cheap way of making Christians of our children. Nothing but to practically live for it makes it sure. To be Christians ourselves—ah! there is the difficulty. How can an unchristian, or only non-christian spirit reigning in the house, quicken the spirit of life and holiness in the hearts subjected to its sway? Even if our false modes of nurture are mistakes, who can expect that mistakes will be as good as verities? O, thou, blessed Son of God, advocate and friend of the little ones, rid us of our falsities, and set us in thy own true spirit, that we may fitly discharge these most sacred and tenderest duties!

IV

THE ORGANIC UNITY OF THE FAMILY

" The children gather wood, and the fathers kindle the fire, and the women knead dough, to make cakes to the queen of heaven, and to pour out drink offerings unto other gods, that they may provoke me to anger." —*Jeremiah* vii. 18.

In this lively picture, you have the illustration of a great and momentous truth—*the Organic Unity of the Family.* If it be an idolatrous family, worshipers of the moon, for example, such is the organic relation of the members, that they are all involved together, and the idol worship is the common act of the house. The children gather wood, the fathers kindle the fire, the women prepare the cakes for an offering, and the queen of heaven receives it, as one that is the joint product of the whole family. The worship is family worship; the god of one is the god of all; the spirit of one, the spirit of all.

And so it is with all family transactions and feelings. They implicate ordinarily the whole circle of the house, young and old, male and female, fathers and mothers, sons and daughters. Acting thus together, they take a common character, accept the same delusions, practice the same sins, and ought, I believe, to be sanctified by a common grace.

This most serious truth is one that is exceedingly

remote from the present age, and from no part of the
Christian world more remote than from us. All our
modern notions and speculations have taken a bent
toward individualism. In the state, we have been
engaged to bring out the civil rights of the individual,
asserting his proper liberties as a person, and vindica-
ting his conscience, as a subject of God, from the
constraints of force. In matters of religion, we have
burst the bonds of church authority, and erected the individual mind into a tribunal of judgment within itself;
we have asserted free will as the ground of all proper
responsibility, and framed our theories of religion so as
to justify the incommunicable nature of persons as
distinct units. While thus engaged, we have well nigh
lost, as was to be expected, the idea of organic powers
and relations. The state, the church, the family, have
ceased to be regarded as such, according to their proper
idea, and become mere collections of units. A national
life, a church life, a family life, is no longer conceived,
or perhaps conceivable, by many. Instead of being
wrought in together and penetrated, to some extent, by
historic laws and forces common to all the members,
we only seem to lie as seeds piled together, without
any terms of connection, save the accident of proximity,
or the fact that we all belong to the heap. And thus
the three great forms of organic existence, which God
has appointed for the race, are in fact lost out of mental
recognition. The conception is so far gone that, when
the fact of such an organic relation is asserted, our
enlightened public will stare at the strange conceit,

and wonder what can be meant by a paradox so absurd.

My design, at the present time, is to restore, if possible, the conception of one of these organic forms, viz: the family. For though we have gained immense advantages, in a civil, ecclesiastical, and religious point of view, by our modern development of individualism, we have yet run ourselves into many hurtful misapprehensions on all these subjects, which, if they are not rectified, will assuredly bring disastrous consequences. And no where consequences more disastrous than in the family, where they are already apparent, though not fully matured; for the very change of view, by which we have cleared individual responsibility, in our discussions of free will, original sin, and kindred subjects, has operated, in another direction, to diminish responsibility, where most especially it needs to be felt; that is, in Christian families.

What then do we mean by the organic unity of the family? It will be understood, of course, that we do not speak of a physical or vascular connection; for, after birth, there is no such connection existing, any more than there is between persons of different families. In so far, however, as a connection of parentage, or derivation has affected the character, that fact must be included, though it can not be regarded as a chief element in the unity asserted. Perhaps I shall be understood with the greatest facility, if I say that the family is such a body, that a power over character is exerted therein *which can not properly be called influence.* We commonly use the term *influence* to denote a persuasive power, or a governmental power, exerted purposely, and with a conscious design to effect some result in the subject. In maintaining the organic unity of the family, I mean to assert, that a power is exerted by parents over children, not only when they teach, encourage, persuade, and govern, but without any purposed control whatever. The bond is so intimate that they do it unconsciously and undesignedly—they must do it. Their character, feelings, spirit, and principles, must propagate themselves, whether they will or not. However, as influence, in the sense just given, can not be *received* by childhood prior to the age of reason and deliberative choice, the control of parents, purposely exerted, must be regarded, during that early period, as an absolute force, not as influence. All such acts of control therefore must, in metaphysical propriety, and as far as the child is concerned, be classed under the general denomination of *organic* causes. And thus whatever power over character is exerted in families one side of consent, in the children, and even before they have come to the age of rational choice, must be taken as organic power, in the same way as if the effect accrued under the law of simple contagion. So too when the child performs acts of will, under parental direction, that involve results of character, without knowing or considering that they do, these must be classed in the same manner.

In general, then, we find the organic unity of the

family, in every exertion of power over character, which is not exerted and received as influence ; that is, with a *design* to address the choice on one side, and *a sense* of responsible choice on the other. Or, to use language more popular, we conceive the manners, personal views, prejudices, practical motives, and spirit of the house, as an atmosphere which passes into all and pervades all, as naturally as the air they breathe. This, however, not in any such absolute or complete sense as to leave no room for individual distinctions. Sometimes the two parents will have a very different spirit themselves, though the grace of God is pledged to make the better, if it be truly right, and hindered by no gross inconsistencies, victorious. Sometimes the child, passing into the sphere of other causes, as in the school, the church, neighboring families, or general society, will emerge and take a character partially distinct—partially, I say ; never wholly. The odor of the house will always be in his garments, and the internal difficulties with which he has to struggle, will spring of the family seeds planted in his nature.

Having carefully stated thus what I mean by the organic unity of the family, I next proceed to inquire whether any such unity exists ? And here it is worth noticing—

1. That there is nothing in this view which conflicts with the proper individuality of persons and their separate responsibility. We have gained immense advantages, in modern times, as regards society, govern-

ment, and character, by liberating and exalting the individual man. Far be it from me to underrate these advantages, or to bring them into jeopardy. But a child manifestly can not be a proper individual, before he is one. Nothing can be gained by assuming that he is; and, if it is not true, much is sure to be lost. Besides, we are never, at any age, so completely individual as to be clear of organic connections that affect our character. To a certain extent and for certain purposes, we are individuals, acting each from his own will. Then to a certain extent and for certain other purposes, we are parts or members of a common body, as truly as the limbs of a tree. We have an open side in our nature, where a common feeling enters, where we adhere, and through which we are actuated by a common will. There we are many—here we are one.

It is remarkable too how often, without knowing it, and, as it were instinctively, we assume the fact, and act upon it. We do it, for example, as between nations, where it is not so much the moral life as the national that constructs the supposed unity. One nation, for instance, has injured or oppressed another— sought to crush, or actually crushed another by invasion. A century or more afterwards, the wrong is remembered, and the injured nation takes the field, still burning for redress. The history of Carthage and Rome gives us an example. But, suppose it had been said—"This is very absurd in you Carthaginians. The Romans, who did you the injury, are all dead, and those who now bear the name are their children's children. They have done you no injury any more than the people of Britain or India. Neither is it the walls, or streets, or temples of Rome that have injured you. The Roman territory is mere land, and this has not injured you. Why then go to war with the Romans? How absurd to think of redressing your old injuries by a war with men who have done you no harm!" Now, it was by just this kind of sophistry that Mr. Jefferson proved that a public debt is obligatory for only one generation, and possibly the Carthaginians might have been speculatively stumbled by such reasonings. Still, they could not have been quite satisfied, I think, of their validity. Against all speculation, they would still have felt that the proposed war was somehow reconcilable with reason. The question is not whether, on Christian principles, they were right, but whether, on natural principles, they were absurd. This probably no reader of the history has ever felt. For, whether it squares with our speculative notions or not, we do all tacitly assume the organic unity of nations. The past we behold, living in the present, and all together we regard as one, inhabited by the common life. How much more true is this (though in a different way) in families, where the common life is so nearly absolute over the members; where they are all inclosed within the four walls of their dwellings, partakers in a common blood, in common interests, wants, feelings, and principles.

2. We discover the organic unity of families, in the

fact that one generation is the natural offspring of another. And so much is there in this, that the children
almost always betray their origin in their looks and
features. The stamp of a common nature is on them,
revealed in the stature, complexion, gait, form, and
dispositions. Sometimes we seem to see remarkable
exceptions. But, in such cases, we should commonly
find, if we could bring up to view the ancestors of remo-
ter generations, that the family bond is still perpetuated,
only by a wider reach of connection. There are said to
be two maiden sisters, the last of a distinguished family,
now living in England, who, having no resemblance to
any near ancestor, have yet a very striking resemblance to the portrait, still hanging in the family
mansion, of an ancestor seven generations back. Indeed, I have myself distinguished, by their looks, the
relationship of two persons, connected by a common
derivation eight generations back, and who more closely
resembled each other in their persons, than either his
nearest kindred. So that, in cases where there seems to
be no transmission of resemblances, there is yet a probable transmission, only one that is covert and more comprehensive. Now, strong external resemblances may
coexist with marked external differences, and therefore
do not prove a coincidence of character. And yet it
can not be denied that, as far as they go, they argue a
transmission of capacities and dispositions, which enter
into character, as remote causes or occasions. Nor
does it make any difference, as regards the matter in
question, whether souls or spiritual natures come into

being through propagation, or not.   If they are created,
as some fancy, by the immediate inbreathing of God,
still they are measured by the house they are to live in,
and the outward man is, in all cases, a fit organ for the
person within.   The dispositions, tempers, capacities—
the natural, and, to a great extent, the moral character,
have the outward frame, as a fit organ of use and expression.   It will even be observed too that, in cases
where there is a remarkable change of character, it will
be signified, in due time, by a change of manner, aspect,
and action.

Besides, it is well understood that qualities received
by training, and *not* in themselves natural, do also pass
by transmission.   It is said, for example, that the dog
used in hunting was originally trained by great care
and effort, and that now almost no training is necessary;
for the artificial quality has become, to a great extent,
natural in the stock.   We have also a most ominous
example of this fact in the human species.   I speak of
the Jewish race.   The singular devotion of this race to
money and traffic is even a proverb.   But their ancestors, of the ancient times, were not thus distinguished.
They were a simple, agricultural people, remarkable
for nothing but their religious opinions, and, in a late
period of the commonwealth, for their fanatical heroism
and obstinacy.   Whence the change?   History gives
the mournful answer, showing them to view, for long
ages, as a hated and down-trodden people, allowed no
rights in the soil, shut up within some narrow and foul
precinct in the cities, compelled to subsist by some

meager traffic, denied every possession but money, and suffered to keep in security not even that, save as they could hide it in secret places, and cloak the suspicion of wealth under a sordid exterior. They have thus been educated to be misers by the extortions and the hatred of Christendom; till finally an artificial nature, so to speak, has been formed in the race, and we take it even as the instinct of a Jew, to get money by small traffic and sharp bargains. So there is little room to doubt that every sort of character and employment passes an effect and works some predisposition in those who come after.

Could we enter into the mental habits of those children, who are spoken of in my text, and trace out all the threads of their inward character and disposition, we should doubtless find some color of idolatry in the fiber of their very being. They are not such as they would be, if their parents, of this and remote generations, had been worshipers of the true God. Their talents, dispositions, propensities are different. The idol god is in their faces and their bones, and his stamp is on their spirit. Not in such a sense that the sin of idolatry is in them—that is inconceivable; for no proper sin can pass by transmission—but that they have a vicious, or prejudicial infection from it, a damage accruing from their historical connection and that of their progenitors with it.

Nor, with these familiar laws of physiology before us, is it reasonable to doubt that, where there is a long line of godly fathers and mothers, kept up in regular succession for many generations, a religious temperament may at length be produced, that is more in the power of conscience, less wayward as regards principles of integrity, and more pliant to the Christian motives. More could be said with confidence, if the godly character were less ambiguous and more thoroughly sanctified.

3. We shall find that there is a law of connection, after birth, under which power over character is exerted, without any design to do it. For a considerable time after birth, the child has no capacity of will and choice developed, and therefore is not a subject of influence, in the common sense of that term. He is not as yet a complete individual; he has only powers and capacities that prepare him to be, when they are unfolded. They are in him only as wings and a capacity to fly are in the egg. Meantime, he is open to *impressions* from every thing he sees. His character is forming, under a principle, not of choice, but of nurture. The spirit of the house is breathed into his nature, day by day. The anger and gentleness, the fretfulness and patience—the appetites, passions, and manners—all the variant moods of feeling exhibited round him, pass into him as impressions, and become seeds of character in him; not because the parents will, but because it must be so, whether they will or not. They propagate their own evil in the child, not by design, but under a law of moral infection. Before the children begin to gather wood for the sacrifice, the spirit of the idol and his faith has been communicated. The airs and feelings

and conduct of idolatry have filled their nature with impressions, which are back of all choice and memory. Go out to them then, as they are gathering faggots for the idol sacrifice, ask them what questions they have had about the service of the god? what doubts? whether any unsatisfied debate or perplexing struggle has visited their minds? and you will probably awaken their first thoughts on the subject by the inquiry itself. All because they have grown up in the idol worship, from a point back of memory. They received it through their impressions, before they were able to receive it from choice. And so it is with all the moral transactions of the house. The spirit of the house is in the members by nurture, not by teaching, not by any attempt to communicate the same, but because it is the air the children breathe.

Now, it is in the twofold manner set forth, under this and the previous head of my discourse, that our race have fallen, as a race, into moral corruption and apostasy. In these two methods, the race have been subjected, as an organic unity, to evil; so that when they come to the age of proper individuality, the damage received has prepared them to set forth, on a course of blamable and guilty transgression. The question of original or imputed sin has been much debated in modern times, and the effort has been to vindicate the personal responsibility of each individual, as a moral agent. Nor is any thing more clear, on first principles, than that no man is responsible for any sin but his own. The sin of no person can be transmitted as a sin, or charged to the account of another. But it does not therefore follow, that there are no moral connections between individuals, by which one becomes a corrupter of others. If we are units, so also are we a race, and the race is one—one family, one organic whole; such that the fall of the head involves the fall of all the members. Under the old doctrines of original sin, federal headship, and the like, cast away by many, ridiculed by not a few, there yet lies a great and momentous truth, announced by reason as clearly as by Scripture—that in Adam all die; that by one man's disobedience many were made sinners; that death hath passed upon all men, for that all have sinned. Not that this original scheme of unity is any disadvantage. I firmly believe and think I could show the contrary even. Enough that so the Scriptures speak, and that so we see, by inspection itself. There can be no greater credulity, than for any man to expect that a sinful and death-struck being, one who has fallen out of the harmony of his mold by sin, should yet communicate no trace of evil from himself, no diseased or damaged quality, no moral discolor, to the generations that derive their existence from him. To make that possible, every law of physiology must be adjourned, and, what is more, all that we see with our eyes, in the eventful era of impressions, must be denied.

I am well aware that those who have advocated, in former times, the church dogma of original sin, as well as those who adhere to it now, speak only of a taint derived by natural or physical propagation, and do not include the taint derived afterwards, under the law of family infection. It certainly can be no heresy to include the latter; and, since it is manifest that both fall within the same general category of organic connection, it is equally manifest that both ought to be included, and, in all systematic reasonings, must be. If, during the age of impressions in the child, and previous to the development of will, a power is exerted over character—exerted necessarily, both as regards the sinful parent and the child, and that as truly as if it fell within the laws of propagation itself—it can not be right to attribute the moral taint wholly, or even principally, to propagation. Until the child comes to his will, we must regard him still as held within the matrix of the parental life; and then, when he is ripe for responsible choice, as born for action—a proper and complete person. Taking this comprehensive view of the organic unity of successive generations of men, the truth we assert of human depravation is not a half-truth exaggerated, (which many will not regard as any truth at all,) but it is a broad, well-authenticated doctrine, which no intelligent observer of facts and principles can deny. It shows the past descending on the present, the present on the future, by an inevitable law, and yet gives every parent the hope of mitigating the sad legacy of mischief he entails upon his children, by whatever improvements of character and conduct he is able to make—a hope which Christian promise so far clears to his view, as even to allow him the presumption that his child may be set forth into responsible action, as a Christian person.

In offering these thoughts, it will be seen that I have not digressed from my subject, but have extended the proof of my doctrine rather, discovering within its scope, the fall of man itself. As a farther proof of the organic unity of the family, I allege—

4. The fact that, in all organic bodies known to us— states, churches, sects, armies—there is a common spirit, by which they are pervaded and distinguished from each other. And we use this word *spirit*, in such cases, to denote a power interfused, a comprehensive will actuating the members, regarding also the common body itself, as a larger and more inclusive individual. How different, for example, is the spirit of France from the spirit of England? the spirit of both from that of the United States? and that from the spirit of the Spartan or Athenian republic? This national spirit, too, is, as it were, a common power in each, by which the subordinate individual members are assimilated, and made to have a kind of organic character. And so much is there in this, that an Englishman can not make to himself a French character, or any one of us an English character. We can not act the character one of another; for so distant are the feelings, prejudices, and temperaments of each, that they can not even be accurately conceived and reproduced, unless we are actually enveloped in them as an atmosphere.

In the same manner, there is a peculiar spirit in every church. Whether you take the larger divisions, the

Jewish, the Greek, the Roman, the Episcopal, the Presbyterian, the Baptist, the Congregational, or descend to the particular churches of a given city, you will find something characteristic in each—a common power, which gives a common stamp to the members peculiar to themselves. Or, if you visit a Quaker settlement, where a few men and women are gathered into a kind of church family, you will discover that the members are pervaded, all, by a peculiar spirit, as distinct from the world around them as if they were a new discovered people. And these Quaker settlements may be taken as a kind of intermediate link between the church-state and the family.

Passing then to families, you are not surprised to discover the same thing. This is specially evident where the family is isolated, and does not mingle extensively with the world. You can scarcely open the door, and take a seat in their house, least of all can you go to their table, or spend a night in their hospitality, without being impressed by the fact. And this family spirit will sometimes be exceedingly opposite to the spirit of goodness. Here it is money, money, written on every face; here it is good living; here show; here scandal and detraction. Sometimes the sense of religion and of spiritual things will seem to be nearly lost, or obliterated. Sometimes a positive hatred of God and all good men and principles will constitute the staple of family feeling. Sometimes a dull and sullen contempt of such things will hold the place of open animosity.

It is very true that the family spirit does not always

perfectly master and assimilate all the members. You will find a Christian son or daughter, here and there, in spite of the ruling spirit of the house. This, however, because families are to some extent intermingled; in which it comes to pass that children often fall under the power of another spirit, that masters the spirit reigning at home. The children go into other families, where they are visited by other feelings. They go into the church of God, where the church spirit breathes another atmosphere. In the school, they are penetrated by the school spirit. In the shop, or in the transactions of trade, the same is true. Were it not for this, the family spirit might almost uniformly rule the character of the members. Who ever expects that an idolatrous religion, in the house, will not uniformly produce idolaters? So the Mohammedan spirit makes only Mohammedans. In like manner, a thievish house perpetuates a race of thieves. Consider also the ductility and the perfect passivity of childhood. Early childhood resists nothing. What is given it receives, making no selection. To expect therefore that a child will form to himself a spirit opposite to the spirit of the family, without once feeling the power of a counteractive spirit, would be credulous in the highest degree. Doubtless he has a conscience, which is the law of God, in his breast, and he has a will free to choose what his conscience requires. But his passions are unfolded before his discretion, his prejudices bent before he assumes the function of self-government. He breathes the atmosphere of the house. He sees the world through his

parents' eyes. Their objects become his. Their life
and spirit mold him. If they are carnal, coarse, passionate, profane, sensual, devilish, his little plastic
nature takes the poison of course. Their very motions,
manners, and voices, will be distinguishable in him.
He lives and moves and has his being in them.

I do not say, of course, that he will exactly resemble
them in character. Were he to receive a contagious
disease, he would, doubtless, be differently handled
under it, from the person who gave the infection. I
only say, that the moral disease of the family he assuredly will take, and that, probably, without even a question, or a cautious feeling started. If some other spirit,
from other families, or the church, or the world, do not
reach him, the organic spirit of the house will infallibly
shape and subordinate his character.

5. We are led to the same conclusions, by considering what may be called the organic *working* of a family.
The child begins, at length, to develop his character, in
and through his voluntary power. But he is still under
the authority of the parent, and has only a partial control of himself, in the development of which, he is gradually approaching a complete personality. Now, there
is a perpetual working in the family, by which the wills,
both of the parents and the children, are held in exercise, and which, without any design to affect character
on one side or conscious consent on the other, is yet
fashioning results of a moral quality, as it were by the
joint industry of the house. And these results are to
be taken, according to our definition, as included in the

organic unity of the family. I except, of course, all the voluntary actings that are designed to influence the child, and are yielded to by him, as consciously right or wrong.

The truth here brought to view is graphically set forth in my text. Whatever working there is in the house, all work together. If the fathers kindle the fire, and the women knead the cakes, the children will gather the wood, and the idol worship will set the whole circle of the house in action. The child being under the law of the parents, they will keep him at work to execute their plans, or their sins, as the case may be; and, as they will seldom think of what they do, or require, so he will seldom have any scruple concerning it. The property gained belongs to the family. They have a common interest, and every prejudice or animosity felt by the parents, the children are sure to feel even more intensely. They are all locked together, in one cause—in common cares, hopes, offices, and duties; for their honor and dishonor, their sustenance, their ambition, all their objects are common. So they are trained of necessity to a kind of general working, or coöperation, and, like stones, rolled together in some brook or eddy, they wear each other into common shapes. If the family subsist by plunder, then the infant is swaddled as a thief, the child wears a thief's garments, and feeds the growth of his body on stolen meat; and, in due time, he will have the trade upon him, without ever knowing that he has taken it up, or when he took it up. If the father is intemperate, the children must go on errands to procure his supplies, lose the shame that might be their safety, be immersed in the fumes of liquor in going and coming, and why not rewarded by an occasional taste of what is so essential to the enjoyment of life? If the family subsist in idleness and beggary, then the children will be trained to lie skillfully, and maintain their false pretences with a plausible effrontery—all this, you will observe, not as a sin, but as a trade.

Nor does what I am saying hold, only in cases of extreme viciousness and depravity. Whatever fire the fathers kindle, the children are always found gathering the wood—always helping as accessaries and apprentices. If the father reads a newspaper, or a sporting gazette, on Sunday, the family must help him find it. If he writes a letter of business on Sunday, he will send his child to the office with the letter. If the mother is a scandal-monger, she will make her children spies and eaves-droppers. If she directs her servant to say, at the door, that she is not at home, she will sometimes be overheard by her child. If she is ambitious that her children should excel in the display of finery and fashion, they must wear the show and grow up in the spirit of it. If her house is a den of disorder and filth, they must be at home in it. Fretfulness and ill-temper in the parents are provocations, and therefore somewhat more efficacious than commandments, to the same. The proper result will be a congenial assemblage, in the house, of petulence and ill-nature. The niggardly parsimony that quarrels with a child, when asking for a book needful for his proficiency at school, is teaching him that money is worth more than knowledge. If the parents are late risers, the children must not disturb the house, but stay quiet and take a lesson that is not to assist their energy and promptness in the future business of life. If they go to church only half of the day, they will not send their children the other half. If they never read the Bible, they will never teach it. If they laugh at religion, they will put a face upon it, which will make their children justify the contempt they express. This enumeration might be indefinitely extended. Enough that we see, in the working of the house, how all the members work together. The children fall into their places naturally, as it were, and unconsciously, to do and to suffer exactly what the general scheme of the house requires. Without any design to that effect, all the actings of business, pleasure, and sin, propagate themselves throughout the circle, as the weights of a clock maintain the workings of the wheels. Where there is no effort to teach wrong, or thought of it, the house is yet a school of wrong, and the life of the house is only a practical drill in evil.

Having sufficiently established, as I think, by these illustrations, the organic unity of families, it remains to add some practical thoughts of a more specific nature. And—

1. It becomes a question of great moment, as connected with the doctrine established, whether it is the

design of the Christian scheme to take possession of the organic laws of the family, and wield them as instruments, in any sense, of a regenerative purpose? And here we are met by the broad principle, that Christianity endeavors to make every object, favor, and relation, an instrument of righteousness, according to its original design. What intelligent person ever supposed that the original constitution, by which one generation derives its existence and receives the bent of its character from another, was designed of God to be the vehicle only of depravity? It might as well be supposed that men themselves were made to be containers of depravity. The only supposition that honors God is, that the organic unity, of which I speak, was ordained originally for the nurture of holy virtue in the beginning of each soul's history; and that Christianity, or redemption, must of necessity take possession of the abused vehicle, and sanctify it for its own merciful uses. That an engine of so great power should be passed by, when every other law and object in the universe is appropriated and wielded as an instrument of grace, and that in a movement for the redemption of the race, is inconceivable. The conclusion thus reached does not carry us, indeed, to the certain inference that the organic unity of the family will avail to set forth every child of Christian parents, in a Christian life. But if we consider the tremendous power it has, as an instrument of evil, how far short of such an opinion does it leave us, when computing the reach of its power as an instrument of grace?

Passing next to the Scriptures, we find such reasonings justified, as explicitly as we can desire. I am not disposed to press the language of Scripture, which is popular, to extreme conclusions. But I observe that Christ is called a second Adam and a last Adam: language, to say the least, that suits the idea of a proposed union with the race, under its organic laws—as if, entering into the Christian family, his design were to fill it with a family spirit, which shall controvert and master the old evil spirit. The declaration corresponds, that, as by one man's disobedience many were made sinners, so by the obedience of one shall many be made righteous—language that measures the grace by the mischief, and shows it flowing in a parallel, but fuller stream. It may not be easy to settle, beyond dispute, the relation of the old covenant to the new; but there can be no question that the church, under Abraham, was measured, in some sense, by the organic unity of the family of Abraham. The covenant was a family covenant, in which God engaged to be the God of the seed, as of the father. And the seal of the covenant was a seal of *faith*, applied to the whole house, as if the continuity of faith were somehow to be, or somehow might be maintained, in a line that is parallel with the continuity of sin, in the family. Nor was the result to depend on mere natural generation, however sanctified, but on the organic causes also, that are involved in family nurture, after birth. For we are expressly informed, (Gen. xviii. 19,) that God rested his covenant, or engagement, on the conduct of Abraham—"for I know him,

that he will command his children and his household
after him, and they shall keep the way of the Lord, to
do justice and judgment, that the Lord may bring upon
Abraham that which he hath spoken of him." And thus
we see that the old church, beyond any possible question, was to have its grounds of perpetuity, in and by the
same terms of organic unity, which sin has made the
vehicle of depravity. Descending then to the New Testament, Jesus the world's Redeemer is declared to have
suffered, "that the blessing of Abraham might come on
the Gentiles," and the Gentiles are said to be "graffed in."
The new "seed," viz., "Christ," are said to be "the seed
of Abraham," and "heirs of the promise" made to him.
The old rite of proselyte baptism, which made the families receiving it Jewish citizens and children of Abraham, was applied over directly to the Christian uses, and
the rite went by "households;" even as the New Testament promise also was—"to you and to your children."
Even the old Jewish law, that one Jewish parent made a
Jewish child, is brought into the church, and one believing
parent "sanctifies" the child. In all of which, it seems
to be clearly held that grace shall travel by the same
conveyance with sin; that the organic unity, which I
have spoken of chiefly as an instrument of corruption,
is to be occupied and sanctified by Christ, and become
an instrument also of mercy and life. And thence it
follows that the seal of faith, applied to households, is
to be no absurdity; for it is the privilege and duty of
every Christian parent that his children shall come forth
into responsible action, as a regenerated stock. The or-

ganic unity is to be a power of life. God engages, on his part, that it may be, and calls the Christian parent to promise, on his part, that it shall be. Thus the church has a constitutive element from the family in it still, as it had in the days of Abraham. The church life—that is, the Holy Spirit—collects families into a common organism, and then, by sanctifying the laws of organic unity in families, extends its quickening power to the generation following, so as to include the future, and make it one with the past. And so the church, in all ages, becomes a body under Christ the head, as the race is a body under Adam the head—a living body, quickened by him who hath life in himself, fitly joined together and compacted by that which every joint supplieth.

2. The theological importance of our doctrine of organic unity, when brought up to this point, is exhibited in many ways, and especially in the fact that it gives the only true solution of the Christian church and of baptism as related to membership. I hardly dare attempt to speak of the "sacramental grace," supposed to attend the rite of baptism, under the priestly forms of Christianity; for I have never been able to give any consistent and dignified meaning to the language, in which it is set forth. That there is a grace attendant, falling on all the parties concerned, is quite evident, if they are doing their duty; for no person, whether laic or priest, can do, or intend what is right, without some spiritual benefit. But the child is said to be "regenerate, spiritually united to Christ, a new creature in Christ

Jesus," under the official grace of baptism. Then this language, so full of import, is defined, after all, to mean only that the child is in the church, where the grace of God surrounds him—translated (not internally, but externally) from the sphere of nature into a new sphere, where all the aids of grace, available for his salvation, are furnished. Sometimes it is added that his sins are remitted, though no man is likely to believe that he has any sins to remit; or, if the meaning be that the corrupted quality, physiologically inherent in his nature, is washed away, he will show in due time that it is not; and no one, in fact, believes that it is. Then if it be asked, whether the new sphere of grace will assuredly work a gracious character? "no," is the answer. "If the child is not faithful, or hinders the grace, he will lose it"—that is, he will not stay regenerate. And then as the child, in every case, is sure, in some bad sense, not to be faithful, he is equally sure to lose the grace, and be landed in a second state that is worse than the first. And thus it turns out, after all, as far as I can see, that the grace magnified in the beginning, by words of so high an import, is a thing of no value—it is nothing. It is, in fact, one of our most decided objections to this scheme of sacramental grace, (paradoxical as it may seem,) that, really and truly, there is not enough of import in it to save the meaning of the rite. The grace is words only, and an air of imposture is all that remains, after the words are explained. The rite is fertile only in maintaining a superstition. Practically speaking, it only exalts a prerogative. By a motion of his hand, the priest breaks in, to interrupt and displace all the laws of character in life—communicating an abrupt, ictic grace, as much wider of all dignity and reason, than any which the new light theology has asserted, as the regenerative power is more subject to a human dis pensation. A superstitious homage collects about his person. The child looks on him as one who opens heaven by a ceremony! The ungodly parent hurries to him, to get the regenerative grace for his dying child. The bereaved parent mourns inconsolably, and even curses himself, that he neglected to obtain the grace for his child, now departed. The priest, in the eye, displaces the memory of duty and godliness in the heart. A thousand superstitions, degrading to religion and painful to look upon, hang around this view of baptism. Not to produce them, the doctrine must yield up its own nature.

In all this, I speak constructively, as reasoning from the doctrine asserted, and as I am able to understand it. Constructive results are never more than partially verified by historic facts; for great truths, blended with the error, qualify and mitigate its effects.

Now the true conception is, that baptism is applied to the child, on the ground of its organic unity with the parents; imparting and pledging a grace to sanctify that unity, and make it good in the field of religion. By the supposition, however, the child still remains within the known laws of character in the house, to receive, under these, whatever good may reach him; not snatched away by an abrupt, fantastical, and therefore incredible grace. He is taken to be regenerate, not historically speaking, but presumptively, on the ground of his known connection with the parent character, and the divine or church life, which is the life of that character. Perhaps I shall be understood more easily, if I say that the child is *potentially* regenerate, being regarded as existing in connection with powers and causes that *contain* the fact, before time and separate from time. For when the fact appears historically, under the law of time, it is not more truly real, in a certain sense, than it was before. And then the grace conferred, being conferred by no casual act, but resting in the established laws of character, in the church and the house, is not lost by unfaithfulness, but remains and lingers still, though abused and weakened, to encourage new struggles.

Thus it will be seen that the doctrine of organic unity I have been asserting, proves its theologic value, as a ready solvent for the rather perplexing difficulties of this difficult subject. Only one difficulty remains, viz, that so few can believe the doctrine.

3. It is evident that the voluntary intention of parents, in regard to their children, is no measure, either of their merit or their sin. Few parents are so base, or so lost to natural affection, as really to intend the injury of their children. However irreligious, or immoral, they more commonly desire a worthy and correct character for their children, often even a Christian character. But, in the great and momentous truth now set forth, you perceive it is not what you intend for your children,

so much as what you are, that is to have its effect.
They are connected, by an organic unity, not with your
instructions, but with your life.   And your life is more
powerful than your instructions can be.   They might
be jealous of intended corruption, and withstand it;
but the spirit of the house, which is your spirit, the
whole working of the house, which is actuated by you,
is what no exercise of will, even if they had more of it
than they have, could well resist.   Therefore, what you
are, they will almost necessarily be; and then, as you
are responsible for what you are, you must also be responsible for the ruin brought on them.   And, if you
desired better things for them, as you probably say,
the more guilty are you that, knowing and desiring
better things, you thwarted your desires by your own
evil life.

So there are Christians who intend and do many things
for their children, and thus acquit themselves of all
blame in regard to their character.   Here, alas! is the
perpetual error of Christian parents, so called, that they
endeavor to make up, by direct efforts, for the mischiefs of a loose and neglectful life.   They convince
themselves that teaching, lecturing, watch, discipline,
things done with a purpose, are the sum of duty.   As
if mere affectations and will-works could cheat the laws
of life and character ordained by God!   Your character
is a stream, a river, flowing down upon your children,
hour by hour.   What you do here and there to carry
an opposing influence is, at best, only a ripple that you
make on the surface of the stream.   It reveals the

sweep of the current; nothing more. If you expect
your children to go with the ripple, instead of the
stream, you will be disappointed. I beseech you then,
as you love your children, to admit other and worthier
thoughts, thoughts more safe for them and certainly for
you. Understand that it is the family spirit, the organic life of the house, the silent power of a domestic
godliness, working, as it does, unconsciously and with
sovereign effect—this it is which forms your children to God. And, if this be wanting, all that you
may do beside, will be as likely to annoy and harden as
to bless.

4. It seems to be a proper inference from the doctrine
I have exhibited, that Christian parents ought to speak
freely to their children, at times, of their own faults and
infirmities. If they are faithful, if they live as Christians, if the spirit of Christ bears rule in the house, they
will yet have faults, and they ought to make no secret
of the fact. The impression should be made, that they
themselves are struggling with infirmities; that they are
humbled under a sense of these infirmities; that there
is much in them for God to pardon, much for their
children to overlook, or even to forgive; and that God
alone can assist them to lead themselves and their family
up to a better world. Instead of lecturing their children, always, on their peccadilloes and sins, it would be.
better, sometimes, to give a lecture on their own. This,
if rightly done, would attract the friendly sympathy of
their children, guard them against the injurious impressions they make when they trip themselves, and unite

the whole family in a common struggle heavenward. There is no other way to correct the mixture of evil you will blend with the family spirit, but to deplore it, and make it an acknowledged truth, that you, too, are only a child in goodness. But if you take a throne of papal infallibility in your family, and endeavor to fight out, with the rod, what you fail in by your misconduct, you may make your children fear you and hate you, but you will not win them to Christ. Alas! there are too many Christian families that are only little popedoms. The rule itself is tyranny—infallibility assumed, then maintained, by the holy inquisition of terror and penal chastisement! God will not smile on such a kind of discipline.

5. It is evident what rule should regulate the society and external intercourse of children. It is a very great mercy, as I have said, that the children of a bad or irreligious family are sometimes permitted to be inmates elsewhere; to go into virtuous and Christian families, where a better spirit reigns. There they see, perhaps, the genuine demonstrations of order, of purity, and of good affections; they hear the voice of prayer, they come where the spirit of heaven breathes. It is a new world, and they are filled with new impressions. So, if a child may go to a school where order, right principle, virtuous manners, and the love of knowledge reign, and find a respite there from the shiftlessness, vice, and brutality at home, how great is the privilege! In this view, a good school is almost the only mercy that can be extended to the hapless sons and daughters

of vice. Their good—most dismal thought!—is to be delivered from their home; to escape the spirit of hell that encompasses their helpless age, and feel, though it be but a few hours a day, the power of another spirit!

But I was speaking of the rule to be observed in the society of children. Let every Christian beware how he makes his children inmates in an irreligious family. It will do, sometimes, to allow the children of an irreligious family to be inmates, temporarily, in your own. You may do it for their advantage; and if you can enlist the hearts of your children in the merciful intentions you cherish, it may even be a good exercise for them. But it is a very different thing to place your children within the atmosphere of another house. Send them not where the spirit of evil reigns. Understand how plastic their nature is, how easily it receives the contagion of another spirit. You yourselves may have intercourse with ungodly persons; it may be your duty to seek it for their benefit; but you may well be cautious how far you subject your children, especially in early years, to the intercourse of irreligious families.

And what shall I say to parents, who are themselves irreligious? Perhaps you make it your boast that you give your children their liberty; that you mean to allow them to be just as religious as they please. And is that enough, do you think, to discharge your duties to them? Is it enough to breathe the spirit of evil and sin into them and around them every hour, to give them no Christian counsel, to train them up in a prayerless house, drill them into conformity with all your worldly ways, and then say that you allow them full liberty to be Christians? Having them under your law, determining yourselves that organic spirit, which is to be the element, the very breath of their moral existence, will you then boast that you mean to allow them to be as virtuous as they please? Ah, if there be any argument, which might compel you to be Christians yourselves, it is these arguments of affection that God has given you. But if you will not be Christians yourselves, then, at least, show your children some degree of mercy, by delivering them, as much as possible, from yourselves! Send them, as often as you may, where a better spirit reigns. Make them inmates with Christian families, as you have opportunity. Let them go where they will hear a prayer and see a Christian Sabbath. Send them, or take them with you, to the church of God, and the Sabbath-school. Give them a respite often from the family spirit and the organic law of the house. If you yourselves will not fashion them for the skies, let others, more faithful than you, and more merciful, do it for you.

V

INFANT BAPTISM, HOW DEVELOPED

"For the promise is unto you and to your children, and to all that are afar off, even as many as the Lord our God shall call."—*Acts*, ii. 39.

IT is a matter of wonder, with many professed disciples of Jesus in our time, that if the baptism of children and their qualified introduction into the church is any genuine part of the Christian economy, there is so little authority for it, by express mention in the New Testament writings. And yet, over opposite to this, it is quite as fair a subject of wonder that in Peter's first sermon, on the day of Pentecost, when addressing only the adult sinners of the assembly, in terms appropriate to their age, he should yet have given out, as it were unconsciously, a declaration that can signify nothing but the engagement of Christ, in his new and more spiritual economy, to identify children with their parents, even as they had been identified in the coarser provisions of the Old. "To you and to your children," says the apostle, and here, covertly as it were to himself, are hid infant baptism, infant church relations, potentially present but as yet undeveloped, even in what may be fitly called the seed sermon of the Christian church. This was no time to be thinking of infants, or children, as related to church polity; probably

there is not one present in the great assembly. It will
be soon enough to settle the church position of children, when the question rises practically afterwards.
These converted pilgrims, Parthians, Medes, Elamites,
and strangers of all names, may not even so much as
think of the question till they reach their homes again.
But the language, we can see, is Jewish; language of
promise, or covenant, only with a Christian addition—
" And to them that are afar off, even as many as the
Lord our God shall call"—and Peter, as we know, did
not really come into the meaning of this language himself till years after, when the great sheet let down from
heaven three times, and the actual ministering to a
Gentile convert, showed him whither, and how far off,
the call of the Lord might be going, in these times, to
run. Let it not surprise us then, that the facts of infant baptism, and of infant church relations, covered,
as they are, by Peter's language in this first sermon,
are still not yet developed, even to himself—any more
than the fact of Christ's call to the Gentiles.

And when our Baptist brethren reiterate the formula,
" believe and be baptized," " believe and be baptized,"
which they assume to be absolutely conclusive and final
on the question of infant baptism because infants can
not believe, they have only to make due allowance
for the fact that Christianity must needs make its chief
address, at the outset, to adult persons, and their argument vanishes. Christianity will of course address itself
to the subjects addressed ; and, telling them what they
must do to be saved, it will not of course tell them, at

the same breath, every thing else that is fit to be known. In this manner its language was naturally shaped, for a considerable time, so as to meet only the conditions of adult minds. When at length it shall begin to be inquired, what is the condition of immature, or infant minds? it will be soon enough to say something appropriate to them.

Besides, the formula has another side—" He that believeth not shall be damned." Does it therefore follow, because it is so continually given to adults as the fixed law of salvation—he that believeth shall be saved, and he that believeth not shall be damned—that infants dying in infancy, and too young to believe, must therefore be inevitably damned? No, it will be answered, even by our Baptist brethren themselves; for the language referred to was evidently designed only for adult persons, and is of course to be qualified so as to meet the demands of reason, when we come to the case of childhood. And why not also the language " believe and be baptized?" Say not that the child is not old enough to believe, and therefore can not be baptized. If he is not old enough to believe, how can he better be saved? Is it a greater, and higher, and more difficult thing to be admitted to baptism, than to be admitted to eternal glory?

Now I can most readily admit that the subject of infant baptism is not as definitely mentioned and formally prescribed in the New Testament, as we might, without any great extravagance, expect. For many will never notice how great a thing it is for Christianity to pass from the first stage of mere propagation, to the stage of a fixed institution. What worlds of modification, correction, new arrangement, are necessary to the transition, they have never observed. They see the real figure of Christianity in the day of Pentecost, having never a conception, it may be, that this figure is most intensely occasional and casual, and the whole scene one that has scarcely a vestige of Christian institution in it.

What I propose, then, is to go over some of the incidents of this Pentecostal scene and show you how it will drop out one point after another, as Christianity becomes a fixed institution; which institutional character, again, will, by a necessary law, bring in other elements whereby to shape itself and complete its organization.

First of all, we are delighted here at the picture given of a new form of society, and a thing so beautiful, so wonderfully hopeful and peculiar, we are ready to think must be the very essence of the new institution itself. "And all that believed were together and had all things common; and sold their possessions and goods and parted them to all men, as every man had need. And they, continuing with one accord in the temple and breaking bread from house to house, did eat their meat with gladness and singleness of heart, praising God and having favor with all the people. And the Lord added daily to the church such as should be saved." What a picture, taken as a mere external description! Saying nothing of internal experiences, it goes to the simple outward demonstrations, and by these it paints the spring-time, or first blossoming of the Christian love. The beauty of the scene consists in the fact, that the disciples hardly know, as yet, what their love signifies. Assembled as pilgrims, from all parts of the world, the Christian love has fallen upon them, and they find, what is altogether new and strange, that rich and poor, honorable and base, despite of all distinctions, they love one another as brethren! Not knowing what to make of it, or, apparently, whether they are hereafter to have any thing to do but to love one another, they give themselves wholly up to love, as children to a play—come what will, they are all agreed in this, that they want only fellowship with each other, fellowship in doctrine, fellowship in praise, fellowship in bread, and why not also in goods?

How sad, that a scene so amiable and lovely could not continue, and that all Christian disciples, to the end of the world, could not fall into the same delightful picture in their conduct! Just as sad, I answer, as it is that children can not always be children; for these are the children of love, acting out the simple instinct of love, and wholly ignorant, as yet, of the cares, labors, and confused struggles, in which their Christian spirit is to have its trial. Doubtless we are to regret, as a loss, whatever departure we may have suffered from the spirit of these first disciples; for the spirit of Christian life is one and the same, in all diversities of form and conduct. But it is plain to any one, who will exercise the least consideration, that it was just as im-

possible to perpetuate these first demonstrations, as it
is to preserve the infantile airs of children after childhood is passed, carrying them still on through the
sturdy toils and cares of a mature age. The moment
we leave these first scenes, following the pilgrims off
to their homes, see them entering into the duties of
home, see the Christian churches getting body and form
in so many places and becoming incorporated as fixed
elements of human society, we shall discover that
almost all the modes and hospitalities of the Pentecostal society are inevitably discontinued.

But we must go deeper into the history and show,
by distinct specification, how intensely casual much
that belongs to the scene of the Pentecost was even
designed to be, and how many things are to be added
to give the new gospel a permanently instituted life.
We begin with the things casual that were designed to
cease.

The doctrine of the Holy Spirit was here to be inaugurated, as a Divine Force, entered systematically into
the world, to work subjectively in men all the characters of love and beauty that are shown objectively in
the life of Jesus. He is to be, in other words, a perpetual indwelling Christ in men's hearts. In times
more ancient, good men had been wont to pray for
spiritual help in a manner correspondent, but now the
kingdom of Help, that kingdom which is righteousness
and peace and joy in the Holy Ghost, is to be set up
as a Christly dispensation. But, at the beginning, there
must be something done before the senses, to waken

sensuous impressions. Otherwise, whatever power the Spirit might exert in the recesses of the human soul, it would probably occur to no one to refer the effects wrought to a Divine Agency. Hence the wondrous character of the scene, which here bursts upon the world—a sound from heaven, a rushing, mighty wind sweeping through the hall, lambent tips of fire resting on the heads of the assembly, wondrous utterances or tongues.

Now, the physical incidents of this scene had nothing to do with its substantial import, save as they were added to suggest the idea of a Divine Agency. They hold the same mechanical relation, as a vehicle, to the Spirit, that the human nature of Jesus held to the Divine Word. They are the body, the sensible show of the Spirit, the smoke by which the fire was revealed. So of the tongues. They were the sign of a power that was playing the action of the inner man, and making audible, as it were, the activity within, of a Divine Influence. All these, like the miraculous gifts so conspicuous in the subsequent history, were *manifestations* of the Spirit, given to profit withal; but being only accidents or exponents, were, of course, to be discontinued, when the doctrine of a spiritual influence from God was sufficiently developed—discontinued and never restored, unless perhaps in cases where the sense of the Spirit is so nearly lost as to require a kind of new development. Accordingly as these fall off, the spiritual influence inaugurated by such tokens, may be expected, for much the same reasons, to move upon the

world in a less imposing method; to remit, in some
degree, the extraordinary, and, as life is itself ordinary,
become, to the human spirit, what the air is to the
body—a Perpetual Element of inbreathing love; to
dwell in the families, to follow the individual, and
whisper holy thoughts in solitary places and silent
hours. He is to fill the world, and be a Spirit of Life
and love, present to all human hearts. He will produce the same exercises, produced in the first disciples,
in the scene of the Pentecost. Sometimes, too, he will
glorify himself in scenes of social effect and power.
But the grand reality revealed is an Abiding Spirit—
not a Scene Spirit, but an Abiding Spirit—accordantly
with Christ's own promise—"He shall give you
another Comforter, that he may abide with you forever." When the sound, therefore, which then shook
the air is hushed to be heard no more; when the rushing, mighty wind that typified so powerfully the breath
of the arriving Spirit of God has dropped into calm;
when the fire-tips have ceased to burn on the heads
of all assemblies, and all the Pentecostal signs are over;
then is there seen to be left as a result, the fixed conviction of a Jesus unlocalized, a Spirit of Jesus present in all places, working in all hearts, present, in conscious manifestation, to all discerning souls, as the life
of their life. How very casual, in this view, is the
scene of the Pentecost. And that is very soon discovered. One year afterwards, not even the persons
present in that scene look upon it as being, in any sense,
a properly institutional element of Christianity. The

Spirit inaugurated is institutional, the life of all holy institutions, but nothing in the forms of the scene is regarded as having a perpetual character.

Again, it will be found that the preaching of the day of Pentecost, powerful as the sermon of Peter appears to have been upon the assembly at that time, was not such, either in style or substance, as could be continued after the first day or two of the gospel proclamation, and was in fact superseded, in a very short time, by the sturdier methods of argument and instruction. We see this in all the epistles, and as truly in those of Peter as of Paul. The infant churches had scarcely begun to be institutions, before this change was apparent.

And yet we have many, in our own time, who do not appear to see this, even though the manner of Peter's sermon is so completely gone by, that one can hardly imagine how it had any power at all. "See," they say, "how simple it was, how easy of apprehension—nothing but a recitation of facts—and then what power it had!" As if the telling, over and over, of old news, announcing again facts that have been known to every reader of the New Testament from his childhood up, as familiarly as he knows his right hand, could have the same value and be means to ends for producing the same effects! Most of us have a better understanding of the subject, perceiving, as clearly as possible, that while Peter's sermon was good for the occasion, it was good for almost no occasion since. It was one of the first things, of which there can not, by

the supposition, be many. A camp meeting, or a band
of pilgrims gathered for a single week, a thousand
miles from home, may well enough desire such kind
of preaching as will serve the zest of the occasion.
But it is no design of Christianity to get by the need
of intelligence, and fashion a sanctity that has no fellowship with dignity. A regularly instituted Christian
congregation, who are to live and grow up on the
same spot, from age to age, it has long ago been discovered, must be compelled to gird up the loins of their
mind. They must reject the mere gospel drinks and
betake themselves to meat. Their life, it will be found,
depends, not on scenes and machineries, not on storms
and paroxysms, but on a capacity rather to receive instruction; to be exercised in high argument, to bear
with patience the discovery how little they know, and
on a good healthful appetite for Christian food. To be
able to burn in a fire decides nothing. They must know
how to supply the fuel of devotion out of their own
exercise in God's truth. They must love a ministry
of doctrine, or intellectual teaching. Neither is it doctrine, as many fancy, when they complain of a want
of doctrinal preaching, to get a few stale dogmas impounded in the head, or stuck in the brain, as dead flies
in ointment: all the rich treasures of thought, and high
motive, and solemn contemplation, garnered up in
God's word, must be brought out, seen, understood, and
fall upon the soul, as manna from the skies. Like
manna, too, it must be the supply of to-day only. A
new shower must be gathered for to-morrow, and the

mind of the people must be kept in active and pro-
gressive motion.

Such a kind of preaching will feed the intelligence
of the hearers, and raise up pillars in the churches.
And here is the great distinction between the preaching
proper to the scene of the Pentecost, and that of an
established Christian congregation. It is the difference
between Peter, giving news to the pilgrims, and Paul of-
ering some "things hard to be understood," to churches
of organized disciples. Such preaching is required, in
an established congregation, as will exert an educating
power. And yet it will, in that way, be a converting
power, as efficacious as any other, if only it is expected
to be. When the community is more deeply moved
by spiritual things, it will, of course, vary its tone and
its subjects to suit the occasion, perhaps multiply its
efforts; but never as being in a hurry, lest the grace
of the occasion may be capriciously withdrawn, never
over-preaching, or preaching out, as if nothing were to
be done by thought in the hearers, but all by the power
of a commotion round them; for it is not the same
thing to fall out of dignity and self-possession as to get
rid of sin, neither is a fever or a whirlwind any proper
instrument of sanctification. Mournful proofs have we
to the contrary. Better is it to reserve a power for the
ordinary, even when we are in the extraordinary. It
is not wisdom to overwork the harvest, so that we have
no strength left for the bread. Rather let the preacher
believe in the Abiding Spirit, and count upon a kind
of perpetual harvest. Let him think to gain many to

Christ imperceptibly, by keeping alive the interest of
God's truth, and letting it distill upon the hearers as a
dew, and through them on the rising families. Whatever he gains in this way will assuredly remain; for it
is not the birth of an occasion, but of quiet conviction.
It partakes the nature of habit. It is the fruit of a
godly training. Seldom, therefore, will it fall away, or
disappoint expectation.

There is yet another class of incidents, or demonstrations, in the scene of the Pentecost, which are referable
to the fact that these first converts are not at home, and
all these must, of course, be modified, or discontinued
by their simple return. They are pilgrims at the
feasts; Parthians, Medes, Elamites—Jewish emigrants,
who have returned from every most distant clime of the
world, to enjoy the great festivals of their religion.

Their property, their business, and, more commonly,
their families, are left behind. Many of them are poor
persons, wholly unable to support the expense even of
a short stay at Jerusalem. The others can not, of course,
leave them to suffer. So they divide their resources
with the poor; and some, who belong at Jerusalem, are
moved by the overflowing love of Christ in their hearts,
to part with their whole property, that they may relieve the necessities of the brotherhood. Only a few
days or weeks are thus spent together. Probably,
within three months, they are, every man, at home in
his own house, providing for his own family, out of the
increase of his own industry and property. During
their short stay at Jerusalem, they had nothing to do

but to exercise their religion. Accordingly they gave themselves wholly up to it. Now the religious occasion is past; the extraordinary is over, and the ordinary has returned. By this time, they have learned, probably, and received it even as a Christian maxim, that one who does not provide for *his own*, denies the faith, and is worse than an infidel.

Again, these first disciples had not yet been called to blend their piety with the common cares and duties of life. Quite likely, they did not, for some time, consider whether they should hereafter have any thing more to do with these gross and earthly callings. But we, at least, have learned what they must also have learned very soon, that though we can not live by bread alone, it is yet difficult to live without bread. We have learned that the very church of God itself is perpetuated, in part, by industry and production, that it can not live by expenditure, that we have something therefore to do, besides breaking bread from house to house; six days to labor, a spectacle of thrift to present to mankind, as a proof that Christian virtue has its blessings. We must shine as good citizens, neighbors, parents, friends. Life is no mere camp-meeting scene; but the greatest of all Christian attainments, we find, is precisely that which the first disciples had not yet thought of, the learning how to blend the spiritual and economical or industrial together; to live in the world, and not be of it; to labor in earthly things, and maintain a conversation in heaven; to unite thrift with charity, and separate gain from greediness; to use property, and not worship it; to prepare comfort, without pursuing pleasure. For it is, by just this kind of trial, that all spiritual strength is gotten, and the Christian life becomes a light to men.

Having glanced, in this manner, at some of the types and conditions of the scene of Pentecost that were, and were inevitably to be, discontinued, let us notice briefly, some of the matters that must also as inevitably be added in the process by which Christianity becomes an institution.

Thus, first of all, as Christ and his evangelists had given the new facts to the world, so it was inevitable that a grand process of thinking or mental elaboration should begin to work out the import or doctrinal interpretation of those facts. In this process, diverse opinions, formulas, sects, controversies, must be developed— consequently new modes of duty.

The simplicity of mere love, displayed, as it was, in the first scenes of the gospel, could not continue, however desirable it may seem. Men must think, as well as love, and thought must make its inroads on mere relations of feeling. And thus a long process of forming and reforming must go on, till the Christ of the head becomes as catholic as the Christ of the heart. Meantime, all must stand for the truth, and there must be no countenance given to error. The happy days of Christian childhood are left far behind, and every church is set in relations of duty that are partly antagonistic. It must take a form required by its new necessities. What

to do for the truth, whom to acknowledge, when to resist and when to forbear, how much consequence to
attribute to opinions, over what errors to spread the
mantle of charity, how to maintain a polemic attitude
in the unity of the Spirit—these are the grave questions
that are to occupy ministers and churches, and, in the
right exercise of which, they are to justify their Christian name. And on this will depend the power of
religion, quite as much as on the duties done to those
who are aliens and unbelievers.

Next we pass on to a field where the new creating
power of the gospel is displayed yet more distinctly.
The first disciples had no thought but to swim in the
strange joy they felt, as forgiven of God and filled with
the love of Jesus. Of Christianity, as a fixed institution, taking the whole society of man into its bosom,
and becoming the school of the race, they had probably,
at first, no conception. Passing thence to the modern
Christian faith, how great is the change! What a variety of means, instruments and arrangements has it
created, maintaining all from age to age, by a sacrifice,
compared with which, the casual contributions to poor
saints at Jerusalem were far less significant in their
effects, and, perhaps, not more to be commended, as
proofs of a Christian spirit.

First, a house of worship; and, in order to this, the
new spiritual life must become a holder of real estate,
and be acknowledged as such in the laws. To make the
place worthy of the cause, genius and taste are to be called
into exercise, and a new Christian art developed.

To maintain expenses and repairs, and collect and disburse charities, there must be officers created, such as deacons and committees of various kinds, and this requires elections, bye-laws, records, and a full organized institutional state.

Mere forms and sacraments being insufficient, preachers of the word must be carefully trained for the service, and installed therein, to feed the intelligence of the flock, and lead them in the truth. Their official rights and duties must be ascertained, and, correspondently, the rights and duties of the flock—matters all how distant from the scene of the Pentecost!

The times and forms of worship need to be settled; for, whether a liturgy is used or not, no organic action can be maintained without forms of some kind, to serve as laws of concert and rules of order.

Christian music, as a new art, must be created, and the children and youth must be trained therein, so that all may bear their part in the worship, and the worship exercise and inspire a devout feeling in all.

There must be a punctual and regular attendance somehow established and made obligatory; for the habit of worship is necessary, to its value, as a power over character. Hence there must be a common responsibility—all must be enlisted. There must be a church spirit, and, in order to this, a fraternal spirit in the members, verified by mutual sympathy and aid under the common burdens of life—a kind of service, I will add, which is often far more beneficent than a community of goods would be; for this latter might be only a

premium given to idleness, while the other is but a good
encouragement to the ingenuous struggles of industry.
There must, however, be some Christian provision for
the poor, that they also may have their part in the
Christian flock, and the blessings of charity descend
upon it and dwell in it.

Nor is the article of dress, in a Christian assembly,
too insignificant to be a subject of care. Probably no
one had a thought of this in the Pentecostal assembly;
but we find the apostles, not long after, giving serious
lectures to the disciples upon their dress. Dress and
manners, manners and morals, morals and piety, are all
connected by an intimate or secret law. A people,
therefore, who are careful to appear before God, in a
well-chosen, modest, and appropriate dress—one that is
neither careless nor ostentatious, one that indicates sobriety, neatness, good sense, and a desire to be approved
of God more than to be seen of men—will avoid barba-
rous improprieties of every sort. Their manner will
express reverence to God. What they express, they
will be likely to feel; and if they become true disciples
of Christ, as there is greater reason to hope, their manner will have a nicer propriety, and their whole de-
meanor will be more thoughtful, consistent, and lovely.

It may, by-and-bye, become evident that, in order
to maintain the full power of religion, and to gain
the neglected youth or children, and such children as
would grow up otherwise in the power of vice, that a
parish school must be instituted, as in Scotland, in connection with every church. And then, at a much later

day, it may become evident that Sunday-schools require
to be instituted in the same way, and that these, enlist-
ing the more capable and devoted of the churches in
Christian studies, and good works—works, that is, of
teaching and attention to the poor—are finally regarded
every where, though wholly unknown to the apostles
and the Pentecostal assembly, as being among the best
means for the training of a practically Christian character, and the gathering in of the outcast families to God.

So far we proceed without difficulty; all these things,
though never preached by apostles, must finally come,
we perceive, as outgrowths of the Christian church.
Pentecostal incidents will disappear, and these will as
certainly grow apace in their time.

But the particular point for which I have drawn this
sketch has been purposely left behind.   Infant baptism,
the relation of the seminal and undeveloped first period
of human existence to Christ and his flock, that which
appears only implicitly in the sermon of Peter, on the
day of Pentecost—where is this, and what is to come,
in the way of development, here?   There was no reason,
or even room, among the scenes of the Pentecost, for so
much as thinking on this subject of infants and their
church relations, and scarcely more for a considerable
time afterward.   It could not become a subject of attention, until the church itself began to settle into forms
of order and structural organization; and how soon
that came to pass we do not definitely know.   It should
therefore be no subject of wonder that infant baptism,

figures somewhat indistinctly, for so long a time at least; and scarcely more, that it shows itself only by implication and a kind of tacit development, for a brief time afterwards.

Furthermore, if it came to pass by a transference of Jewish ideas into Christian spheres, Jewish modes and conditions into the Christian order and economy— just as Peter's Jewish language, when he said, in his Pentecostal speech, "to you and to your children," finally came back to him in its Christian power,—it would make no bold and staring figure any where. If the Christian teachers looked to see all the better mercies of the old economy transferred into the Christian, and exalted there into some higher and more perfect meaning, we ought certainly not to expect any debate, or any thing but a silent, scarcely conscious flow of transition, when infants are taken to be with their parents, in the church, the covenant, the Christian Israel of their faith. And in just this way the defect of any bold declarations on the subject of infant baptism in the writings of the New Testament, and the fact that it appears only in a few historic glimpses, and occasional modes of speech that are subtle implications of the fact, is sufficiently accounted for.

But we are inquiring after the mode in which this rite became an accepted element of the Christian organization, and a part of the church practice, as we certainly know that it did at sometime afterward. Peter probably conceived as little what his language might infer* respecting it, as he certainly did, what hidden

import there was in his testimony, by the same words,
of a grace to the Gentiles; for he spoke in prophetic ex-
altation, as the ancient prophets did, not knowing what
the spirit of Christ that was in them did signify. But
suppose one of these adult converts at the Pentecost to
have set off, after the few happy weeks of his sojourn
are ended, for his home in some remote region of Ara-
bia, Parthia, or Greece. He carries Christ with him, he
is a new man, filled with a strange joy, burning with a
strange, all-sacrificing love to the cause of his new
Master, and to every sinner of mankind. He begins to
preach the Christ he loves to his friends, tells them all
he knows of the new gospel, speaks to them as one
whom Christ has endowed with power to speak. He
gathers a little circle, which we may call a church,
around him, perhaps converts a little obscure synagogue
into a church. He knows that he himself was baptized as a token of his faith, and he has heard, a thousand times repeated, Christ's word, "he that believeth
and is baptized," "except a man be born of water and
of the Spirit," and he does not scruple to baptize all his
new fellow disciples. Then comes the question, what
of the families? what of the infants we have, who are
not old enough to believe? This, on the supposition
that he had heard nothing of infant baptism before he
left Jerusalem, which may or may not be true. But he
has heard the whole story of Christ's life many times
over, including the fact of his beautiful interest in
children, and his declaration—"of such is the kingdom."
He recollects also the ancient religion of his people;

how it identified always the children with the fathers,
and included them in the covenant of the fathers, raising doubtless the question, whether the gospel in its nobler, wider generosity and completer grace, would fall
short even of the old religion in its tenderness to the
family affections, and its provisions for the religious
unity of families.   And just here, we will suppose, the
words of Peter, in that first sermon flash on his recollection—"For the promise is to you and to your children."   They meant almost nothing, it may be, when
they were spoken, but how full and clear the meaning
they now take.   It is like a revelation.   The doubt
struggling in his bosom is over, the question is settled.
"My children," he says, "are with me, one with me in
my faith, included with me in all my titles and hopes, and
as I came in, out of the defilements of sin, and was baptized in token of my cleansing, so too are they to share
my baptism and be heirs together with me in the grace
of life.

Thus instructed, he will baptize his children, and
make his religion a strictly family grace, expecting them
to grow up in it; others also consenting with him in the
same conclusion, and offering their children to God in
the same manner.   And, as the result, they will no
more be Christians with families, but Christian families—
all together in the church of God.   In this manner the
Pentecost itself, when the seeds that are in it are developed, will almost certainly issue the adult baptism there
begun, the baptism of the three thousand, in the common baptism of the house.

And here we have, in small, just what would most naturally take place in the development of Christianity itself. Taken as connected with its own precedent history and preparations, the church could hardly be held back from infant baptism, except by some specific revelation.

VI

APOSTOLIC AUTHORITY OF INFANT BAPTISM

"And I baptized also the household of Stephanas."—1 *Corinthians*, i. 16.

WE have traced the conditions under which infant baptism would almost certainly be developed. But we do not leave the question here. We have many and distinct evidences for the rite, which are abundantly decisive; some from the nature of the family state, some from the New Testament, and some from the subsequent history of the church. These I will now undertake to present in the briefest manner possible. And

1. The organic unity of the family makes a ground for it, and sets it in terms of rational respect. The child that is born, is really not born, in the higher sense of that term, till he has breathed a long time. He does not live in his own will, but is in the will and life of his parents. To bring him forward into his own will and responsibility is the problem of years. He is in the matrix still of parental character, where all the graces, faiths, prayers, promises, of the parents are his also. He lives and breathes in them, and is of them, almost as truly as they are of themselves. What we call the house, is the organic life that grows him as a mind or agent, tempers him, works him into his habits, fashions him as by a pre-

cedent power to be born, and finally take dominion of himself. Why then should religion make no recognition of a fact so profoundly religious? Why not assume that the child is just where he is; in the faith of the house, to grow up there? It would even be a supposition against nature to suppose that he will not. It is very true that he may not, because the faith of the house is no faith, or so mixed with sense and passion as to have none of the true power. Still, when the discipleship is assumed to be made by faith, it must also be assumed that, being so made, it will have all the power of faith, shaping the parental life in the molds of that power, and just as certainly including or inclosing in those molds, there to be also shaped, the infant life of the offspring. The father and mother are not merely a man and a woman, but they are a man and woman having children; and accordingly it is the father and mother, that is, the man and woman *and* their children, that are to be baptized.

2. It is precisely this great fact of an organic unity that is taken hold of and consecrated, in the field of religion, by the Abrahamic and other family covenants. And the whole course of revelation, both in the Old and New Testament, is tinged by associations, and sprinkled over with expressions that recognize the religious unity of families, and the inclusion of the children with the parents. All the promises run—"to you and to your children;" for Peter's language here is only an inspired transfer and reassertion of the Jewish family ideas, at the earliest moment, in the field of Christianity

itself. It recognizes the fact that Christianity is just what we know it to be, nothing but a continuation and fuller development of the old religion. It widens out the scope of the old religion, so as to include all nations, even as the prophets foretold, and raises all the rites and symbols into a higher spiritual sense, as they were appointed from the first to be raised. Taken all together, the old and the new constitute a perfect whole or system, and the process is neither more nor less than God's way of developing and authenticating a universal religion. In this universal religion, therefore, we are to look for the continuance onward of the old family character and the inclusive oneness of fathers with their children. The only difference will be that the oneness will be raised into a more spiritual and higher sense, just as every thing else was raised. The children are thus looked upon to be presumptively as believing in the faith, and regenerated in the regeneration of the fathers. And here again,

3. Circumcision comes to our aid, as another and distinct evidence. For it was given to be " a seal of the righteousness of faith," and the application of it, as a seal, to infant children, involves all the precise difficulties—neither more nor less—that are raised by the deniers of infant baptism. Let the point here made be accurately understood. The argument is not that infant baptism was directly substituted for circumcision. Of this there is no probable evidence. Such a substitution could not have been made without remark, discussion, oppositions of prejudice, and the raising of contentions

that would have required distinct mention, many times over, in the apostolic history. But the argument is this: that the Jewish mind was so familiarized by custom with the notion of an inclusive religious unity in families, (partly by the rite of circumcision,) that Christian baptism, being the seal of faith, was naturally and by a kind of associational instinct, applied over to families in the same manner. Not to have made such an application would have required some authoritative interposition, some dike of positive hindrance, to turn aside the current of Jewish prepossessions. And if there had risen up, somewhere, a man of Baptist notions, to ask, where is the propriety of applying baptism, given as a rite for believers, to infants, who we certainly know are not old enough to believe? he could not even have begun to raise an impression by it. Was not circumcision given to Abraham to be the seal of faith? and has it not been applied from his time down to the present, in this way—applied to infant children eight day's old? True it is the doctrine of Christ, "he that believeth and is baptized shall be saved," and our apostles too are saying, "if thou believest with all thy heart thou mayest." So we all say and think, as relating to adult persons; but do we not all know that what is given to the father includes the children, and that his faith is the faith of the house? Nothing, in short, is plainer than that every argument raised to convict infant baptism of absurdity, holds, in the same manner, as convicting circumcision of absurdity, and all the religious polity of the former ages.

Every such argument, too, mocks the religious feeling and conviction of all these former ages, in a way of disrespect equally presumptuous.

It is very true, as declared by the apostle Paul, in his epistle to the Romans, that circumcision, seal of faith as it was, did not always have its meaning fulfilled; "for all are not Israel that are of Israel." Esau and Edom, his posterity, became, thus, an apostate race; and this, in a certain sense, by Providential appointment. But the scope of God's providential purpose, as every intelligent Christian ought to know, does not correspond with the scope of his grace or the measures of his gifts and promises. For the Providential plan takes in all the perversities of human action, while the grace-plan or promise corresponds with the aims and measures of God's paternal goodness. He means and offers, in other words, more than human perversity will take; gives a presumption of good, on his part, which he knows that human wrongs will not allow to be actualized. Then, as his Providential purposes and plan are graduated to what will actually be, not to what he means, wishes, and promises, it follows that the facts or issues of his Providential order do not answer to the scope of his gracious intention. And thus it comes to pass that, while he gives a seal of faith, which ought to be answered, by a result in which all are Israel that are of Israel, the fact is different. Had Israel ruled his house as he ought, had Rebekah been an honest woman, loving both her sons impartially, and seeking the true welfare of both—not conspiring with one to rob and cheat the other—Esau might have been a different man, and Edom might have been a family of Israel. In circumcision, as a seal of faith, God gave, on his part, the pledge and presumption that so it should be. But Edom was thrown off into apostasy by courses of human perversity that disappointed the seal. And the same is true of infant baptism in all those cases where the faith is narrowed, or denied, by parental misconduct. There is yet no falsity in the circumcision, or the baptism, because all which it signified was true; viz., that God, on his part, sought and meant and would have made actual, the whole promise of it. How often is adult baptism itself applied to such as have no faith at all; but this does not affect the inherent truth of the rite, and if they should live so as not to allow it any correspondence with fact, when applied to their children, does it any more affect the truth of it there? The rite measures God's intent and promise, and refuses to narrow itself by the perversity of the subjects. It says, "this child shall grow up in faith—so it is given." Then if, by unbelief and graceless conduct in the parents, it grows up to be the stem of an Edomitish stock, it will not disappoint God's providential order and plan, and as little will it disprove God's promise and truth in the baptism. God is honored, and the rite is honored still. It is only the parental faith and life that are not.

4. It appears that Christian baptism was not a rite wholly new, but a reapplication of proselyte baptism. The custom had been, as the Gentile was an unclean

person, to baptize him, as a token of cleansing, when he was received to be a Jew; and his family, of course, were baptized with him, to make the lustration complete. So Christ proposes baptism, as the token of that lustration, which is to purify such as become citizens in the kingdom of heaven. And the conversation of Christ with Nicodemus evidently supposes such a rite, previously existing and familiarly known by him. This being true, all that he says of baptism, or the lustration by water and the Spirit, supposes a baptism also of children with their parents, according to the custom. The civil regeneration of the proselyte and his family by such ceremonies will be answered, in reapplying the rite, by the spiritual regeneration of the convert and his family. If infants were, in this case, to be excepted, or not baptized, the exception required to be expressly made; for otherwise, the very transfer of the rite to a spiritual use must, of itself, carry infant baptism with it. Thus Lightfoot says with great force, "the Baptists object—it is not commanded that infants should be baptized, therefore they should not be baptized. But I say it is not prohibited that infants should be baptized, therefore they should be baptized; for since the baptism of children was familiarly practiced in the admission of proselytes, there was no need that it should be confirmed by express precept, when baptism come to be an evangelical sacrament. For Christ took baptism as he found it, and the whole nation knew perfectly well that little children had always been baptized. On the contrary, if he had intended that the custom should be

abolished, he would have expressly prohibited it."
Wetstein also says, in the same manner—"I do not see
how it could enter into their thoughts to expunge boys
and infants from the list of disciples, or from baptism,
unless they had been excluded by the express injunction of Christ, which we no where find."*

5. Christ comes very near to a specific and formal
command of infant baptism, when we put together, side
by side, what he says of baptism in the third chapter
of John, and what he says concerning infants elsewhere.
There he recognizes baptism as a token of one's entrance into the *kingdom of God;* elsewhere he says—
suffer little children to come unto me and forbid them
not for of such is the *kingdom of heaven.* These terms,
"kingdom of God," and "kingdom of heaven," denote,
externally, the church; and the church is also presented
under the figure of a school, as here of a kingdom, in
all those cases where becoming "a disciple" or learner is
spoken of. In this latter view or figure, baptism is conceived to be one's enrollment openly as a disciple; and
what is more fit than that children should be learners—
brought in by their parents to be learners with them—
of the Christian grace? This, in fact, was the general
significance of faith in those times; they were called
believers who so recognized the truth of Christ's person
that they were ready to become learners under him.
And the Baptists themselves act on this same principle,
never holding the necessity that baptism should actually

---

*This subject of proselyte baptism has been spoken of also in the
second Sermon, and need not be further dwelt upon here.

follow faith, in the high and complete sense of spiritual conversion. Probably half their members, in the church, come into doubt, before they die, of the time when they were really born of the Spirit; and, in cases of open apostasy, where there is a recovery, and the disciple openly testifies that he was not before a truly converted person, he is not rebaptized. It is enough that, by his baptism, he has openly signified his wish to be a disciple in the school of Christ; where, if he has never learned before, it is only the more necessary that he be a true learner now; which if he become, the great law, "he that believeth and is baptized," is sufficiently fulfilled. Just so with the child of a Christian parentage; whatever doubts may be entertained of his certainly growing up in the faith, there is a much better presumption that he will, if the parents are faithful, than there is, in the case of persons converted from the world, that they will prove to be true believers; and if he should not grow up in the faith, but afterwards becomes a Christian, there is just as much greater propriety in his baptism as an infant, and no more reason why he should be rebaptized, than there is in the case of apostate professors who become truly converted.

6. What is said in the New Testament of household baptism, or the baptizing of households, is positive proof that infants were baptized in the times of the apostles—baptized, that is, in and because of the supposed faith of the parents. The fact of such baptism is three times distinctly mentioned; in the case of "the household of Stephanas," of Lydia "and her house-

hold," and the jailor "and all his." In the first case, nothing is said of faith at all, though doubtless he was baptized as a believer. In the second, every thing turns on the personal faith of Lydia—"if ye have judged *me* to be faithful." In the third, it seems to be said, according to an English translation, that all the house believed—"*he* rejoiced, believing in God, with all his house." But the participle, believing, is singular and not plural in the original, and the phrase— "with all his house"—plainly belongs to the verb and not to the participle. Rigidly translated, the passage would read—"he rejoiced with all his house, himself believing."

It is often objected that, in all these three cases, for aught that appears, the households were made up of adult persons, who were baptized because they all believed. But the chance that this should be true of the only three households said to be baptized, and that there should be three households, as households were commonly made up in that time, in which there were no young children or infants, is not even one in a million, as computed by what is called the doctrine of chances. Besides, if it was a thing understood that infants were never to be baptized, it is important to observe that no such way of speaking could ever come into use. What Baptist could ever be induced, with his view of baptism, to say inclusively, and without some kind of qualification, that he had baptized the household of Richard or Mary? We need not stop, in this view, to ask whether certainly there were infants in any one of these households; the mode of speaking itself shows that baptism went by households, and that when the head was judged to be faithful, his baptism carried the presumptive faith and consequent baptism of all. Of this, too,

7. We have a distinct indication, in what is said of children, where but one of the parents believes. Thus Paul distinctly teaches, " For the unbelieving husband is sanctified by the wife, and the unbelieving wife is sanctified by the husband; else were your children unclean, but now are they holy." It is not meant here that the children are actually and inwardly holy persons, but that only having one Christian parent is enough to change their presumptive relations to God; enough to make them Christian children, as distinguished from the children of unbelievers. So strong is the conviction, even, in these apostolic times, of an organic unity sovereign over the faith and the religious affinities of children that, where but one parent only believes, that faith carries presumptively the faith of the children with it. And upon this grand fact of the religious economy, baptism was, from the first, and properly, applied to the children of them that believe. Hence, too—

8. It was that the children of believers were familiarly addressed with them as believers; as in the epistles of Paul to the Ephesians and Colossians. These epistles are formally inscribed to churches or Christian brotherhoods—" to the saints, which are at Ephesus, and to the faithful in Christ Jesus "—" to the saints and

faithful brethren, which are at Colosse." And yet in both, the children are particularly addressed—" Children obey your parents in the Lord, for this is right "— Children obey your parents in all things; for this is well pleasing unto the Lord. In this manner, children are formally included among the "faithful in Christ Jesus." The conception is that children are, of course, included in the religion of their parentage, grow up faithful with their faithful or believing parents. On the ground of this same presumption, they were properly baptized with them, or on their account. Again—

9. It is a point of consequence to notice that such as reject all these and similar evidences from the Scripture, on the ground that infant baptism can not be rightly practiced, because it is not directly and specifically appointed in the Scripture, do yet make nothing of their own argument in other observances familiarly accepted. Why infant baptism was not and should not be required to have been specifically commanded, I have shown already ; how, for example, it was necessarily developed, as from a point distinctly referred to in Peter's first sermon, and how the very institution of baptism carried, of necessity, infant baptism with it, apart from any express mention. In the meantime, it will be found that the objectors themselves are admitting and practicing, without difficulty, observances that have comparatively no specific authority at all. At the sacrament of the Supper, they use leavened bread without scruple, when they know that it was not used by Christ himself, and was solemnly forbidden at the

festival, he was there, in fact, reappointing for the Christian uses of his disciples in all future ages. Where then is the authority given for a change even in the element of the Holy Supper itself? The Christian Lord's day, too, accepted in the place of the Jewish Sabbath, and that even against a specific command of the decalogue—how readily, and with how little scruple, do they accept this Lord's day and let the ancient Sabbath go, when it is only by the faintest, most equivocal, or evanescent indications they can make out a shadow of authority for the change? "Direct proof! positive command! specific injunction!" they say, "without these, infant baptism has no right." Where then do they get their authority for these other observances; one of them never referred to in Scripture at all, and the other so doubtfully that infant baptism has, in comparison, the clear evidence of day?

Lastly, it remains to glance at the evidences from church history, or the history of times subsequent to the age of the apostles. It has been the mood of Christian learning, in the generation past—for the learned men have moods and phases, not to say fashions, like others in the less thoughtful conditions—to make large concessions in the matter of baptism, both as regards the manner and the subjects. But a reaction is now begun, and it is my fixed conviction that it will not stop, till the encouragement heretofore given to the Baptist opinions is quite taken away.

It has never been questioned, however, that infant baptism, became the current practice of the church at a very early date. It is mentioned, incidentally and otherwise, in the writings of the earliest church fathers after the age of the apostles.

Thus it is testified by Justin Martyr, who was probably born before the death of the apostle John—" There are many of us, of both sexes, some sixty and some seventy years old, who were made disciples from their childhood." And the word *made disciples* is the same that Christ himself used when he said, " Go *teach* [i. e. disciple] all nations, baptizing," &c. ; the same that was currently applied to baptized children afterwards.

Ireneus, born a few years later, writes—" Christ came to redeem all by himself; all who through him are regenerated unto God; infants and little children, and young men, and older persons. Hence, he passed through every age, and for the infants he became an infant, sanctifying infants; among the little children, he became a little child, sanctifying those who belong to this age; and at the same time, presenting them an example of well doing, and obedience; among the young men he became a young man, that he might set them an example, and sanctify them to the Lord." In the phrase, " regenerated to God," which is thus applied to infants, expressly named as distinguished from little children, he refers, it can not be doubted, to baptism; which, being the outward sign of such inward grace, was naturally and very commonly called regeneration. Infants plainly could be regenerated to God in no other sense ; and therefore his language can not even be supposed to have any meaning, if this be rejected.

Tertullian follows, urging the delay of baptism, and, in fact, advocating the disuse of infant baptism altogether. But his appeal supposes the current practice of such baptism at the time, and in that way rather augments than diminishes the weight of historic evidence. And the more so that he urges the delay of baptism on grounds that are false and even superstitious, viz. : that baptism carries the forgiveness of sins, and should therefore be postponed to a later period, because the sins committed after baptism must otherwise be cleared by a more purgatorial method.

Origen, who was born near the close of the second century, or about a hundred years after the time of the apostles, testifies—"According to the usage of the church, baptism is given to infants." And again—"The church received an order from the apostles to baptize infants."

Somewhere in these first two centuries, the ancient writing called the "Shepherd," or the "Shepherd of Hermas," because it purports to have been written by a teacher of that name, declares the opinion that—"All infants are in honor with the Lord, and are esteemed first of all—the baptism of water is necessary to all." Who this Hermas was, and when he lived, is not ascertained, but he is supposed by many to be the very same person mentioned by Paul, Rom. xvi. 14. He is acknowledged by Neander, as one who "had great authority in the first centuries."

It is a remarkable evidence, too, that inscriptions are found on the monuments of children, considered by antiquarians to be of a very early age, probably of the first two or three centuries, in which they are called *fideles*, that is *faithfuls ;* just as children are addressed by Paul among the "faithful brethren" of Ephesus and Colosse. The following is an example—(Buonarotti, 17 Fabretti, Cap. 4,) "A faithful among faithfuls, here lies Zosimus. He lived two years one month and twenty-five days." How far they carried the presumption of infant baptism, that children are to grow up in the grace of their parents, is here seen.

It signifies little, therefore, as respects this question, after the authorities cited, that the Bishops of the North African Church, in a council called by Cyprian, about the middle of the third century, decided that baptism should not of course be delayed for eight days, according to the law of circumcision, which many supposed to govern the rite.

So clear, in short, and decided was the authority of infant baptism, that Pelagius, a man of great learning, who had traveled in Britain, France, Italy, Africa Proper, Egypt, and Palestine, declared, in his controversy with Augustine, about the beginning of the fifth century, that "he had never heard of any impious heretic or sectary, who had denied infant baptism." "What," he also asked, "can be so impious as to hinder the baptism of infants?"

Augustine himself also testifies—"The whole church of Christ has constantly held that infants were baptized. Infant baptism the whole church practices. It was not instituted by councils, but was ever in use."

Infant baptism, therefore, is a fact of church history not to be fairly questioned. And accordingly the argument may be summed up thus: beginning at a point previous, we find customs and associations that would almost certainly be issued in such a rite of family religion; in the discourses of Christ and the apostolical writings we find that it actually was; and then we find the facts of church history correspondent. On the whole, while it may be admitted that baptism itself is a little more positively authenticated, it can not be denied that infant baptism is authenticated by all sufficient evidence.

VII

CHURCH MEMBERSHIP OF CHILDREN

"To the saints and faithful brethren in Christ which are at Colosse."—*Colossians*, i. 2.

THESE "saints and faithful brethren," it will be seen, include young children; for the apostle makes a distribution of them afterwards, in the third chapter of the epistle, addressing the class of wives, the class of husbands, the class of fathers, the class of servants, the class of masters, and, among all these, the class of children—"Children obey your parents in all things; for this is well pleasing unto the Lord." The Epistle to the Ephesians, too, is inscribed, in the same way—"to the saints which are at Ephesus, and to the faithful in Christ;" and this, again, makes a like distribution; addressing the classes of husbands, wives, fathers, mothers, children, servants, and masters, all as being included in the church at Ephesus—"children obey your parents in the Lord; for this is right. Honor thy father and mother; for this is the first commandment with promise." Where also it is made clear that he is speaking to quite young children; for he turns immediately to the fathers, exhorting them to bring up their children in the nurture and admonition of the Lord.

They are children so young, therefore, as to be subjects of nurture, and yet are addressed among the faithful brethren.

The explanation, then, is not that such children were believers, in the sense of being converts entered into the fold by an adult experience, and distinguished from other children not thus converted. When Lydia speaks of herself as one adjudged to be "faithful," it is probably in this sense. But when Titus, in ordaining elders, is directed to choose such as have "faithful children, not accused of riot, or unruly," it would be very singular, if he was permitted to ordain only such as have all their children thus formally converted. Paul obviously means that the elders shall be such as are under no scandal on account of their families; whose children are growing up in the Christian way and grace; sober, well-behaved, hopefully Christian children. We can see, too, in the language employed, that Paul includes the Colossian and Ephesian children among the faithful brethren of the two cities, in this more presumptive or merely anticipative way. For when he says, "children obey your parents in the Lord," it is not "children in the Lord," or "children obey in the Lord, your parents," but it is "obey them who are parents in the Lord;" as if their very parentage itself, in the flesh, were a parentage also in the Spirit, communicating both a personal and a Christian life. So, also, when the parents are required to give a nurture in the Lord, we may see that the children are expected to be grown as saints and faithfuls, and to be presumptively in the Lord, apart from all expectations and processes of adult conversion.

And it was out of such uses that the term "*faithful*" grew into the peculiar kind of church use, in which it denotes all the supposed members of the Christian body, whether adults, or only baptized children; as, for example, in that very ancient inscription cited by Buonarotti, where the child "two years, one month, and twenty-five days old," is described as lying among his Christian kinsmen—"a faithful among faithfuls." The very language supposes a membership in the church, or among the faithful brethren, by virtue of baptism and mere Christian nurture; such as on the footing of strict individualism, held by our Baptist brethren, could never even be thought of.

What I propose then, at the present time, is a full and careful discussion of this great subject, *the church membership of baptized children.*

And as it has fallen out, in the extreme individualism of our modern era, that multitudes are unable to conceive it as being any thing less than a kind of absurdity, or self-evident monstrosity, I shall be obliged to show the nature and kind of this membership.

As it is very commonly disrespected on the ground of its practical insignificance, I must also show the reasons why it should exist.

And then, since it is to the same extent, disowned as a rightful part of the true church economy, I must also establish the fact of its existence.

I. I am to show the nature and extent of this membership.

All those classes of Christian disciples who practice infant baptism conceive it, of course, to have a certain common character with adult baptism, and so to create a supposed, or somehow supposable membership in the church. And yet they often have it as a question, suppressed, or openly put without satisfaction—"who is a member of Christ's body, but one who is able to act and choose for himself, and in that manner to believe?" Many preachers, too, quite pass over the fact of any assignable reality in this relationship, publishing a call of salvation that practically ignores it as having any meaning at all; addressing young persons and children who have been baptized, in a way that as steadily and unqualifiedly assumes their unregenerate state, as if they were the children of heathenism. The opposers of infant baptism are bolder and more positive, of course, insisting always on the manifest absurdity of this nondescript, unintelligible, unintelligent membership; which makes a child a church member, not to be a voter nor a subject of discipline; which puts the initiatory rite of faith upon him, when he does not believe any thing, or even know that there is any to believe; creating thus a membership that has no rational meaning and no sound verity, but supposes a faith that does not exist, and constitutes a relationship that brings into no relation.

What, then, is this infant membership? what conception can we take of it, which will justify its Christian

dignity? A great many persons who are very sharp at
this kind of criticism, appear to have never observed
that creatures existing under conditions of growth, allow
no such terms of classification as those do which are
dead, and have no growth; such, for example, as
stones, metals, and earths. They are certain that gold
is not iron, and iron is not silver, and they suppose that
they can class the growing and transitional creatures,
that are separated by no absolute lines, in the same manner. They talk of colts and horses, lambs and sheep,
and it, possibly, not once occurs to them, that they can
never tell when the colt becomes a horse, or the lamb
a sheep; and that about the most definite thing they
can say, when pressed with that question, is that the
colt is potentially a horse, the lamb a sheep, even from
the first, having in itself this definite futurition; and,
therefore, that, while horses and sheep are not all to be
classed as colts and lambs, all colts and lambs may be
classed as horses and sheep. And just so children are
all men and women; and, if there is any law of futurition
in them to justify it, may be fitly classed as believing
men and women. And all the sharp arguments that
go to cover their membership, as such, in the church,
with absurdity, or turn it into derision, are just such
arguments as the inventors could raise with equal point,
to ridicule the horsehood and sheephood of the young
animals just referred to. The propriety of this membership does not lie in what those infants can or can not
believe, or do or do not believe, at some given time,
as, for example, on the day of their baptism; but it lies

in the covenant of promise, which makes their parents, parents in the Lord; their nurture, a nurture of the Lord; and so constitutes a force of futurition by which they are to grow up, imperceptibly, into "faithfuls among faithfuls," in Christ Jesus. Perhaps no one can tell when they become such, and it may be that some initiating touch of grace began to work inductively in them, by a process too delicate for human observation, even from their earliest infancy, or from their baptismal day. For there is a nurture of grace, as well as a grace of conversion; that for childhood, as this for the age of maturity, and one as sure and genuine as the other.

The conception, then, of this membership is, that it is a potentially real one; that it stands, for the present, in the faith of the parents and the promise which is to them and to their children, and that, on this ground, they may well enough be accounted believers, just as they are accounted potentially men and women. Then, as they come forward into maturity, it is to be assumed that they will come forward into faith, being grown in the nurture of faith, and will claim for themselves, the membership, into which they were before inserted.

Nor is this a case which has no analogies, that it should be held up as a mark of derision. It is generally supposed that our common law has some basis of common sense. And yet this body of law makes every infant child a citizen; requiring, as a point of public order, the whole constabulary and even military force of the state to come to the rescue, or the redress of his wrongs, when his person is seized or property invaded by conspiracy. This infant child can sue and be sued; for the court of chancery will appoint him a guardian, whose acts shall be the child's acts; and it shall be as if he were answering for his own education, dress, board, entertainments, and the damages done by his servants, precisely as if he were a man acting in his own cause. Doubtless it may sound very absurdly to call him a citizen. What can he do as a citizen? He can not vote, nor bear arms; he does not even know what these things mean, and yet he is a citizen. In one view, he votes, bears arms, legislates, even in his cradle; for the potentiality is in him, and the state takes him up in her arms, as it were, to own him as her citizen.

In a strongly related sense, it is, that the baptized child is a believer and a member of the church. There is no unreality in the position assigned him; for the futurition of God's promise is in him, and, by a kind of sublime anticipation, he is accepted in God's supernatural economy as a believer; even as the law accepts him, in the economy of society, to be a citizen. He is potentially both, and both is actually to be, in a way of transition so subtle and imperceptible that no one can tell, when he begins to be, either one, or the other.

Nor is it any objection that there might be some difficulty in the exercise of a regular church discipline over baptized children; or that, if this can not be done, they are really not church members in any sense that ought to be implied in the terms. Is then a child no citizen, because he is not held responsible in the law

in precisely the same manner as adults; responsible, in
a private action, for slander; or responsible, in a public, for murder and treason? The church membership
is, of course, to be qualified and shaded by the gradations of age; just as the law contrives to shade the
progress of the citizen child into the citizen man. All
the logical or theological bantering we hear, therefore,
on one side or the other, showing that the child, being
a church member, ought to be held subject to discipline;
or, if he is not held subject to discipline, that he is
really no church member, is without reason or any
proper show of practical dignity.

It was proposed—

II. To show the reasons why this relation of infant
membership should exist, or be appointed. And here
it is very obvious—

First of all, that, if there is really no place in the
church of God for infant children, then it must be said,
and formally maintained, that there is none. And what
could be worse in its effect on a child's feeling, than to
find himself repelled from the brotherhood of God's
elect, in that manner. What can the hapless creature
think, either of himself or of God, when he is told that
he is not old enough to be a Christian, or be owned by
the Saviour as a disciple?

Again, it would be most remarkable, if Christianity,
organizing a fold of grace and love, in the world and
for it, had yet no place in the fold for children. It
spreads its arms to say—" For God so loved the world,"

and even declares that publicans and harlots shall flock
in, before the captious priests and princes of the day;
and yet it has no place, we are told, for children; children are out of the category of grace! Jesus himself
was a child, and went through all the phases and conditions of childhood, not to show any thing by that
fact, as the Christian Fathers fondly supposed; he said,
too, "Suffer little children," but this was only his human feeling; he had no official relationship to such,
and no particular grace for them! They are all outside
the salvation-fold, hardening there in the storm, till
their choosing, refusing, desiring, sinning power is sufficiently unfolded to have a place assigned them within!
Is this Christianity? Is it a preparation so clumsy, so
little human, so imperfectly graduated to man as he is,
that it has no place for a full sixth part of the human
race; a part also to which the other five-sixths are
bound, in the dearest ties of love and care, and all but
compulsory expectation? It would seem that any Christian heart, meeting Christianity at this point, and sur-
veying it with only a little natural feeling, would even
be oppressed by the sense of some strange defect in it,
as a grace for the world. In this view it gives to little
children the heritage only of Cain, requiring them to
be driven out from the presence of the Lord, and grow
up there among the outside crew of aliens and enemies. Let no one be surprized that, under such treatment, they stiffen into alienated, wrathful men, ripened
for wickedness, by the ranges of all but reprobate exclusion in which they have been classed.

Nor, again, is it any breach on their liberty, that children are entered into this qualified membership by their parents. What is it but a being entered into privilege? Is it a hard thing for human parents to enter their child into the lot of wealth and high society, and a station of family dignity, because it does not leave them to acquire the wealth and the position of honor in society, by their own original exertion, unassisted? When the order of the Cincinnati took their sons into the grand society of revolutionary honor with them, was it a breach on the liberty of the children? Or we may take another view of the question. The church of God is a school, and the members are disciples, or learners. Does not every parent choose the school for his children, giving them no choice in the matter, and taking it to be his own unquestionable right? This, too, on the ground that they are to have the benefit of his maturer judgment, and his more competent choice. Where then is the encroachment, when Christian parents baptize their child into the same discipleship with themselves, and set it in the school of Christ? It is only a part of their ordinary charge as parents, for it is given them to have the child in their own character, so to speak, and be themselves discipled with it and for it, (and why not it with them?) in all the honors and hopes of the heavenly kingdom.

Consider again the remarkable and certainly painful fact that, in the view which excludes infant baptism and the discipleship of children, the conversion itself of a parent operates a kind of dissolution in the family state, than which nothing could be more unnatural. It is much as if our process of naturalization in the state, were to naturalize the parents and not the children; leaving these to be foreigners still, and aliens. God's effectual calling is no such unnatural grace; it will never call the parents away from the children; to be themselves included in the great family of salvation, and look out, in their joy, to see their children fenced away! No—"The promise is to you and to your children;" not, to you without your children. Come in hither, then, ye guilty families of man, parents to be parents in the Lord, children to obey in the Lord, all to be circled by the common grace of life and the common fellowship of the saints. Why should we think that our Great Father who has been refusing, ever since the world began, to so much as put into any bird of the air, an instinct that will draw it away from its nest, may yet, as a matter of celestial mercy, be engaged by his Spirit, in the gathering of human parents away from their young!

It is a matter, too, of great consequence to parents, as respects their own fidelity in their office, that their children are not put away, by the Saviour, to hold rank with heathens outside of the fold, but are brought in with them, to be heirs together with them in the grace of life. What will justify, or will naturally produce, a more sullen remissness of duty in parents, than to feel that, for the present, God has shut away, and is holding away their children, and that they are never to be dis-

ciples of the fold, till after they have been passed round
into it, through long detours of estrangement and ripen-
ing guiltiness? If there is nothing better for them
than to be converted just as heathens are, why should
they, as parents, be greatly concerned for their own example, and the faithfulness of their training, when the
conversion is to be every thing and will have power to
remedy every defect?

How refreshing the contrast, when the children, giv-
en to God in baptism, are accounted members of the
church with them, as being included in their faith, and
having the seal of it upon them. They look upon it
now as their privilege to be parents in the Lord. Their
prayers, they understand, are to keep heaven open upon
their house. Their aims are to be Christian. Their
tastes and manners to be flavored by the Christian hope
in which they live. There is to be a quickening element in the atmosphere they make. They will set all
things upon a Christian footing for their children's sake;
and their children, growing up in such nurture of the
Lord, will, how certainly, unfold what their nurture
itself has quickened.

It is still another consideration, that the church itself,
having this infant membership in it, will unfold other
aims and tempers, and exert a finer quality of power.
It will not be a dry convention of simply grown up
men and women; the men will, some of them, be fathers, the women mothers, and the children being also
gathered with them in the fold, they will all be gentled
together by the tender brotherhood of the little ones.

The parents will learn from the children quite as much as they teach, and will do their teaching fitly, just because they learn.   The church prayers will have a certain paternity and maternity in them, and the children will feel the grace of these prayers warming always round them.   Even the church life itself, two, or three, or more, generations deep, will be qualified by the grandfather and grandmother spirit, and the father and mother spirit, and the reverent manners of the little ones, and the whole volume of religious life will be unfolded thus, by taking into itself the whole volume of nature and family feeling.

Such are some of the reasons, briefly and faintly presented, which determine, as I conceive, God's appointment of the great fact of an infant membership in his church.   And yet the reasons, taken by themselves, are hardly a sufficient evidence of the fact.   They set us in the mood of respect, and even put us in the expectation of it, but they leave the inquiry still upon our hands—

III. Whether the supposed infant membership is a real and true fact?   That it is, may be seen from the following proofs:—

1. Those declarations of Scripture which assert or assume the fact.   Thus, when the Saviour commands— "Suffer little children to come unto me and forbid them not, for of such is the kingdom of heaven," it would be very singular if they could not come in with the disciples, when they may so freely come to the Master him-

self. And if Christ had been calling his disciples themselves into fraternity with him, what more could he have said for them, than that of such is the kingdom of heaven? Nor is it any objection, as respects the children, that, except a man be born again, he can not be entered into this kingdom; for potentially, at least, they are thus born again; and so are as fitly to be counted citizens of the kingdom, as they are to be citizens of the state. Besides, there is still less in that kind of objection, that the kingdom of God, taken in its lower sense as identical with the church, is expressly likened by the Saviour to a net that gathers of every kind. And what again does it signify, as regards the apostolic ideas of this matter of infant membership, that the great apostle to the Gentiles, in at least two of his epistles to Christian churches, addresses, directly, children, as being included among the saints and faithful in Christ Jesus? I allege as proof,

2. The analogy of circumcision. This was given to be the seal of faith, and the church token, in that manner, of a godly seed. Baptism can certainly be the same with as little difficulty, or as little charge of absurdity. True, they were not all Israel that were of Israel, and so all may not be Israel that are baptized. Enough that God gives the possibility, in both cases, in giving the rite itself; and then it is to be seen, whether the parents will be parents in the Lord, as it is formally permitted them to be. Let the true point here be carefully observed; some kind of presumption must be given by God, in respect to the church position of

children; for they must either be taken into the church, or else they must be excluded till they are old enough to be admitted on the ground of a religious experience—there is no other alternative. If they are excluded, then it is taken for granted, that they are to grow up as unbelievers and aliens, which is only their public consignment to evil. If they are taken to be in the faith, presumptively, as in the nurture of their parents, and so accepted, then every kind encouragement is given to them, and every pledge of divine help is graciously given to their parents. Which of the two methods is most consonant to nature, and worthiest of God's beneficence, it is not difficult to see. God, on his part, gives no presumption, either to the parents or their child, that he is to be only a transgressor and alien, but he gives the seal of the faith, as a pledge, to raise their expectation of what he will do for them, and to throw the blame of a godless childhood and youth, if such there is to be, on themselves.

3. The church connection of children is virtually assumed, as we may see, by the apostle Paul, when he teaches that the believing wife sanctifies the unbelieving husband, and the believing husband the unbelieving wife—"else were your children unclean, but now are they holy." He refers, in this matter, it is plain, to the effect of a parental faith, on the church position of children. He does not, of course, use the term "sanctify," in any spiritual sense, as affirming the regeneration of character in the children; but he alludes only to the church ideas of clean and unclean, affirming

that the unclean state of a godless father, or mother, is
so far taken away by the clean state of a godly mother,
or father, that the children are accounted clean, or
holy—so far holy, that is, that they are of the fold, and
not aliens, or unclean foreigners without the fold, as the
Jews were accustomed to regard all the uncircumcised
races.   One believing parent, he declares, puts the children in the church classification of believers.

4. All the reasons I have given for the observance
of infant baptism, go to establish also the fact of infant membership in the church.   And this holds good,
especially of that which discovers the origin of the rite
in proselyte baptism.   For as foreigners, becoming proselytes, were baptized and so made clean, thus to be accounted natural born citizens, so Christ, reapplying the
rite to a spiritual use, makes it the token of that regeneration which enters the soul into his heavenly kingdom, and gives a divine citizenship there.   In which
you may see how my comparison of infant membership
in the church, to the well-known citizenship of infants
in the state, is borne out by Christian authority itself.
Their very baptism is the figure of their citizenship;
wherein they are shown to be "fellow-citizens of the
saints, and of the household of God."

Now it is to be conceded, as respects all these proofs
from the Scripture, that the church membership of children is not formally asserted in them.   According to
a certain coarse way of judging, therefore, they are not
as strong as they might be.   And yet, in a more perceptive and really truer mode of judgment, they lack

that kind of strength just because they have too much
of another, which is deeper and more satisfactory, to
suffer it.   So familiar is the idea, to all Jewish minds,
of a religious oneness in parents and their offspring,
that a church institution of any kind, arranged to include parents and not their offspring, would even have
been a shocking offense to the nation.   Children were
as much expected to be with their parents in their
religion, as they were to be in their sustentation.   Does
any one doubt that children were citizens in the old
theocracy?   And yet I recollect no passage where that
sort of membership with their parents is instituted, or
formally asserted.   And the reason, is that it is a fact
too familiar, too close to the sentiment or sense of na
ture, to be asserted.   We can even see for ourselves
that they look upon religious faith itself as a kind of
hereditament in the family, descending on the child by
laws of family connexion, where it is not hindered by
some bad fault in the manners and walk of the parents.
Thus we hear even Paul himself, the man who knew
as well as any other, and taught as powerfully, the significance of Christian faith, addressing his young brother
Timothy, as having the greater confidence in his faith
because it is hereditary—" When I call to remembrance
the unfeigned faith that is in thee, which dwelt first in
thy grandmother Lois, and thy mother Eunice, and I
am persuaded that in thee also."   This unfeigned, this
certainly true Christian faith, he conceives to have even
leapt the gulf between the old religion and the new,
and so to have come down upon him, through at

least two generations of godly motherhood under the
law and before the coming of Jesus. When such notions of family grace are familiar, what does it signify
that the church membership of children is not formally
asserted? How could that be instituted by an apostolic decree, which no apostle, or man, or woman, had
ever thought could be otherwise?

Over and above these more direct evidences, for the
church membership of baptized children, there is still
another kind of evidence to be adduced, which has, and
very properly should have, much weight. I allude to
the opinions of the church and her most qualified
teachers, from the apostolic era downward. In one
sense, the mere opinions of men regarding such a question are of little consequence. But where they coin-
cide with the known practice of the church from the
earliest times downward, and show the practice to be
grounded in the same reasons of organic unity and
presumptive grace that we are now asserting, they
both show that our doctrine is no novelty, and contribute a powerful evidence in support of its original
authenticity.

Thus I have cited already in support of infant baptism, passages from Justin Martyr, Ireneus, Tertullian,
Origen, the Shepherd of Hermas, and others, which not
only show the fact of infant baptism, but discover also,
in their phraseology, the same views of church membership that I am now asserting. This whole view of
infant membership, as it stood in the first three centu-

ries of the church history, appears to be well summed up, both as regards the facts and the reasons, in the following statement of Neander:—

"It is the idea of infant baptism that Christ, through the divine life which he imparted to, and revealed in, human nature, sanctified that germ from its earliest development. The child born in a Christian family was, when all things were as they should be, to have this advantage over others, that he did not come to Christianity out of heathenism or the sinful natural life, but from the first dawning of consciousness unfolded his powers under the imperceptible, preventing influences of a sanctifying, ennobling religion; that with the earliest germinations of the natural self-conscious life, another divine principle of life, transforming the nature, should be brought nigh to him, ere yet the ungodly principle could come into full activity, and the latter should, at once, find here its powerful counterpoise. In such a life, the new birth was not to constitute a new crisis, beginning at some definable moment, but it was to begin imperceptibly, and so proceed through the whole life. Hence baptism, the visible sign of regeneration, was to be given to the child at the very outset: the child was to be consecrated to the Redeemer from the very beginning of its life."*

A more popular and practical view of Christianity, as seen in the domestic life of families, and one, at the same time, wholly coincident, is given by Cave:—

" Gregory Nazianzen peculiarly commends his mother,

---

* Neander's Church History, Torrey's translation, pp. 311, 312.

that not only she herself was consecrated to God, and brought up under a pious education, but that she conveyed it down, as a necessary inheritance, to her children; and it seems her daughter Gorgonia was so well seasoned with these holy principles, that she religiously walked in the steps of so good a pattern; and did not only reclaim her husband, but educated her children and nephews in the ways of religion, giving them an excellent example while she lived, and leaving this, as her last charge and request when she died. * * * This was the discipline under which Christians were brought up in those times.   Religion was instilled into them betimes, which grew up and mixed itself with their ordinary labors and recreations. * * * * So that Jerome says, of the place where he lived, you could not go into the field, but you might hear the plowman at his hallelujahs, the mower at his hymns, and the vine-dresser singing David's Psalms."*

I can not answer for an exact agreement of my doctrine with that of Calvin.   It must be sufficient that he recognizes the valid possibility of a regenerate character, existing long before it is formally developed, and the propriety of infant baptism as the initiatory rite of membership.   He says:—

"Christ was sanctified from his earliest infancy, that he might sanctify in himself all his elect.   But how, it is inquired, are infants regenerated who have no knowledge either of good or evil?   We reply that the work of God is not yet without existence because it is not

---

* Primitive Christianity, pp. 173, 174.

observed or understood by us. Now it is certain
that some infants are saved, and that they are previously regenerated by the Lord is beyond all doubt.
They are baptized into future repentance and faith;
for though these graces have not yet been formed in
them, the seeds of both are nevertheless implanted in
their hearts by the secret operations of the Spirit."*

The mercurial mind of Baxter penetrates directly
into all the subtleties of the question, asserting the organic unity of children who stand accepted in the covenant of their fathers; showing how regenerate character is to begin, seminally, in the children of them that
believe, and get the start of sin by a kind of gracious
anticipation; and so that, in this view, nurture and
growth are God's way of unfolding grace in the church,
as preaching and conversion are his method of grace
with them that are without. Which three points are
successively asserted in the following passages:—

" *Q.*—Why then are they baptized who can not
covenant?

"*A.*—As children are made sinners and miserable by
the parents, without any act of their own, so they are
delivered out of it by the free grace of Christ, upon a
condition performed by their parents. Else they who
are visibly born in sin and misery should have no certain or visible way of remedy. Nature maketh them,
as it were, *parts of* their parents, or so near as causeth
their sin and misery. And this nearness supposed,
God, by his free grace, hath put it in the power of the

---

* Ins. cap. xvi. § 17, 18, 20.

parents to accept for them the blessings of the covenant, and to enter them into the covenant of God, the parents' will being instead of their own, who have yet no will to choose for themselves."*

"Of those baptized in infancy, some do betimes receive the secret seeds of grace, which, by the blessings of a holy education, is stirring in them according to their capacity, and working them to God by actual desires, and working them from all known sin, and entertaining further grace, and turning them into actual acquaintance with Christ, as soon as they arrive at full natural capacity, so that they *never were* actual ungodly persons."†

"Ungodly parents do serve the devil so effectually, in the first impressions on their children's minds, that it is more than magistrates and ministers and all reforming means can afterwards do to recover them from that sin to God. Whereas, if you would first engage their hearts to God by a religious education, piety would then have all those advantages that sin hath now. (Prov. xxii. 6.) The language which you teach them to speak when they are children, they will use all their life after, if they live with those that use it. And so the opinions which they first receive, and the customs which they are used to at first are very hardly changed afterwards. I doubt not to affirm, that a godly education is God's first and ordinary appointed means, for the begetting of actual faith and other graces in the children of believers. Many

---

* Teacher of Householders, fol., vol. ii., p. 135.

† Confirmation, fol., vol. iv., p. 267.

have received grace before; but they can not sooner have actual faith, repentance, love, or any grace than they may have reason itself, in act and exercise. And the preaching of the word by public ministers, is not the first ordinary means of grace, to any but those that were graceless till they come to hear such preaching; that is, to those on whom the first appointed means hath been neglected or proved vain; * * * * therefore it is apparent that the ordinary appointed means for the first actual grace, is parents' godly instruction and education of their children. And public preaching is appointed for the conversion of those only that have missed the blessing of the first appointed means."*

Our New England fathers, coming out as they did from a mode of church economy which made Christian piety itself to be scarcely more than baptism, and passing through great struggles to settle a scheme of church order that should recognize the strict individuality of persons, and the essential personality of spiritual regeneration, fell off for a time, as they naturally might, into a denial of the great underlying principles and facts on which the membership of baptized children in the church must ever be rested. In the Cambridge Platform of 1649, they asserted a view of membership, by which it was to be rigidly confined to such as appear to be renewed persons. Meantime none were allowed to be qualified as voters in the commonwealth, except in the Hartford and Providence colonies, who were not members of the church—the same principle with which

---

* Christian Directory, vol. ii., cap. 6, § 4, fol. p. 516.

they had been familiar in England. The result was, under their individualizing scheme of membership, that they began to find, as soon as their sons were grown to manhood, that many of them, even though baptized, were, in fact, aliens in the state. They could not vote in the state, and, having no pretense of faith, could not baptize their children, not being in the church themselves. Another synod was convened A. D. 1662, to find some way of relieving these difficulties. And they hit upon the rather strange expedient of a half-membership, allowing all baptized persons who live reputably, and give a speculative assent to the gospel, to be so far members that they may be voters and have their children baptized. This decision was stoutly opposed by some of the ablest men in the synod, and great debates followed. And yet as the facts were reported by Cotton Mather, these three positions were asserted and agreed to on all hands—even though the scheme adopted had no systematic and practical agreement with them, or ground of reason in them.

1. That the children of Christian parents, trained in a Christian way, often grow up as spiritually renewed persons, and must indeed be accounted true disciples of Christ, until some evidence conclusive to the contrary is given by their conduct.

"Children of the covenant have *frequently* the beginning of grace wrought in them in younger years, as Scripture and experience show. Instance Joseph, Samuel, David, Solomon, Abijah, Josiah, Daniel, John Baptist, Timothy. Hence this sort of persons, [baptized persons] showing nothing to the contrary, are, in charity, or to ecclesiastical reputation, visible believers."*

2. That baptism supposes an initial state of piety, or some right beginning, in which the child is prepared unto good, by causes prior to his own will.

" We are to distinguish between faith and the *hopeful beginning* of it, the charitable judgment whereof runs upon a great latitude, and faith in the *special exercise* of it, unto the visible discovery whereof, more experienced operations are to be inquired after. The words of Dr. Ames are: 'Children are not to be admitted to partake of all church privileges, till first *increase* of faith do appear, but from those which belong to the *beginning* of faith and entrance into the church they are not to be excluded.' "*

3. That there is a kind of individualism which runs only to evil; that the church is designed to be an organic, vital, grace-giving power, and thus a nursery of spiritual life to its children.

" The way of the Anabaptists, to admit none to membership and baptism but adult professors, is the straitest way; one would think it should be a way of great purity; but experience hath shewed that it has been an inlet unto great corruption. If we do not keep in the way of a *converting, grace-giving covenant*, and keep persons under those church dispensations wherein grace is given, the church will die of a lingering though not violent death. The Lord hath not set up churches only that a *few old* Christians may keep one another warm

---

* Magnalia, book v., fol. p. 72.　　† Magnalia, book v., fol. p. 77.

while they live, and then carry away the church with them when they die; no, but that they might with all care, and with all the obligations and advantages to that care that may be, *nurse* still successively another generation of subjects to our Lord, that may stand up in his kingdom when they are gone."*

Under this half-way covenant, and probably in part because of it, practical religion fell into a state of great debility. The churches lost their spirituality, and had well nigh lost the idea of spiritual life itself; when at length the Great Revival, under Whitfield and Edwards, inaugurated and brought up to its highest intensity the new era of individualism—the same overwrought, misapplied scheme of personal experience in religion, which has continued with some modifications to the present day. It is a religion that begins explosively, raises high frames, carries little or no expansion, and after the campaign is over, subsides into a torpor. Considered as a distinct era, introduced by Edwards, and extended and caricatured by his cotemporaries, it has one great merit, and one great defect. The merit is that it displaced an era of dead formality, and brought in the demand of a truly supernatural experience. The defect is, that it has cast a type of religious individualism, intense beyond any former example. It makes nothing of the family, and the church, and the organic powers God has constituted as vehicles of grace. It takes every man as if he had existed *alone;* presumes that he is unreconciled to God until he has undergone

---

* Magnalia, book v., fol. p. 81.

some sudden and explosive experience in adult years, or after the age of reason; demands that experience, and only when it is reached, allows the subject to be an heir of life. Then, on the other side, or that of the Spirit of God, the very act or *ictus* by which the change is wrought is isolated or individualized, so as to stand in no connection with any other of God's means or causes —an epiphany, in which God leaps from the stars, or some place above, to do a work apart from all system, or connection with his other works. Religion is thus a kind of transcendental matter, which belongs on the outside of life, and has no part in the laws by which life is organized—a miraculous epidemic, a fire-ball shot from the moon, something holy, because it is from God, but so extraordinary, so out of place, that it can not suffer any vital connection with the ties, and causes, and forms, and habits, which constitute the frame of our history. Hence the desultory, hard, violent, and often extravagant or erratic character it manifests. Hence, in part, the dreary years of decay and darkness, that interspace our months of excitement and victory.

Even Edwards himself, fifteen years after the Great Revival, began to be oppressed with sorrowful convictions of some great defect in the matter and mode of it, confessing his doubt whether "the greater part of supposed converts give reason, by their conversation, to suppose that they continue converts;" protesting, also, his special confidence in the fruits of family religion in terms like these—

"Every Christian family ought to be, as it were ·

little church, consecrated to Christ, and wholly influenced and governed by his rules.   And family education
and order are some of the *chief means of grace*.   If these
fail, all other means are likely to prove ineffectual."*

Dr. Hopkins, a pupil of Edwards, had probably been
turned by suggestions from him, to a consideration of
the importance of family nurture and piety, as .con-
nected with the propagation of religion; and, as if to
supply some defect in this direction, he occupied sixty
pages in his System of Divinity, with a careful discussion of the "nature and design of infant baptism."   In
this article, he goes even beyond the notion of a presumptive piety in the children baptized, and says:—
"The church receive and look upon them as holy, and
those who shall be saved.   So they are as visibly holy,
or as really holy, in their view, as their parents are."†

How far his theory of conversion would compel him
to isolate the act of God by which the spiritual renovation of a soul is wrought, I will not undertake to decide.   Enough, that he asserts an organic connection of
character between parents and children, as effectual for
good as for evil; nay, that they may as truly, and in
the same sense, transmit holiness as they transmit *existence*.   Thus, after asserting, not more clearly or decidedly than I have done, the impossibility that parents
should spiritually renew their children, considered as
acting by themselves, he says:—

"But it does not follow from this, that God has not
so constituted the covenant of grace, that holiness shall

---

* Vol. i. p. 90.   † Vol. ii. p. 319.

be communicated, by Him, to the children, in consequence of the faithful endeavors of their parents; so
that, in this sense, and by virtue of such a constitution,
they do by their faithful endeavors convey saving blessings to their children. In this way they give existence
to their children. God produces their existence by his
own Almighty energy; but, by the constitution he has
established, they receive their existence from their parents, or by their means. By an established constitution, parents convey moral depravity to their children.
And if God has been pleased to make a constitution
and appoint a way, in his covenant of grace with man,
by which pious parents may convey and communicate
moral rectitude or holiness to their children, they, by
using the appointed means, do it as really and effectually
as they communicate existence to them. In this sense,
therefore, they may convey and give holiness and salvation to their children."*

Dr. Witherspoon, a cotemporary of Dr. Hopkins,
held opinions on this subject that were in a high degree
coincident, though presented in a more popular and less
doctrinal shape. He says:—

"I will not enlarge on some refined remarks of
persons as distinguished for learning as piety, some
of whom have supposed that they [children] are capable of receiving impressions of desire and aversion, and
even of moral temper, particularly of love or hatred, in
the first year of their lives. * * * When the gospel comes to a people that have long sitten in darkness,

* Pages 334, 335.

there may be numerous converts of all ages; but when the gospel has long been preached, in plenty and purity, and ordinances regularly administered, few but those who are called in early life are called at all. A very judicious and pious writer, Richard Baxter, is of opinion that in a regular state of the church, and a tolerable measure of faithfulness and purity in its officers, family instruction and government are the usual means of conversion, public ordinances of edification. This seems agreeable to the language of Scripture; for we are told that God hath set in the church apostles, prophets, evangelists, pastors and teachers, (not for converting sinners, but) for the perfecting of the saints, for the work of the ministry, for the edifying of the body of Christ."*

From all these citations, which could be multiplied without limit, it will be seen that the children of Christian parents have been looked upon as being heirs of the parental faith, and presumptively included in that faith; and so, either with or without a distinct assertion of the proper church membership of children, such opinions have been held in all ages respecting them, as make the denial of their membership a clear impropriety and even a kind of offense against nature.

It is hardly necessary to add, in closing this subject, that if children baptized are so far accepted as members of the Christian church, it must be a great fault and a most hurtful dereliction of duty that nothing is practically made of this membership, and that really it passes

---

* Witherspoon, vol. ii., pp. 395, 397.

for a thing of no significance. The rite is appointed because it has a meaning and a value, and then, when it is passed, it is treated in a way that even indicates the possible absurdity of it. That the children will see any thing in such a mode of practice is impossible. And it requires but the smallest possible perception, to see that the rite will, in this manner, be regularly sinking into discredit, till it is quite done away, and the value it might have in the church is lost. To accomplish all that is needed to give full effect to the rite—

Baptized children ought to be enrolled by name in the catalogue of each church, as composing a distinct class of candidate, or catechumen, members; and to see that they are held in expectancy, thus, by the church, as presumptively one with them in the faith they profess.

Then, when they come forward to acknowledge their baptism, and assume the covenant in their own choice, they ought not to be received as converts from the world, as if they were heathens coming into the fold, but there should be a distinction preserved, such as makes due account of their previous qualified membership; a *form of assumption* tendered in place of a *confession*—something answering to the Lutheran *confirmation*, passed without a bishop's hands.

Children, as soon as they are well out of their infancy, ought to be taken also to the stated meetings of fellowship and prayer, drawn into all the moods of worship, praise, supplication, reproof, as being rightfully concerned in them, on the score of their membership.

There ought to be a great deal made of singing too in such meetings, that they may join their voices and play into expression their own tribute of feeling and Christian sentiment.

Whenever there are orphan children, that have been baptized, the church ought to look after them, as being members; see, if possible, that they are not neglected, but trained up in a Christian manner; provided, if need be, with a godly fatherhood and motherhood in the church itself; led into the church and out into the world, as disciples beloved according to their years.

Meantime, it is a matter of prime significance that the Christian father and mother should live so as to indicate a sense of their privilege and responsibility; even as Abraham did when he sojourned in the land of promise, as in a strange country, dwelling in tents with Isaac and Jacob, *heirs with him of the same promise.* It is one thing to live for a family of children, as if they were going possibly to be converted, and a very different to live for them as church members, training them into their holy profession; one thing to have them about as strangers to the covenant of promise, and another to have them about as heirs of the same promise, growing up into it, to fulfill the seal of faith already upon them. One great reason why the children of Christian parents turn out so badly is, that they are taken to be the world, and the manner and spirit of the house are brought down to be of the world too, and partly for their sake. Take them as disciples of Jesus, to be carefully trained for Him; prepared to no mere worldly tastes, and fashions, and pleasures, but kept in purity, saved from the world, and led forth under all tender examples of obedience and godly living; and it will be strange if that nurture of the Lord does not show them growing up in the faith, to be sons and daughters, indeed, of the Lord Almighty.

VIII

THE OUT-POPULATING POWER OF THE CHRISTIAN STOCK

"And did he not make one? Yet had he the residue of the Spirit. And wherefore one? That he might have a godly seed."—*Malachi*, ii. 15.

THE prophet is enforcing here a strict observance of marriage. And he adverts, in his argument, to the single and sole state of the first human pair, as a standing proof against polygamy, inconstancy, and all similar abuses of the marriage state. God was not spent, he says, in creating a single man, Adam, and a single woman, Eve, but he had such a residue, or overplus of creative energy left, that he could have created millions if he would. Wherefore then did he cease, producing only just one man and woman, and no more? The answer is—That he might have a godly seed. In that lies the reason, he declares, of God's economy in this family institution. We perceive, accordingly,

That God is, from the first, looking for a godly seed; or, what is nowise different, inserting such laws of population that piety itself shall finally over-populate the world.

To be more explicit, there are, too, principal modes by which the kingdom of God among men may be, and is to be extended. One is by the process of conversion, and the other by that of family propagation; one by gain-

ing over to the side of faith and piety, the other by the
populating force of faith and piety themselves.   The
former is the grand idea that has taken possession of the
churches of our times—they are going to convert the
world.   They have taken hold of the promise, which
so many of the prophets have given out, of a time when
the reign of Christ shall be universal, extending to all
nations and peoples; and the expectation is that, by
preaching Christ to all the nations, they will finally
convert them and bring them over into the gospel fold.
Meantime very much less, or almost nothing, is made
of the other method, viz: that of Christian population.
Indeed, as we are now looking at religion, or religious
character and experience, we can hardly find a place for
any such thought as a possible reproduction thus of
parental character and grace in children.   They must
come in by choice, on their own account; they must be
converted over from an outside life that has grown to
maturity in sin.   Are they not individuals, and how
are they to be initiated into any thing good by inheritance and before choice?   It is as if they were all so
many Melchisedecs in their religious nature, only not
righteous at all—without father, without mother, without
descent.   Descent brings them nothing.   Born of faith,
and bosomed in it, and nurtured by it, still there is yet
to be no faith begotten in them, nor so much as a contagion even of faith to be caught in their garments.

What I propose, at the present time, is to restore, if
possible, a juster impression of this great subject; to
show that conversion over to the church is not the only

way of increase; that God ordains a law of population in it as truly as he does in an earthly kingdom, or colony, and by this increase from within, quite as much as by conversion from without, designs to give it, finally, the complete dominion promised.

Nor let any one be repelled from this truth, or set against it, by the prejudice that piety is and must be a matter of individual choice. The same is true of sin. Many of us have no difficulty in saying that mankind are born sinners. They may just as truly and properly be born saints—it requires the self-active power to be just as far developed to commit sin, as it does to choose obedience. This individual capacity of will and choice is one that matures at no particular tick of the clock, but it comes along out of incipiencies, grows by imperceptible increments, and takes on a character, in good or evil, or a mixed character in both, so imperceptibly and gradually, that it seems to be, in some sense, prefashioned by what the birth and nurture have communicated. We may fitly enough call this character a propagated quality—in strictest metaphysical definition, it is not; in sturdiest fact of history, or practical life, it is.

Nor let any one be diverted from the truth I am going to assert, by imagining that a propagated piety is, of course, a piety without regeneration, dispensing with what Christ himself declared to be the indispensable need of every human creature. For aught that appears, regeneration may, in some initial and profoundly real sense, be the twin element of propagation itself. The parentage may, in other words, be so thoroughly wrought in by the Spirit of God, as to communicate the seeds or incipiencies of a godly, just as it communicates the seeds of a depravated and disordered, character. In one view, the child will be regenerate when he is born; in another view, he will not be, till the godly life is developed in his own personal choice and liberty.

Dismissing these, and other like prepossessions, let us go on to examine some of the evidences by which this doctrine of church population is to be substantiated.

1. I name, as an evidence, the very important fact that in the matter of infant baptism and infant church membership, grounded as they are in the assumption that a believing parentage sanctifies the offspring, God is seen to frame the order of church economy, so as to bring in the law of increase, or family propagation; looking to the populating principle for growth, just as the founder of a new colony, on some foreign shore, would look. He declares that parents are to be parents in the Lord, and children to grow up in the nurture of the Lord. The whole scheme of organic unity in the family and of family grace in the church, is just what it should be, if the design were to propagate religion, not by conversions only, but quite as much, or more, by the populating force embodied in it—just that force which, in all states and communities, is known to be the most majestic and silently creative force in their history.

2. It is a matter of consequence to observe, that the Abrahamic order and covenant stood upon this footing, formally proposing and promising to make the father of the faithful a blessing to mankind, by and through the

multitude of his offspring. "Look now," says the word
of promise, "toward heaven and tell the stars, if thou be
able to number them. So shall thy seed be." Again,
"I will make thee a father of many nations." And
again, "All the nations of the earth shall be blessed in
him." Neither was it to be the only blessing, that
Jesus, the Saviour of mankind, was to be born of this
honored family. "I will make thee exceeding fruitful," was the form of the promise; and the blessing, as
we may see, by all the modes of expression used, was
to turn as much on the wonderful populousness of the
stock, overspreading the world, as it was, on the new-
creating grace to be unfolded in it. For if it be matter
of debate, in what precise manner, the Christian church
has connection with this more ancient and apparently
mere family bond, there is certainly no doubt in the
mind of the great Christian apostle, that there is a real
and valid connection of some kind, such that the promise passes and spreads, and is to get its fulfillment, only
when the godly seed has filled the world. The spread
of Christianity is, in his view, the blessing of Abraham
come on the Gentiles, through Jesus Christ. These
Gentile converts, too, he calls the seed of Abraham—
"And if ye be Christ's, then are ye Abraham's seed and
heirs according to the promise." He looks, you will
perceive, on the Gentile converts as being grafted in
upon the ancient stock; which also he expressly says,
in another place, counting them to be so unified with
Abraham, as to be the outgrowth of his person. Just
as the proselytes were taken to be sons and daughters

of Abraham, naturalized into his stock, so are these converts to become the channel of his over-populating force, till such time as the natural branches, broken off, are grafted in again. And, in this view, it is that the Gentile converts are called "*a seed*," that being the word that contemplates the fact of their multiplication as a family of God.

3. It is an argument which ought to be convincing, that the universal spread of the gospel, and the universal reign of Christian truth—that which prophets and apostles promise, and which we, in these last times, have taken up as our fondest, most impelling Christian hope—plainly enough never can be compassed by the process of adult conversions, but must finally be reached, if reached at all, by the populating forces of a family grace in the church. We expect that, in that day, all flesh shall see the salvation of God, and that every thing human will be regenerated by it; that the glory of God will cover the earth like a baptism of water—even as the waters cover the sea. These are to be the times of the restitution of all things. God, we believe, will put his laws now in the mind, and write them on the heart, and "all shall know him from the least to the greatest." I do not care to press these epithets *least* and *greatest*—perhaps there is no reference to children in them. It would scarcely make the text more significant if there were; for this universal triumph of the word, in which we all believe, this imprinting of it on men's hearts, all over the world, in such manner as to make the day of glory—that great

day of light which figures so grandly in the visions of God's prophets and apostles, and is promised by Christ himself—such a day, I say, can plainly enough never be reached, as long as the children of the world grow up in sin, as we now assume to be the fact, still to be called and prayed for as now and preached into the kingdom. When the little child shall lead forth in pairs the wolf and the lamb, the leopard and the kid, the calf and the young lion; when the sucking child shall play on the hole of the asp unstung, and the weaned child shall put his hand unbitten on the cockatrice's den; we not only take hold of it as the prophet's meaning that there is to be a great universal mitigation of the ferocities of appetite, and prey, and passion, in the world, but that the little ones are to have their part in the joy, and be raised in dominion by that all-renewing grace which has now restored and imparadised the world. Otherwise our day of glory would be such a kind of jubilee as shows ·the adult souls only of the race to be gathered into the kingdom, while the poor, unripe sinners of childhood, a full fourth in the total number, are in no sense, in it, but are waiting their conversion-time on the outside! This is not our millennial day; we have no such hope.

We conceive that Christ will then overspread all souls with his glory, and that children, filled according to their age and measure with the divine motions of grace, will be unfolding the heavenly beauty, as they advance in years, even as the flowers unfold their colors in the sun. These colors no one sees in the root, and the clear, transparent sap it circulates, and yet the color is there. Just so will God, in that great day of grace, bring out of infancy and childhood, sanctifyingly touched by his Spirit, what creates them children of God, as truly as their parents, though too subtle to be seen, or defined, till it has blushed into color, in the sunlight of their intelligence in the truth. Such a day of glory then contemplates a great in-birth of sanctification, or renewing life. Conversions from without are to have their part in preparing it, but the consummation hoped for is even impossible, as regards a third or fourth part of the race, save as it is reached by a populating process which enters them into life itself, through the gate of a sanctified infancy and childhood.

4. Consider a very important fact in human physiology which goes far to explain, or take away the strangeness and seeming extravagance of the truth I am endeavoring to establish, viz., that qualities of education, habit, feeling, and character, have a tendency always to grow in, by long continuance, and become thoroughly inbred in the stock. We meet humble analogies of this fact in the domestic animals. The operations to which they are trained, and in which they become naturalized by habit, become predispositions, in a degree, in their offspring; and they, in their turn, are as much more easily trained on that account. The next generation are trained still more easily, till what was first made habitual, finally becomes functional in the stock, and almost no training is wanted. That which was inculcated by practice passes into a ten-

dency, and descends as a natural gift, or endowment. The same thing is observable, on a large scale, in the families of mankind. A savage race is a race bred into low living, and a faithless, bloody character. The instinct of law, society, and order is substituted, finally, by the overgrown instinct of prey, and the race is lost to any real capacity of social regeneration; unless they can somehow be kept in ward, and a process of training, long enough to breed in what has been lost. A race of slaves becomes a physiologically servile race in the same way. And so it is, in part, that civilization descends from one generation to another. It is not merely that laws, social modes, and instrumentalities of education descend, and that so the new sprung generations are fashioned after birth, by the forms and principles and causes into which they have been set, but it is that the very type of the inborn quality is a civilized type. The civilization is, in great part, an inbred civility. There is a something functional in them, which is itself configured to the state of art, order, law, and property.

The Jewish race are a striking and sad proof of the manner in which any given mode of life may, or rather must, become a functional property in the offspring. The old Jewish stock of the Scripture times, whatever faults they may have had, certainly were not marked by any such miserably, sordid, usurious, garbage-vending propensity, as now distinguishes the race. But the cruelties they have suffered under Christian governments, shut up in the Jews' quarter of the great cities, dealing in old clothes and other mean articles for their gains, hiding these in the shape of gold and jewels in the crevices of their cellars, to prevent seizure by the emissaries of the governments, and disguising their prosperity itself by the squalid dress of their persons— these, continued from age to age, have finally bred in the character we so commonly speak of with contempt. Our children, treated as they have been for so many generations, would finally reveal the marks of their wrongs in the same sordid, miserly instincts.

Now if it be true that what gets power in any race, by a habit or a process of culture, tends by a fixed law of nature to become a propagated quality, and pass by descent as a property inbred in the stock; if in this way whole races of men are cultivated into properties that are peculiar—off into a savage character, down into a servile or a mercenary, up into civilization or a high social state—what is to be the effect of a thoroughly Christian fatherhood and motherhood, continued for a long time in the successive generations of a family? What can it be but a general mitigation of the bad points of the stock, and a more and more completely inbred piety. The children of such a stock are born, not of the flesh only, or the mere natural life of their parentage, but they are born, in a sense most emphatic, of the Spirit also; for this parentage is differed, as we are supposing, age by age, from its own mere nature in Adam, by the inhabiting grace of a supernatural salvation. Physiologically speaking, they are tempered by this grace, and it is all the while tending to become, in some sense, an inbred quality. Hence the very frequent remark—"How great a privilege and order of nobility to be descended of a pious ancestry!" It is the blessing that is to descend to the thousandth generation of them that love God and keep his commandments.

In this view it is to be expected, as the life of Christian piety becomes more extended in the earth, and the Spirit of God obtains a living power, in the successive generations, more and more complete, that finally the race itself will be so thoroughly regenerated as to have a genuinely populating power in faith and godliness. By a kind of ante-natal and post-natal nurture combined, the new-born generations will be started into Christian piety, and the world itself over-populated and taken possession of by a truly sanctified stock. This I conceive to be the expectation of Christianity. Not that the bad heritage of depravity will cease, but that the second Adam will get into power *with* the first, and be entered seminally into the same great process of propagated life. And this fulfills that primal desire of the world's Creator and Father, of which the prophet speaks—"That he might have a godly seed."

And let no one be offended by this, as if it supposed a possible in-growth and propagation of piety, by mere natural laws and conditions. What higher ground of supernaturalism can be taken, than that which supposes a capacity in the Incarnate Word, and Sanctifying Spirit, to penetrate our fallen nature, at a point so deep as to cover the whole spread of the fall, and be a grace of life, traveling outward from the earliest, most latent germs of our human development. It is only saying, with a meaning—"My substance was not hid from Thee, when I was made in secret, and curiously wrought in the lowest parts of the earth." Or, in still another view, it is only conceiving that those sporadic cases of sanctification from the womb, of which the Scripture speaks, such as that of Samuel, Jeremiah, and John, are to finally become the ordinary and common fact of family development.

In such cases, the faith or piety of a single pair, or possibly of the mother alone, begets a heavenly mold in the predispositions of the offspring, so that, as it is born of sin, it is also born of a heavenly grace. If then we suppose the heavenly grace to have such power, in the long continuing process of ages, as to finally work the general stock of parentage into its own heavenly mold, far enough to prepare a sanctified offspring for the world, what higher, grander fact of Christian supernaturalism could be asserted? Nor is it any thing more of a novelty than to say, that "where sin abounded, grace did much more abound." The conception is one that simply fulfills what Baxter, Hopkins, and others, were apparently struggling after,* when contriving how to let the grace of God in our salvation, match itself by the hereditary damage, or depravation, that descends upon us from our parentage, and the organic unity of our nature as a race. And probably enough they were put upon this mode of

---

* See quotations from these writers in the last Discourse.

thought, by the familiar passage of Paul just referred to.

Christianity then has a power, as we discover, to prepare a godly seed. It not only takes hold of the world
by its converting efficacy, but it has a silent force
that is much stronger and more reliable ; it moves, by
a kind of destiny, in causes back of all the eccentric
and casual operations of mere individual choice, preparing, by a gradual growing in of grace, to become
the great populating motherhood of the world. In this
conviction, we shall be strengthened—

5. By the well known fact, that the populating
power of any race, or stock, is increased according to
the degree of personal and religious character to which
it has attained. Good principles and habits, intellectual
culture, domestic virtue, industry, order, law, faith—
all these go immediately to enhance the rate and capacity of population. They make a race powerful, not
in the mere military sense, but in one that, by century-
long reaches of populating force, lives down silently
every mere martial competitor. Any people that is
physiologically advanced in culture, though it be only
in a degree, beyond another which is mingled with it
on strictly equal terms, is sure to live down and finally
live out its inferior. Nothing can save the inferior
race but a ready and pliant assimilation.

The promise to Abraham depended, doubtless, on
this fact for its fulfillment. God was to make his
family fruitful, above others, by imparting Himself to
it, and so infusing a higher tone of personal life.

Hence also the grand religious fact that this race unfolded a populating power so remarkable. Going
down into Egypt, as a starving family, it begins to be
evident in about four hundred years, that they are over-
populating the great kingdom of Egypt itself. "The
children of Israel were fruitful and increased abundantly, and multiplied and waxed exceeding mighty,
and the land was filled with them." Till finally the
jealousy of the throne was awakened, and the king
began to say—"Behold the people of the children of
Israel are more and mightier than we!"

Afterwards little Palestine itself was like a swarm of
bees; building great cities, raising great armies, and
displaying all the tokens, age upon age, of a great and
populous empire. So great was the fruitfulness of the
stock, compared with other nations of the time, owing
to the higher personality unfolded in them, by their
only partial and very crude training, in a monotheistic
religion.

And again, at a still later time, when the nation itself
is dismembered, and thousands of the people are driven
off into captivity, we find that when the great king of
Persia had given out an edict of extermination against
them, and would like to recall it but can not, because
of the absurd maxim that what the king has decreed
must not be changed, he has only to publish another
decree, that they shall have it as their right to stand for
their lives, and that is enough to insure their complete
immunity. "They gathered themselves together in their
cities, and throughout all the provinces, and no man

could withstand them, for the fear of them fell upon all people." In which we may see how this captive race had multiplied and spread themselves, in this incredibly short time, through all the great kingdom of the Medo-Persian kings.

Or we may take a more modern illustration, drawn from the comparative history of the Christian and Mohammedan races. The Christian development begins at an older date, and the Mohammedan at a later. One is a propagation by moral and religious influences, at least in part; the other a propagation by military force. Both have religious ideas and aims, but the main distinction is that one is taken hold of by religion as being a contribution to the free personal nature of souls; and the other is taken hold of by a religion whose grip is the strong grip of fate. For a time, this latter spread like a fire in the forest, propagated by the terrible sword of predestination, and it even seemed about to override the world. But it by-and-bye began to appear, that one religion was creating and the other uncreating manhood; one toning up a great and powerful character, and the other toning down, steeping in lethargy, the races it began to inspire; till finally we can now see as distinctly as possible, that one is pouring on great tides of population, creating a great civilization, and great and powerful nations; the other, falling away into a feeble, half-depopulated, always decaying state, that augurs final extinction at no distant period. Now the fact is that these two great religions of the world had each, in itself, its own law of population from the beginning, and it was absolutely certain, whether it could be seen or not, that Christianity would finally live down Mohammedanism, and completely expurgate the world of it. The campaigning centuries of European chivalry, pressing it with crusade after crusade, could not bring it under; but the majestic populating force of Christian faith and nurture can even push it out of the world, as in the silence of a dew-fall.

What a lesson also could be derived, in the same manner, from a comparison of the populating forces of the Puritan stock in this country, and of the inferior, superstitions, half Christian stock and nurture of the South American states. And the reason of the difference is that Christianity, having a larger, fuller, more new-creating force in one, gives it a populating force as much superior.

How this advantage accrues, and is, at some future time, to be more impressively revealed than now, it is not difficult to see. Let the children of Christian parents grow up, all, as partakers in their grace, which is the true Christian idea, and the law of family increase they are in, is, by the supposition, so far brought into the church, and made operative there. And then comes in also the additional fact, that there are causes and conditions of increase now operative in the church which exist nowhere else.

Here, for example, there will be a stronger tide of health than elsewhere. In the world without, multitudes are perishing continually by vice and extravagance, and, when they do not perish themselves, they are always entailing the effects of their profligacy on the half-endowed constitution of their children. Meantime, in the truly Christian life, there is a good keeping of temperance, a steady sway of the passions, a robust equability and courage, and the whole domain of the soul is kept more closely to God's order; which again is the way of health, and implies a higher law of increase.

Wealth, again, will be unfolded more rapidly under the condition of Christian living than elsewhere; and wealth enough to yield a generous supply of the common wants of life, is another cause that favors population. True piety is itself a principle of industry and application to business. It subordinates the love of show and all the tendencies to extravagance. It rules those licentious passions that war with order and economy. It generates a faithful character, which is the basis of credit, as credit, of prosperity. Hence it is that upon the rocky, stubborn soil, under the harsh and frowning skies of our New England, we behold so much of high prosperity, so much of physical well-being, and ornament. And the wealth created is diffused about as evenly as the piety. A true Christian society has mines opened, thus, in its own habits and principles. And the wealth accruing is power in every direction, power in production, enterprise, education, colonization, influence, and consequent popular increase.

There will also be more talent unfolded in a Christian people, and talent also takes the helm of causes every where. Christian piety is itself a kind of holy development, enlarging every way the soul's dimensions.

It will also be found that Christian families abound
with influences, specially favorable to the awakening of
the intellectual principle in childhood.   Religion itself
is thoughtful.   It carries the child's mind over directly
to unknown worlds, fills the understanding with the
sublimest questions, and sends the imagination abroad
to occupy itself where angels' wings would tire.   The
child of a Christian family is thus unsensed, at the earliest moment, and put into mental action; this, too, under the healthy and genial influence of Christian principle.   Every believing soul, too, is exalted and empow-
ered by union to God.   His judgment is clarified, his
reason put in harmony with truth, his emotions swelled
in volume, his imagination fired by the object of his
faith.   The church, in short, is God's university, and it
lies in her foundation as a school of spiritual life, to
energize all capacity, and make her sons a talented and
powerful race.

Here, too, are the great truths, and all the grandest,
most fruitful ideas of existence.   Here will spring up
science, discovery, invention.   The great books will be
born here, and the highest, noblest, most quickening
character will here be fashioned.   Popular liberties and
the rights of persons will here be asserted.   Commerce
will go forth hence, to act the preluding of the Christian
love, in the universal fellowship of trade.

And so we see, by this rapid glance along the inven-
tories of Christian society, that all manner of causes are
included in it, that will go to fine the organization, raise
the robustness, swell the volume, multiply the means,

magnify the power of the Christian body. It stands among the other bodies and religons, just as any advanced race, the Saxon for example, stands among the feebler, wilder races, like the Aborigines of our continent; having so much power of every kind that it puts them in shadow, weakens them, lives them down, rolling its over-populating tides across them, and sweeping them away, as by a kind of doom. Just so there is, in the Christian church, a grand law of increase by which it is rolling out and spreading over the world. Whether the feebler and more abject races are going to be regenerated and raised up, is already very much of a question. What if it should be God's plan to people the world with better and finer material? Certain it is, whatever expectations we may indulge, that there is a tremendous overbearing surge of power in the Christian nations, which, if the others are not speedily raised to some vastly higher capacity, will inevitably submerge and bury them forever. These great populations of christendom—what are they doing, but throwing out their colonies on every side, and populating themselves, if I may so speak, into the possession of all countries and climes? By this doom of increase, the stone that was cut out without hands, shows itself to be a very peculiar stone, viz: a growing stone, that is fast becoming a great mountain, and preparing, as the vision shows, to fill the whole earth.

We are not, of course, to suspend our efforts to convert the heathen nations—we shall never become a thoroughly regenerate stock, save as we are trained up into such eminence, by our works of mercy to mankind. It is for God to say what races are to be finally submerged and lost, and not for us. Meantime, we are to gain over and save as many as possible by conversion, and so to hasten the day of promise. And what feebler and more pitiful conceit could we fall into, than to assume that we have the grand, over-populating grace in our own stock, and sit down thus to see it accomplish by mere propagation, that which of itself supposes a glorious inbred habit of faith, and sacrifice, and heavenly charity. I only say that, when we set ourselves to the great work of converting the world, we are to see that we do not miscondition the state of childhood, and throw quite away from us, meantime, all the mighty advantages that God designs to give us, in this other manner; viz., in the religious nurture and growth of the godly seed.

Once more, it is a consideration that will have great weight with all deeply, thoughtful persons, that the vindication of God in sin, suffering, punishment, and all evil pertaining to the race, probably depends, to a great degree, on just the truth I am here endeavoring to establish. How constantly is the question raised, why God, as an infinitely good and gracious Father, should put on foot such a scheme of existence as this; one that unites such oppressive disadvantages, and is to be such a losing concern? We begin life, it is said, with constitutions depravated and poisoned, and come thus into choice with predispositions that are damaged even beforehand. Idolatry, darkness, and guilt, overspread the world, in this manner, from age to age, and the vast majorities of the race, rotting away thus into death under sin, are being all the while precipitated into a wretched eternity, which is their end; for they go hence in a state visibly disqualified for the enjoyment, either of themselves, or of God. The picture is a very dark one, though I feel a decided confidence that every single part of God's counsel in it can be sufficiently vindicated. But this is not a matter in the compass of my present inquiry, except so far as the general difficulty is relieved by the possibility and prospect of great future advantages that are to accrue, in the fact of a grand over-populating righteousness, which is finally to change the aspect of the whole question. We are not to assume, with many, that the world is now just upon its close, but to look upon it as barely having opened its first chapter of history. Its real value, and what is really to come of it, probably does not even yet begin to appear. When its propagations cease to be mere propagations of evil, or of moral damage and disaster, and become propagations of sanctified life, and ages of life; when the numbers, talents, comforts, powers of the immense godly populations are increased to more than a hundred fold what they now are; and when, at some incomputable distance of time, whose rate of approach is only hinted by the geologic ages of the planet, they look back upon us as cotemporaries almost of Adam, and forward through ages of blessing just begun, beholding so many worlds-full of regenerated mind and character, pouring in from hence to over-people, as it were, eternity itself; they will certainly have a very different opinion of the scheme of existence from that which we most naturally take up now. Then it will be confessed that the nurture of the Lord has meaning and force enough to change the aspect of every thing in God's plan. Our scheme of propagated and derivative life is no longer a scheme of disadvantage, but a mode of induction that gives to every soul the noblest, safest beginning possible. On the other hand, if we cling to the present way and state as the measure of all highest possibilities, and expect to go on converting over, out of heathenism and death, the sturdy, grown-up aliens of depravity, it will be a most difficult—always growing more and more difficult—thing to vindicate the ways of God in what he has put upon the world. Shall we miss, and give it to the future ages to miss, a a vindication of God's way so inspiring in itself and so often promised in his word?

Having reached this closing point or consummation of the doctrine of nurture, we are able, I think, to see something of the dignity there is in it. How trivial, unnatural, weak, and, at the same time, violent, in comparison, is that overdone scheme of individualism, which knows the race only as mere units of will and personal action; dissolves even families into monads; makes no account of organic relations and uses; and expects the world to be finally subdued by adult conversions, when growing up still, as before, in all the younger tiers of life, toward a mere convertible state

of adult ungodliness. Such a scheme gives a most un-
genial and forlorn aspect to the family. It makes the
church a mere gathering in of adult atoms, to be increased only by the gathering in of other and more
numerous adult atoms. It very nearly makes the
scheme of existence itself an abortion; finding no great
law of propagative good and mercy in it, and taking
quite away the possibility and prospect of that sublime
vindication of God which is finally to be developed, and
by which God's way in the creation is to be finally
crowned with all highest honors of counsel and beneficence. Opposite to this, we have seen how it is God's
plan, by ties of organic unity and nurture, to let one
generation extend itself into and over another, in the
order of grace, just as it does in the order of nature;
to let us expect the growing up of children in the Lord,
even as their parents are to be parents in the Lord, and
are set to bring them up in the nurture of the Lord;
on this ground of anticipation, permitting us to apply
the seal of our faith to them, as being incipiently in the
quickening of our faith, even before they have intelligence to act it, and consciously choose it; so accepting
them to be members of the church, as being presumptively in the life of the church; in this manner incor-
porating in the church a great law of grace and sanctifying power, by which finally the salvation will become
an inbred life and populating force, mighty enough to
overlive, and finally to completely people the world.
And this is what we call the day of glory. It lies, to a
great degree, in the scheme of Christian nurture itself,

and is possible only as a consummation of that scheme. If I rightly conceive the gospel work and plan, this is the regeneration [παλιγγενεσία] which our Lord promises, viz.: that he will reclaim and resanctify the great principle of reproductive order and life, and people, at last, the world with a godly seed.

The church, as being made up of souls that are born of the Spirit is a new supernatural order thus in humanity; a spiritual nation, we may conceive, that was founded by a colony from the skies. It alights upon our globe as its chartered territory. Can it overspread the whole planet and take possession? We see that it can unfold more of health, wealth, talent, than the present living races of inhabitants. It has within itself a stronger law of population, as well as a mighty power to win over and assimulate the nations. Its people have more truth, beauty, weight of character to exalt their predominance. And, what is more, God is in them by his all-informing, all-energizing Spirit, to be Himself unfolded in their history, and make it powerful. Not to believe that the Heavenly Colony, thus constituted and endowed, will finally overspread and fill the world, is to deny causes, their effects, and to quite invert the natural order of strength and weakness. God, too, has testified in regard to this branch of his planting—"They shall inherit the land."

It is very obvious that this general view of Christian nurture, and its effects is one that, becoming really installed in our faith, and the aims of our piety, would

induce important modifications in our Christian practice, and change, to a considerable degree, the modes
of our religious demonstration. Our over-intense individualism carries with it an immense loss of feeling,
affection, sentiment, which hardens the aspect of every
thing, and dries away the sweet charities and tender
affections that would grace the older generations of
souls, when conceiving that the younger live in them,
and are somehow folded in their personality. We not
only lose our children under this atomizing scheme of
piety, which is a loss we can not afford, but a certain
misproportion is induced, which distempers all our
efforts and demonstrations.

One principal reason why we are so often deficient in
character, or outward beauty, is, that piety begins too
late in life, having thus to maintain a perpetual and
unequal war with previous habit. If it was not true
of Paul, it is yet too generally true, that one born out
of due time will be found out of due time, more often
than he should be afterwards—unequal, inconsistent
with himself, acting the old man instead of the new.
Having the old habit to war with, it is often too strong
for him. To make a graceful and complete Christian
character, it needs itself to be the habit of existence;
not a grape grafted on a bramble. And this, it will be
seen, requires a Christian childhood in the subject.
Having this, the gracious or supernatural character becomes itself more nearly natural, and possesses the peculiar charm of naturalness, which is necessary to the
highest moral beauty.

It results also from our mistaken views of Christian training, that we fall into a notion of religion that is mechanical. We thrust our children out of the covenant first, and insist, in spite of it, that they shall grow up in the same spiritual state as if their father and mother were heathens. Then we go out, at least on certain occasions, to convert them back, as if they actually were heathens. Our only idea of increase is of that which accrues by means of a certain abrupt technical experience. Led away thus from all thought of internal growth in the church, efforts to secure conversions take an external character, becoming gospel campaigns. Accretion displaces growth. The church is gathered as a foundling hospital; and lest it should not be such, its own children are reduced to foundlings. Immediate repentance proclaimed, insisted on, and realized in an abrupt change, proper only to those who are indeed aliens and enemies, is the only hope or inlet of the church. We can not understand how the spiritual nation should grow and populate, and become powerful within itself.

Piety becomes inconstant, and revivals of religion take an exaggerated character from the same causes. If all Christian success is measured by the count of technical conversions from without, then it follows that nothing is done when conversions cease to be counted. The harvest closes not with feasting, but with famine. Despair cuts off Christian motive. The tide is spent; let us anchor during the ebb. It is well indeed to live very piously in the families; still, there is nothing depending on it. The children will be good subjects enough for conversion without. The piety of the church is thus made to be desultory and irregular by system. The idea of conquest displaces the idea of growth. Whereas, if it were understood that Christian education or training in the families, is to be itself a process of domestic conversion; that as a child weeps under a frown and smiles at the command of a smile, so spiritual influences may be streaming into his being from the handling of the nursery and the whole manner and temperament of the house, producing what will ever after be fundamental impressions of his being; then the hearth, the table, the society and affections of the house, would all feel the presence of a practical religious motive. The homes would be Christian, the families abodes of piety.

Here too is the greatest impediment to a true missionary spirit. The habit of conquest runs to dissipation and irregularity. It is as if a nation, forgetting its own internal resources, were scouring the seas, and trooping up and down the world, in pursuit of prize-money and plunder, forsaking the loom and the plow, and all the regular growths of industry. Whereas, if the church were unfolding the riches of the covenant at her firesides and tables; if the children were identified with religion from the first, and grew up in a Christian love of man, the missionary spirit would not throw itself up in irregular jets, but would flow as a river.

We suffer also greatly and even produce a somewhat painful evidence of mistake, in our endeavor to be always operating by an immediate influence of the

Holy Spirit, when we make his mediate influence a matter of little account. For there is, I apprehend, a certain fixed relation between those exertions of spiritual influence which are immediate, and those which flow mediately from the church; else why has not the Spirit left the church behind, and poured itself, as a rushing, mighty wind, into the bosom of the whole world in a day? There needed to be an objective influence, as well as one internal; else the subject of the Spirit would not know or guess to what his internal motions are attributable, and might deem them only nervous or hysteric effects; or possibly, if a heathen, the work of some enchanter or demon. When the church, therefore, grows and manifests the work of God by the beauty of her life, and the heavenly energy of her spirit, when the sanctification she speaks of visibly strikes through—through the body, through the manners and works, into the family state, into the community—that is the mediate influence necessary to another which is immediate. Looking on her demonstrations, the observer is not only impressed and drawn by the assimilating power of her character, but he distinguishes in her the type and form of that into which he is himself to be wrought, and so he is ready for the intelligent reception of the Spirit in himself. If now there is this fixed relation between God's mediate and immediate agency in souls, how great is the mistake, when we virtually assume, in our efforts and expectations, that he will come upon souls, only as the lightning is bolted from the sky. How desultory and irruptive is the grace he ministers, how little respective of the work he has already begun in others, whom he might employ to be the medium of his power! On the other hand, if we are right in this view—if there is a fixed relation between the mediate and immediate influences of the Spirit—such that one measures the other, (and we could urge many additional reasons for the opinion,) then are we brought fairly out upon the sublime conclusion, that the growth or progress of Christian piety in the church, if it shall take place, offers the expectation of a correspondent progress in the development of those spiritual influences that are immediate. The mediate and immediate are both identical at the root. If therefore the church unfolds her piety as a divine life, which is one, the divine life will display its activity as much more potently and victoriously without, which is the other. And as the kingdom of heaven, which was at first as a grain of mustard seed, advances in the last days toward the stature of a tree, the more it may advance; for the Holy Spirit will pour himself into the world, as much more freely and powerfully. Grant, O God! that we may not disappoint ourselves of a hope so glorious, by attempts to extend thy church without that holy growth of piety, on which our success depends! Pour thyself, in thy fullness and as a gale of purity, into our bosom! Expel all schemes that are not begun in Thee! Let there be good desires in us, that our works may be good! And that Thou mayest do thy will in the earth, do it in us perfectly!

PART II—THE MODE

I

WHEN AND WHERE THE NURTURE BEGINS

" When I call to remembrance the unfeigned faith that is in thee, which dwelt first in thy grandmother Lois, and thy mother Eunice, and I am persuaded that in thee also."—2 *Timothy*, i. 5.

THIS faith of Timothy, which is but another name for the grace of life in his character, the apostle speaks of here, it will be seen, as a kind of personal hereditament, or heir-loom in the family. He does not mean to say, as I understand him, that it is literally such, or in what sense, and how far, it is such. He only recognizes a godly parentage, doing godly things in him and for him, for one, two, three, or he knows not how many, generations back. He regards his young friend as born of godliness, nurtured and trained by godliness, and indulges a certain pleasant conviction that his present, full developed faith in Jesus, was a seed somehow planted in him by the believing motherhoods of the past, and began to live and grow in him, thus, long before he knew it himself, or others observed it in him. So by a short method, which includes and covers all, the apostle calls it his heir-loom; complimenting his godly motherhood in the figure, and testifying the greater confidence in his piety, that it was so near to being the inborn nobility of his Christian stock.

I use the text, accordingly, not to draw some definite conclusion or truth, from the evidently well understood indefiniteness of the terms of it, but simply to head a discussion of the question, *when and where, at what point, and how early, does the office of a genuine nurture begin?*

Having settled our conceptions of the scheme, or doctrinal import, of Christian nurture, finding what place it has, and is to have, in the Christian plan, we are come now to a matter farther in advance, and, in one view, more practical, viz: to a consideration of the modes and means, by which the true idea of a godly nurture may be realized in the training of families. And here it becomes our first endeavor to rectify, or expel a whole set of false impressions, that have grown up round the gate of responsibility itself, turning off, and pushing aside all due concern, till the time of greatest facility and advantage is quite gone by. The very common impression is that nothing is to be done for the religious character of children, till they are old enough to form religious judgments, put forth religious choices, take the meaning of the Christian truths, and perceive what is in them as related to the wants of sin, consciously felt and reflected on. There could not be a more sad or, in fact, more desolating mistake, in any matter, either of duty or of privilege. And it is the more wonderful, the closer in appearance to real fatuity, that it holds its ground so firmly, where all the tenderest pressures of affection might be expected to force it aside, and clear the field of its really cruel usurpations.

In discussing the question proposed, I should not properly cover the whole ground of it, and could not really be said to answer it, if I did not—

1. Bring into view the very important, but rather delicate fact, suggested or distinctly alluded to in the apostle's words, that there is even a kind of ante-natal nurture which must be taken note of, as having much to do with the religious preparations or inductive mercies of childhood. We are physiologically connected and set forth in our beginnings, and it is a matter of immense consequence to our character, what the connection is. In our birth, we not only begin to breathe and circulate blood, but it is a question hugely significant whose the blood may be. For in this we have whole rivers of predispositions, good or bad, set running in us—as much more powerful to shape our future than all tuitional and regulative influences that come after, as they are earlier in their beginning, deeper in their insertion, and more constant in their operation. It is a great mistake to suppose that men and women, such as are to be fathers and mothers, are affected only in their souls by religious experience, and not in their bodies. On mere physiological principles it can not be true, for the mind must temper the body to its own states and changes. Living, therefore, in the peace and purity, holding the equilibrium, flowing in the liberty, reigning in the confidence, of a genuine sanctification, the subjects of such grace are penetrated bodily, all through, by the work of the Spirit in their life. Their appetites are more nearly in heaven's order, their passions more

tempered by reason, their irritabilities more sweetened and calmed, and so far they are entered bodily into the condition of health. Where the constitution was poisoned originally by descent, or has since been broken down by excess and abuse, it may not be wholly restored in this life. I do not suppose that it will; but since the soul is acting itself always into and through the body, when it becomes a temple of the Spirit, the body also must be, just as the Scriptures explicitly teach; undergoing, with the soul, a remedial process in its tempers and humors, and prospering in heaven's order, even as the soul prospereth. This being true, it is impossible, on mere physiological principles, that the children of a truly sanctified parentage should not be advantaged by the grace out of which they are born. And, if the godly character has been kept up in a long line of ancestry, corrupted by no vicious or untoward intermarriages, the advantage must be still greater and more positive. Even temporary changes in the Christian state of character and attainment, will have their effect; how much more the godly keeping of a thoroughly and evenly sanctified life; how much more such a keeping of inbred grace and faith, in a long line of godly ancestors.

I might even state the case more strongly, bringing into the comparison a godly and a vicious parentage. Take a parentage that has in it all the dyspeptic woes of gluttony and self-indulgence, one that is stung and maddened by the fiery pains of intemperance, one that is poisoned and imbruted by the excesses of lust, one that is broken by domestic wrongs or exasperated by domestic quarrels, one that is fevered by ambitions, one that is soured by the morbid humors of envy and defeat—lengthen out the catalogue, take in all the sins, which, in some true sense, are also vices and have their effect on the body, how is it possible, on any principle of rational physiology, that the children who are sprung of this distempered heritage, should be as pure in their affinities, as close to the order of truth, as ready for the occupany of all good thoughts, as well governed before all government, as ductile in a word to God, as they that are born of a glorious lineage in faith and prayer and God's indwelling peace. Nothing could be more improbable antecedently, or farther off from the actual fact afterward. On the contrary, it is a most dismal and hard lot, as every one knows, to be in the succession of a bad, or vicious parentage. No heritage of wealth could repay, or more than a little soften the bitterness of it.

It is somewhat difficult to investigate the facts of this subject, because of the complexities induced by unpropitious and exceptional marriages. But when such marriages are reduced by the more general, and finally universal, spread of Christian piety, and when the pitch of Christian sanctification is raised, as it will be, by the fuller inspiration from God, breaking into his saints all over the world, it will be found that children are born as much closer to God, and with predispositions that waft them as much more certainly into the ways of duty and piety. It will be as if the faith-power of the past were descending into the present, flowing on down the future, and the general account of the world will be, that, as it has been corrupted, so also it is in some equally true sense, regenerated from the womb. Precisely that which is named in Scripture, as the fact extraordinary, will become at last the ordinary and even the universal fact.

Here, then, is the real and true beginning of a godly nurture. The child is not to have the sad entail of any sensuality, or excess, or distempered passion upon him. The heritage of love, peace, order, continence and holy courage is to be his. He is not to be morally weakened beforehand, in the womb of folly, by the frivolous, worldly, ambitious, expectations of parents-to-be, concentrating all their nonsense in him. His affinities are to be raised by the godly expectations, rather, and prayers that go before; by the steady and good aims of their industry, by the great impulse of their faith, by the brightness of their hope, by the sweet continence of their religiously pure love in Christ. Born, thus, of a parentage that is ordered in all righteousness, and maintains the right use of every thing, especially the right use of nature and marriage, the child will have just so much of heaven's life and order in him beforehand, as have become fixed properties in the type of his parentage; and by this ante-natal nurture, will be set off in a way of noblest advantage, as respects all safety and success, in the grand experiment he has come into the world to make.

Having called your attention to this very important

but strangely disregarded chapter, in the economy of Christian nurture, I leave it to be more fully and circumstantially developed by your own thoughtful consideration; for it is a matter which will open itself readily, and prove itself by striking and continually recurring facts to such as have it in their hearts to watch for the truth and the duties it requires.   We pass now—

2. To that which is the common field of inquiry, and here we raise again the question, where and how early does the work of nurture begin? here to set forth and maintain still another answer, which antedates the common impression, about as decidedly as the one . just given.   The true, and only true answer is, that the nurture of the soul and character is to begin just when the nurture of the body begins.   It is first to be infantile nurture—as such, Christian; then to be a child's nurture; then to be a youth's nurture—advancing by imperceptible gradations, if possible, according to the gradations and stages of the growth, or progress toward maturity.

There is, of course, no absolute classification to be made here, because there are no absolute lines of distinction.   A kind of proximate and partly ideal distinction may be made, and I make it simply to serve the convenience of my subject—otherwise impossible to be handled, so as to secure any right practical conviction respecting it.   It is the distinction between the age of *impressions* and the age of *tuitional influences;* or between the age of *existence in the will of the parent,* and the age of *will and personal choice in the child.*   If the

distinction were laid, between the age previous to language and the age of language, it would amount to
nearly the same thing; for the time of personal and
responsible choice depends on the measure of intelligence attained to, and the measure of intelligence
is well represented, outwardly, by the degree of development in language. Of course it will be understood that we speak, in this distinction, of that which
is not sharply defined, and is passed at no precise date
or age. The transition is gradual, and it will even be
doubtful, when it is passed. No one can say just where
a given child passes out of the field of mere impression
into the field of responsible action. It will be doubtful,
in about the same degree, when it can be said to have
come into the power of language. We do not even
know that there is not some infinitesimal development
of will in the child's first cry, and some instinct of language struggling in that cry. Our object in the distinction is not to assume any thing in respect to such
matters, but simply to accommodate our own ignorance,
by raising a distribution that enables us to speak of
times and characteristics truly enough to serve the conditions of general accurary, and to assist, in that manner, the purposes of our discussion.

Now the very common assumption is that, in what
we have called the age of impressions, there is really
nothing done, or to be done, for the religious character.
The lack of all genuine apprehensions, in respect to this
matter, among people otherwise intelligent and awake,
is really wonderful; it amounts even to a kind of

coarseness. Full of all fondness, and all highest expectation respecting their children, and having also many
Christian desires for their welfare, they seem never to
have brought their minds down close enough to the
soul of infancy, to imagine that any thing of consequence is going on with it. What can they do, till
they can speak to it? what can it do, till it speaks? As
if there were no process going on to bring it forward
into language; or as if that process had itself nothing
to do with the bringing on of intelligence, and no deep,
seminal working toward a character, unfolding and to
be unfolded in it. The child, in other words, is to
come into intelligence through perfect unintelligence!
to get the power of words out of words themselves,
and without any experience whereby their meaning
is developed! to be taught responsibility under moral
and religious ideas, when the experience has unfolded
no such ideas! In this first stage, therefore, which
I have called the stage of impressions, how very
commonly will it be found that the parents, even
Christian parents, discharge themselves, in the most in-
nocently unthinking way possible, of so much as a conception of responsibility. The child can not talk, what
then can it know? So they dress it in all fineries,
practice it in shows and swells and all the petty airs
of foppery and brave assumption, act it into looks
and manners not fit to be acted any where, provoking
the repetition of its bad tricks by laughing at them,
indulging freely every sort of temper towards it, or, it
may be, filling the house with a din of scolding between

the parents—all this in simple security, as if their child were only a thing, or an ape! What hurt can the simple creature get from any thing done before it, toward it, or upon it, when it can talk of nothing, and will not so much as remember any thing it has seen or heard? Doubtless there is a wise care to be had of it, when it is old enough to be taught and commanded, but till then there is nothing to be done, but simply to foster the plaything kindly, enjoy it freely, or abuse it pettishly, at pleasure!

Just contrary to this, I suspect, and I think it can also be shown by sufficient evidence, that more is done to affect, or fix the moral and religious character of children, before the age of language than after; that the age of impressions, when parents are commonly waiting, in idle security, or trifling away their time in mischievous indiscretions, or giving up their children to the chance of such keeping as nurses and attendants may exercise, is in fact their golden opportunity; when more is likely to be done for their advantage or damage, than in all the instruction and discipline of their minority afterward.

And something like this I think we should augur beforehand, from the peculiar, full-born intensity of the maternal affection, at the moment when it first embraces the newly arrived object. It scarcely appears to grow, never to grow tender and self-sacrificing in its care. It turns itself to its charge, with a love that is boundless and fathomless, at the first. As if just then and there, some highest and most sacred office of motherhood

were required to begin. Is it only that the child demands her physical nurture and carefulness? That is
not the answer of her consciousness. Her maternity
scorns all comparison with that of the mere animals.
Her love, as she herself feels, looks through the body
into the inborn personality of her child,—the man or
woman to be. Nay, more than that, if she could sound
her consciousness deeply enough, she would find a certain religiousness in it, measurable by no scale of mere
earthly and temporal love. Here springs the secret of
her maternity, and its semi-divine proportions. It is
the call and equipment of God, for a work on the
impressional and plastic age of a soul. Christianized
as it should be, and wrought in by the grace of the
Spirit, the minuteness of its care, its gentleness, its
patience, its almost divine faithfulness, are prepared for
the shaping of a soul's immortality. And, to make the
work a sure one, the intrusted soul is allowed to have
no will as yet of its own, that this motherhood may
more certainly plant the angel in the man, uniting him
to all heavenly goodness by predispositions from itself,
before he is united, as he will be, by choices of his own.
Nothing but this explains and measures the wonderful
proportions of maternity.

It will be seen at once, and will readily be taken as
a confirmation of the transcendent importance of what
is done, or possible to be done, for children, in their
impressional and plastic age, that whatever is impressed
or inserted here, at this early point, must be profoundly
seminal, as regards all the future developments of the

character. And though it can not, by the supposition,
amount to character, in the responsible sense of that
term, it may be the seed, in some very important sense,
of all the future character to be unfolded; just as we
familiarly think of sin itself, as a character in blame
when the will is ripe, though prepared, in still another
view, by the seminal damages and misaffections derived
from sinning ancestors. So when a child, during the
whole period of impressions, or passive recipiencies,
previous to the development of his responsible will,
lives in the life and feeling of his parents, and they in
the molds of the Spirit, they will, of course, be shaping
themselves in him, or him in themselves, and the effects
wrought in him will be preparations of what he will
by-and-bye do from himself; seeds, in that manner possibly, even of a regenerate life and character.

That we may conceive this matter more adequately
and exactly, consider, a moment, that whole contour of
dispositions, affections, tempers, affinities, aspirations,
which come into power in a soul after the will is set
fast in a life of duty and devotion. These things, we
conceive, follow in a sense the will, and then become
in turn a new element about the will—a new heart, as
we say, prompting to new acts and a continued life of
new obedience. Now what I would affirm is, that just
this same contour of dispositions and affinities may be
prepared under, and come after, the will of the parents,
when the child is living in their will, and be ready as a
new element, or new heart, to prompt the child's will,
or put it forward in the choice of all duty, whenever it

is so matured as to choose for itself. Of course these regenerated dispositions and affinities, this general disposedness to good, which we call a new heart, supposes a work of the Spirit; and, if the parents live in the Spirit as they ought, they will have the Spirit for the child as truly as for themselves, and the child will be grown, so to speak, in the molds of the Spirit, even from his infancy.

This will be yet more probable, if we glance at some of the particular facts and conditions involved. Thus if we speak of impressions, or the age of impressions, and of that as an age prior to language, what kind of religious impressions can be raised in a soul, it may be asked, when the child is not far enough developed in language to be taught any thing about God, or Christ, or itself, that belongs to intelligence? And the sufficient answer must be, that language itself has no meaning till rudimental impressions are first begotten in the life of experience, to give it a meaning. Words are useful to propagate meanings, or to farther develop and combine meanings, but a child would never know the meaning of any word in a language, just by hearing the sound of it in his ears. He must learn to put the meaning into it, by having found that meaning in his impressions, and then the word becomes significant. And it requires a certain wakefulness and capacity of intelligent apprehension, to receive or take up such impressions. Thus a dog would never get hold of any religious impression at the family prayers, all his lifetime; but a child will be fast gathering up, out of his

little life and experience, impressional states and associations, that give meanings to the words of prayer, as
they, in turn, give meanings to the facts of his experience. All language supposes impressions first made.
The word *light* does not signify any thing, till the eye
has taken the impression of light. The word *love* is
unmeaning, to one who has not loved and received love.
The word *God*, raises no conception of God, till the
idea of such a being has been somehow generated and
associated with that particular sound. How far off is it
then from all sound apprehensions of fact, to imagine
that nothing religious can be done for a child till after
he is far enough developed in language to be taught;
when in fact he could not be thus developed in language at all, if the meanings of language were not
somehow started in him by the impressions derived
from his experience.

Observe, again, how very quick the child's eye is, in
the passive age of infancy, to catch impressions, and
receive the meaning of looks, voices, and motions. It
peruses all faces, and colors, and sounds. Every sentiment that looks into its eyes, looks back out of its
eyes, and plays in miniature on its countenance. The
tear that steals down the cheek of a mother's suppressed
grief, gathers the little infantile face into a responsive sob. With a kind of wondering silence, which is
next thing to adoration, it studies the mother in her
prayer, and looks up piously with her, in that exploring watch, that signifies unspoken prayer. If the child
is handled fretfully, scolded, jerked, or simply laid aside

unaffectionately, in no warmth of motherly gentleness,
it feels the sting of just that which is felt towards it;
and so it is angered by anger, irritated by irritation,
fretted by fretfulness; having thus impressed, just that
kind of impatience or ill-nature, which is felt towards
it, and growing faithfully into the bad mold offered, as
by a fixed law. There is great importance, in this manner, even in the handling of infancy. If it is unchristian, it will beget unchristian states, or impressions.
If it is gentle, even patient and loving, it prepares a
mood and temper like its own. There is scarcely room
to doubt, that all most crabbed, hateful, resentful, passionate, ill-natured characters; all most even, lovely,
firm and true, are prepared, in a great degree, by the
handling of the nursery. To these and all such modes
of feeling and treatment as make up the element of the
infant's life, it is passive as wax to the seal. So that if
we consider how small a speck, falling into the nucleus
of a crystal, may disturb its form; or, how even a mote
of foreign matter present in the quickening egg, will
suffice to produce a deformity; considering, also, on the
other hand, what nice conditions of repose, in one case,
and what accurately modulated supplies of heat in the
other, are necessary to a perfect product; then only do
we begin to imagine what work is going on, in the
soul of a child, in this first chapter of life, the age of
impressions.

It must also greatly affect our judgments on this
point, to observe that, when this first age of impressions is gone by, there is, after that, no such thing any

more as a possibility of absolute control.   Thus far the
child has been more a candidate for personality than
a person.   He has been as a seed forming in the capsule of the parent-stem, getting every thing from that
stem, and fashioned, in its kind, by the fashioning kind
of that.   But now, having been gradually and imperceptibly ripened, as the seed separates and falls off, to
be another and complete form of life in itself, so the
child comes out, in his own power, a complete person,
able to choose responsibly for himself.   Now he is no
more in the power of the parent, as before; the dominion of the older life is supplanted, by the self-asserting
competency of the younger; what can the old stalk do
upon the seed that is already ripe?   The transition here
is very gradual, it is true, covering even a space of
years; and something may be done for the child's character by instruction, by the skillful management of motives, and the tender solicitudes of parental watching
and prayer; but less and less, of course, the older the
child becomes, and the more completely his personal
responsibility is developed.   But how very fearful the
change, and how much it means, that the child, once
plastic and passive to the will of the parent, has gotten
by the point of absolute disposability, and is never
again to be properly in that will!   The perilous power
of self-care and self-assertion has come, and what is to
be the result?   And how much does it signify to the
parent, when he feels his power to be thus growing difficult, weak, doubtful, or finally quite ended!   What a
conception it is, that he once had his child in abso-

lute direction, and the fashioning of his own superior will, to dress, to feed, to handle, to play himself into his sentiments, be the disposition of his dispositions, the temper of his tempers. Was there not something great to be done then, when the advantage was so great—now to be done no more? It will be difficult to shake off that impression; impossible to a really thoughtful Christian soul. And if the will, now matured and gone over into complete self-assertion, rushes into all wildness and profligacy, unrestrained and unrestrainable, the recollection of a time when it was restrainable and could have been molded, even as wax itself, will return with inevitable certainty upon the parents, and taunt, O how bitterly, the neglectfulness and lightness, by which they cast their opportunity away!

I bring into view accordingly, just here, a consideration that goes further to establish the position I am asserting, than any other, and one that is naturally suggested by the topic just adverted to. We call this first chapter of life the age of impressions; we speak of the child as being in a sense passive and plastic, living in the will of the parents, having no will developed for responsible action. It might be imagined from the use of such terms, that the infant or very young child has no will at all. But that is not any true conception. It has no *responsible* will, because it is not acquainted, as yet, with those laws and limits and conditions of choice that make it responsible. Nevertheless it has will, blind will, as strongly developed as any other faculty, and sometimes even most strongly of all. The manifestations of it are sometimes even frightful. And precisely this it is which makes the age of impressions, the age prior to language and responsible choice, most profoundly critical in its importance. It is the age in which the will-power of the soul is to be tamed or subordinated to a higher control; that of obedience to parents, that of duty and religion. And, in this view, it is that every thing most important to the religious character turns just here. Is this infant child to fill the universe with his complete and total self-assertion, owning no superior, or is he to learn the self-submission of allegiance, obedience, duty to God? Is he to become a demon let loose in God's eternity, or an angel and free prince of the realm?

That he may be this, he is now given, will and all, as wax, to the wise molding-power of control. Beginning, then, to lift his will in mutiny, and swell in self-asserting obstinacy, refusing to go or come, or stand, or withhold in this or that, let there be no fight begun, or issue made with him, as if it were the true thing now to break his will, or drive him out of it by mere terrors and pains. This willfulness, or obstinacy, is not so purely bad, or evil, as it seems. It is partly his feeling of himself and you, in which he is getting hold of the conditions of authority, and feeling out his limitations. No, this breaking of a child's will to which many well-meaning parents set themselves, with such instant, almost passionate resolution, is the way they take to make him a coward, or a thief, or a hypocrite, or a mean-spirited and driveling sycophant—nothing in fact is more dreadful to thought than this breaking of a will, when it breaks, as it often does, the personality itself, and all highest, noblest firmness of manhood. The true problem is different; it is not to break, but to bend rather, to draw the will down, or away from self-assertion toward self-devotion, to teach it the way of submitting to wise limitations, and raise it into the great and glorious liberties of a state of loyalty to God. See then how it is to be done. The child has no force, however stout he is in his will. Take him up then, when the fit is upon him, carry him, stand him on his feet, set him here or there, do just that in him which he refuses to do in himself—all this gently and kindly, as if he were capable of maintaining no issue at all. Do it again and again, as often as may be necessary. By-and-bye, he will begin to perceive that his obstinacy is but the fussing of his weakness; till finally, as the sense of limitation comes up into a sense of law and duty, he will be found to have learned, even before-hand, the folly of mere self-assertion. And when he has reached this point of felt obligation to obedience, it will no longer break him down to enforce his com-pliance, but it will even exalt into greater dignity and capacity, that sublime power of self-government, by which his manhood is to be most distinguished.

By a different treatment at the point or crisis just named, that is by raising an issue to be driven straight through by terror and storm, one of two results almost equally bad were likely to follow; the child would either have been quite broken down by fear, the lowest of all possible motives when separated from moral convictions, or else would have been made a hundred fold more obstinate by his triumph. Nature provided for his easy subjugation, by putting him in the hands of a superior strength, which could manage him without any fight of enforcement—to have him schooled and tempered to a customary self-surrender which takes nothing from his natural force and manliness. And so is accomplished what, in one view, is the great problem of life; that on which all duty and allegiance to God, in the state even of conversion, depends.

It only remains to add that we are not to assume the comparative unimportance of what is done upon a child, in his age of impressions, because there is really no character of virtue or vice, of blame or praise, developed in that age. Be it so—it is so by the supposition. But the power, the root, the seed, is implanted nevertheless, in most cases, of what he will be. Not in every case, but often, the seed of a regenerate life is implanted—that which makes the child a Christian in God's view, as certainly as if he were already out in the testimony and formal profession of his faith. I was just now speaking of the dreadful power of will or willfulness, some times manifested even in this first age, that we have called the age of impressions, and of the ways in which, by one kind of mismanagement or another, the character may be turned to vices that are as opposite, as the vices of meanness and the crimes of violence and blood. So it will be found that almost every sort of mismanagement, or neglect, plants some

seed of vice and misery that grows out afterwards into
a character in its own kind. Thus the child by a continually worry of his little life, under abusive words,
and harsh, flashy tempers, grows to be a bed of nettles
in all his personal tempers, and will so be prepared to
break out, in the age of choice, into almost any vice of
ill-nature. A child can be pampered in feeding, so as
to become, in a sense, all body ; so that, when he comes
into choice and responsible action, he is already a confirmed sensualist, showing it in the lines of his face,
even before it appears in his tastes, habits and vices.
Thus we have a way of wondering that the children of
this or that family should turn out so poorly, but the
real fact is, probably, if we knew it, that what we call
their turning out, is only their growing out, in just that
which was first grown in, by the mismanagement of
their infancy and childhood. What they took in as
impression, or contagion, is developed by choice—not
at once, perhaps, but finally, after the poison has had
time to work. And in just the same way, doubtless,
it may be true, in multitudes of Christian conversions,
that what appear to be such to others, and also to the
subjects themselves, are only the restored activity and
more fully developed results of some predispositional
state, or initially sanctified property, in the tempers and
subtle affinities of their childhood. They are now
born into that by the assent of their own will, which
they were in before, without their will. What they
do not remember still remembers them, and now claims
a right in them. What was before unconscious, flames

out into consciousness, and they break forth into praise
and thanksgiving, in that which, long ago, took them
initially, and touched them softly without thanks.   For
there is such a thing as a seed of character in religion,
preceding all religious development.   Even as Calvin,
speaking of the regenerative grace there may be in the
heart of infancy itself, testifies—"the work of God is
not yet without existence, because it is not observed
and understood by us."

By these and many other considerations that might
be named, it is made clear, I think, to any judicious
and thoughtful person, that the most important age of
Christian nurture is the first; that which we have called
the age of impressions, just that age, in which the duties and cares of a really Christian nurture are so commonly postponed, or assumed to have not yet arrived.
I have no scales to measure quantities of effect in this
matter of early training, but I may be allowed to express my solemn conviction, that more, as a general fact,
is done, or lost by neglect of doing, on a child's immortality, in the first three years of his life, than in all his
years of discipline afterwards.   And I name this particular time, or date, that I may not be supposed to lay the
chief stress of duty and care on the latter part of what I
have called the age of impressions; which, as it is a matter somewhat indefinite, may be taken to cover the space
of three or four times this number of years; the development of language, and of moral ideas being only partially accomplished, in most cases, for so long a time.
Let every Christian father and mother understand, when

their child is three years old, that they have done more than half of all they will ever do for his character. What can be more strangely wide of all just apprehension, than the immense efficacy, imputed by most parents to the Christian ministry, compared with what they take to be the almost insignificant power conferred on them in their parental charge and duties. Why, if all preachers of Christ could have their hearers, for whole months and years, in their own will, as parents do their children, so as to move them by a look, a motion, a smile, a frown, and act their own sentiments and emotions over in them at pleasure; if, also, a little farther on, they had them in authority to command, direct, tell them whither to go, what to learn, what to do, regulate their hours, their books, their pleasures, their company, and call them to prayer over their own knees every night and morning, who could think it impossible, in the use of such a power, to produce almost any result? Should not such a ministry be expected to fashion all who come under it to newness of life? Let no parent, shifting off his duties to his children, in this manner, think to have his defects made up, and the consequent damages mended afterwards, when they have come to their maturity, by the comparatively slender, always doubtful, efficacy of preaching and pulpit harangue.

If now I am right in the view I have been trying to establish, it will readily occur to you that irreparable damage may be and must often be done by the self-indulgence of those parents, who place their children mostly in the charge of nurses and attendants for just those years of their life, in which the greatest and most absolute effects are to be wrought in their character. The lightness that prevails, on this point, is really astonishing. Many parents do not even take pains to know any thing about the tempers, the truthfulness, the character generally, of the nurses to whom their children are thus confidingly trusted. No matter—the child is too young to be poisoned, or at all hurt, by their influence. And so they give over, to these faithless and often cruelly false hirelings of the nursery, to be always with them, under their power, associated with their persons, handled by their roughness, and imprinted, day and night, by the coarse, bad sentiments of their voices and faces, these helpless, hapless beings whom they call their children, and think they are really making much of, in the instituting of a nursery for them and their keeping. Such a mother ought to see that she is making much more of herself than of her child. This whole scheme of nurture is a scheme of self-indulgence. Now is the time when her little one most needs to see her face, and hear her voice, and feel her gentle hand. Now is the time when her child's eternity pleads most entreatingly for the benefit of her motherly charge and presence. What mother would not be dismayed by the thought of having her family grow up into the sentiments of her nurse, and come forward into life as being in the succession to her character! And yet how often is this most exactly what she has provided for.

Again, it is very clear that, in this early kind of nurture, faithfully maintained, there is a call for the greatest personal holiness in the parents, and that just those conditions are added, which will make true holiness closest to nature, and most beautifully attractive—saving it from all the repulsive appearances of severity and sanctimony. In this charge and nurture of infant children, nothing is to be done by an artificial, lecturing process; nothing, or little by what can be called government. We are to get our effects chiefly by just being what we ought, and making a right presence of love and life to our children. They are in a plastic age that is receiving its type, not from our words, but from our spirit, and whose character is shaping in the molds of ours. Living under this conviction, we are held to a sound verity and reality in every thing. The defect of our character is not to be made up here, by the sanctity of our words; we must be all that we would have our children feel and receive. Thus, if a man were to be set before a mirror, with the feeling that the exact image of what he *is*, for the day, is there to be produced and left as a permanent and fixed image forever, to what carefulness, what delicate sincerity of spirit would he be moved. And will he be less moved to the same, when that mirror is the soul of his child?

Inducted, thus, into a more profoundly real holiness, we shall, at the same time, grow more natural in it. The family quality of our piety, living itself into our children, will moisten the dry individualism we suffer, relieve the eccentricities we display, set purity in the place of bustle and presumption, growth in the place of conquest, sound health in the place of spasmodic exalt-ations; for when a conviction is felt in Christian fami-lies, that living is to be a means of grace, and as God will suffer it, a regenerating power, then will our piety be-come a domestic spirit, and as much more tender, as it is closer to the life of childhood. Now, we have a kind of piety that contains, practically speaking, only adults, or those who are old enough to reflect and act for themselves, and it is as if we lived in an *adult world*, where every one is for himself. If we could abolish also distinctions of age, and sex, and office, we should only make up a style of religion somewhat drier and farther off from nature than we now have. We can never come into the true mode of living that God has appointed for us, until we regard each generation as hovering over the next, acting itself into the next, and casting thus a type of character in the next, before it comes to act for itself. Then we shall have gentle cares and feelings; then the families will become bonds of spiritual life; example, education and government, being Christian powers, will be regulated by a Christian spirit; the rigidities of religious principle will be soft-ened by the tender affections of nature twining among them, and the common life of the house dignified by the sober and momentous cares of the life to come. And thus Christian piety, being oftener a habit in the soul than a conquest over it, will be as much more respectable and consistent as it is earlier in the birth and closer to nature.

II

PARENTAL QUALIFICATIONS

"For I know him, that he will command his children and his household after him, and they shall keep the way of the Lord."—*Genesis*, xviii. 19.

THE real point of the declaration, here, is not that Abraham will command his children, but that he is such a man, having such qualities or qualifications as to be able to command, certain to command, and train them into an obedient and godly life. The declaration is, you will observe—"For I know *him;*" not simply and directly—"For I know the fact." Every thing turns on what is *in him*, as a father and householder—his qualifications, dispositions, principles, and modes of life—and the declaration is, that what he is to do, will certainly come out of what he is. He will certainly produce, or train a godly family, because it is in him, as a man, to do nothing else or less. The subject raised then by the declaration is, not so much family training and government, as it is—

The personal and religious qualifications, or qualifications of character, necessary to success in such family training and government.

There is almost no duty or work, in this world, that does not require some outfit of qualifications, in order to the doing of it well. We all understand that some kind of preparation is necessary to fill the place of a magistrate, teach a school, drill a troop of soldiers, or do any such thing, in a right manner. Nay, we admit the necessity of serving some kind of apprenticeship, in order to become duly qualified for the calling, only of a milliner, or a tailor. And yet, as a matter of fact, we go into what we call the Christian training of our children, without any preparation for it whatever, and apparently without any such conviction of negligence or absurdity, as at all disturbs our assurance in what we do. Not that young parents, and especially young mothers, are not often heard lamenting their conscious insufficiency for the charge that is put upon them, but that, in such regrets, they commonly mean nothing more than that they feel very tenderly, and want to do better things than, in fact, any body can. It does not mean, as a general thing, that they are practically endeavoring to get hold of such qualifications as they want, in order to their Christian success. After all, it is likely to be assumed that they have their sufficient equipment in the tender instinct of their natural affection itself. So they go on, as in a kind of venture, to command, govern, manage, punish, teach, and turn about the way of their child, in just such tempers, and ways of example and views of life, as chance to be the element of their own disfigured, ill-begotten character, at the time. This, in short, is their sin—the undoing, as it will by-and-bye appear, of their children—that they undertake their most sacred office, without any sacred qualifications; govern without self-government, discharge the holiest responsibilities irresponsibly, and thrust their children into evil, by the evil and bad mind, out of which their training proceeds.

I know not any thing that better shows the utter incompetency of mere natural affection as an equipment for the parental office, or that, in a short way, proves the fixed necessity in it, of some broader competency and higher qualification, than just to glance at the real cruelties, even commonly perpetrated, under just those tender, faithful instigations of natural affection, that we so readily expect to be a kind of infallible protection to the helplessness of infancy. How often is it a fact, that the fondest parents, owing to some want of insight, or of patience, or even to some uninstructed, only half intelligent desire to govern their child, will do it the greatest wrongs—stinging every day and hour, the little defenseless being, committed to their love, with the sense of bitter injustice; driving in the ploughshare of abuse and blame upon its tender feeling, by harsh words and pettish chastisements, when, in fact, the very thing. in the child that annoys them is, that they themselves have thrown it into a fit of uneasiness and partial disorder, by their indiscreet feeding; or that in some appearance of irritability, or insubjection, it has only not the words to speak of its pain, or explain its innocence. The little child's element of existence becomes, in this manner, not seldom, an element of bitter wrong, and the sting of wounded justice grows in, so to speak, poisoning the soul all through, by its immedicable rancor. The pain of such wrong goes deeper,

too, than many fancy. No other creature suffers under
conscious injury so intensely. And the mischief done
is only aggravated by the fact that the sufferer has no
power of redress, and has no alternative permitted, but
either to be cowed into a weak and cringing submission,
or else, when his nobler nature has too much stuff in it
for that, to be stiffened in hate and the bitter grudges
of wrong. I know not any thing more sad to think of,
than the cruelties put upon children in this manner.
It makes up a chapter which few persons read, and
which almost every body takes for granted can not
exist. For the honor of our human nature, I wish it
could not; and that what we call maternal affection, the
softest, dearest, most self-sacrificing of all earthly forms
of tenderness and fidelity, were, at least, sufficient to
save the dishonor, which, alas! it is not; for these
wrongs are, in fact, the cruelties of motherhood, and as
often, I may add, of an even over-fond motherhood, as
any—wrongs of which the doers are unconscious, and
which never get articulated, save by the sobbings of
the little bosom, where the sting of injury is felt.

Here, then, at just the point where we should, least
of all, look for it, viz: at the point of maternal affection itself, we have displayed, in sadly convincing evidence, the need and high significance of those better
qualifications of mind and character, by which the
training of children becomes properly Christian, and
upon which, as being such, the success of that training
depends. Few persons, I apprehend, have any concep-

tion, on the other hand, of the immense number and sweep of the disqualifications that, in nominally or even really Christian parents, go in to hinder, and spoil of all success, the religious nurture of their children. Sometimes the disqualification is this, and sometimes it is that; sometimes conscious, sometimes unconscious; sometimes observable by others and well understood, and sometimes undiscovered. The variety is infinite, and the modes of combination subtle, to such a degree, that persons taken to be eminently holy in their life, will have all their prayers and counsels blasted, by some hidden fatality, whose root is never known, or suspected, whether by others, or possibly by themselves. The wonder that children, whose parents were in high esteem for their piety, should so often grow up into a vicious and ungodly life, would, I think, give way to just the contrary wonder, if only some just conception were had of the various, multifarious, unknown, unsuspected disqualifications, by which modes of nurture, otherwise good, are fatally poisoned.

Sometimes, for example, it is a fatal mischief, going before on the child, but probably unknown to the world, that the parents, one or both, or it may be the mother especially, does not accept the child willingly, but only submits to the maternal office and charge, as to some hard necessity. This charge is going to detain her at home, and limit her freedom. Or it will take her away from the shows and pleasures for which she is living. Or it will burden her days and nights with cares that weary her self-indulgence. Or she is not fond of

children, and never means to be fond of them—they are
not worth the trouble they cost. Indulging these and
such like discontents, unwisely and even cruelly pro-
voked, not unlikely, by the unchristian discontents and
foolish speeches of her husband, she poisons both herself and her child beforehand, and receives it with no
really glad welcome, when she takes it to her bosom.
Strange mortal perversity that can thus repel, as a harsh
intrusion, one of God's dearest gifts; that which is the
date of the house in its coming, and comes to unseal a
new passion, whereby life itself shall be duplicated in
meaning, as in love and duty! This abuse of marriage
is, in fact, an offense against nature, and is no doubt
bitterly offensive to God. Though commonly spoken of,
in a way of astonishing lightness, it is just that sin, by
which every good possibility of the family is corrupted.
What can two parents do for the child, they only submit to look upon, and take as a foundling to their care?
If they have some degree of evidence in them that they
are Christian disciples, they will have fatally clouded
that evidence, by a contest with God's Providence, so
irreverent to Him, and so cruel to their child. If now,
at last, they somewhat love the child, which is theirs
by compulsion, what office of a really Christian nurture
can they fill in its behalf? They are under a complete
and total disqualification, as respects the duties of their
charge. They are out of rest in God, out of confidence
toward Him, hindered in their prayers, lost to that
sweetness of love and peace which ought to be the element of their house. Delving on thus, from such a

point of beginning, and assuming the possible chance
of success, in what they may do in the spirit of such
a beginning, is simply absurd. What can they do in
training a child for God, which they have accepted,
at his hands, only as being thrust upon them by
compulsion?

I might speak of other disqualifications that have a
similar character, as implying some disagreement with
Providence. But it must suffice to say generally, that
there can be no such thing as a genuine Christian nurture that is out of peace with God's Providence—in
any respect. On the contrary, it is when that peace is
the element of the house, and sweetens every thing in
it—pain, sickness, loss, the bitter cup of poverty,
every ill of adversity or sting of wrong—then it is, and
there, as nowhere else, that children are most sure to
grow up into God's beauty, and a blessed and good life.
The child that is born to such keeping, and lovingly
lapped in the peaceful trust of Providence, is born to a
glorious heritage. On the other hand, where the endeavor and life-struggle of the house is, at bottom, a
fight with Providence; envious, eager, anxious, out of
content, out of rest, full of complaint and railings, it
is impossible that any thing Christian should grow in
such an element. The disqualification is complete.

Another whole class of disqualifications require to be
named by themselves; those I mean which are caused
by a bad or false morality in the parties, at some point
where the failure is not suspected, and misses being

corrected by the slender and very partial experience
of their discipleship.

They are persons, for example, who make much of
principles in their words, and really think that they are
governed by principles, when, in fact, they do every
thing for some reason of policy, and value their principles, more entirely than they know, for what they are
worth in the computations of policy. Contrivance,
artifice, or sometimes cunning, is the element of the
house. A subtle, inveterate habit of scheming creeps
into all the reasons of duty; and duty is done, not for
duty's sake, but for the reasons, or prudential benefits
to be secured by it. Even the praying of the house
takes on a prudential air, much as if it were done for
some reason not stated. A stranger in the house, seeing no scandalous wrong, but a fine show of principle,
has a certain sense of coldness upon him, which he can
not account for. How much of true Christian nurture
there may be in such a house, it is not difficult to
judge. Here, probably, is going to be one of the
cases, where everybody wonders that children brought
up so correctly, turn out so badly. It is not understood that such children were brought up to know principles, only as a stunted undergrowth of prudence, and
that now the result appears.

Again there is, in some persons, who appear, in all
other respects, to be Christian, a strange defect of truth
or truthfulness. They are not conscious of it. They
would take it as a cruel injustice, were they only to
suspect their acquaintances of holding such an estimate

of them. And yet there is a want of truth in every sort of demonstration they make. It is not their words only that lie, but their voice, air, action, their every putting forth has a lying character. The atmosphere they live in is an atmosphere of pretense. Their virtues are affectations. Their compassions and sympathies are the airs they put on. Their friendship is their mood and nothing more. And yet they do not know it. They mean, it may be, no fraud. They only cheat themselves so effectually as to believe, that what they are only acting is their truth. And, what is difficult to reconcile, they have a great many Christian sentiments, they maintain prayer as a habit, and will sometimes speak intelligently of matters of Christian experience. But how dreadful must be the effect of such a character, on the simple, trustful soul of a little child. When the *crimen falsi* is in every thing heard, and looked upon, and done, he may grow up into a hypocrite, or a thief, but what shall make him a genuine Christian?

In the same manner, I could go on to show a multitude of disqualifications for the office of a genuine Christian nurture, that are created by a bad or defective morality, in parents who live a credibly Christian life. They make a great virtue, it may be, of frugality or economy, and settle every thing into a scale of insupportable parsimony and meanness. Or, they make a praise of generous living, and run it into a profligate and spendthrift habit. Or, they make such a virtue of honor and magnanimity, as to set the opinions and principles of men in deference, above the principles of

God. Or, they get their chief motives of action out of the appearances of virtue, and not out of its realities. There is no end to the impostures of bad morality, that find a place in the lives of reputably Christian persons. They are generally too subtle to be detected by the inspection of their consciousness, and very commonly pass unobserved by others. And yet they have power to poison the nurture of the house, even though it appears to be, in some respects, Christian. Hence the profound necessity that Christian parents, consciously meaning to bring up their children for God, should make a thorough inspection of their morality itself, to find if there be any bad spot in it; knowing that, as certainly as there is, it will more or less fatally corrupt their children.

We have still another whole class of disqualifications to speak of, that belong, as vices, to the Christian life itself, and will, as much more certainly, be ruinous in their effects. Some of them would never be thought of as disqualifications for the Christian training of children, and yet they are so, in a degree to even cut off the reasonable hope of success. Probably a great part of the cases of disaster, that occur in the training of Christian families, are referable to these Christian vices, which are commonly not put down as evidences of apostasy, or any radical defect of Christian principle, because they are not supposed to imply a discontinuance of prayer, or a fatal subjection to the spirit of this world.

Sanctimony, for example, as we commonly use the term, is one of these vices. It describes what we conceive to be a saintly, or over-saintly air and manner, when there is a much inferior degree of sanctity in the life. There is no hypocrisy in it, for there is no intention to deceive; but there is a legal, austere, conscientiousness, which keeps on all the solemnities and longitudes of expression, just because there is too little of God's love and joy in the feeling, to play in the smiles of gladness and liberty. Now it is the little child's way, to get his first lessons from the looks and faces round him. And what can be worse, or do more to set him off from all piety, by a fixed aversion, than to have gotten such impressions of it only, as he takes from this always unblessed, tedious, look of sanctimony. What can a poor child do, when the sense of nature and natural life, the smiles, glad voices, and cheerful notes of play, are all overcast and gloomed, or, as it were, forbidden, by that ghostly piety in which it is itself being brought up? And yet the world will wonder immensely at the strange perversity of the child that grows up under such a saintly training, to be known as a person mortally averse to religion! Why, it would be a much greater wonder if he could think of it even with patience!

Bigotry is another of these Christian vices, and yet no one will assume his infallible capacity, in the matter of Christian training, as confidently as the bigot. Has he not the truth? is he not opposite, as possible, to all error? has any man a greater abhorrence of all laxity and all variation from the standards? Is he not in a way of speaking out always, and giving faithful testimonies in his house? Yes, that must be admitted; and yet he is a man that mauls every truth of God, and every gentle and lovely feeling of a genuinely Christian character. His intensities are made by his narrowness and hate, and not by his love. He fills the house with a noise of piety, and may dog his children possibly into some kind of conformity with his opinions. But he is much more likely, by this brassy din, to only stun their intelligence and make them incapable of any true religious impressions. There is no class of children that turn out worse, in general, than the children of the Christian bigots.

The vice of Christian fanaticism operates, in another and different way, but with a commonly disastrous effect. The fanatic is a man who mixes false fire with the true, and burns with a partly diabolical heat. He means to be superlatively Christian, but it happens that what he gets, above others, is the addition of something to his passions, which would be more genuine, if it were in his affections. He scorches, but never melts. He is most impatient of what is ordinary and common, and does not sufficiently honor the solid works and experiences of that goodness which is fixed and faithful. This kind of character makes a fiery element for childish piety to grow in. What can the child become, or learn to be, where every thing is in this key of excess? It is as if there were a simoon of piety blowing through the house, and it dries away all gentle longings and holiest sympathies of the child's affectionate nature, so that all attractions God-ward are suspended. A certain violence and harshness in the parental fanaticism, wakens often the sense of injustice too, or hate, and makes the superlative piety appear to be no better, after all, than it might be.

Another Christian vice is created by a censorious habit. Not by that habit of judging and condemning, which takes a pleasure in condemnation itself—that is the vice of a Christless character, not of a Christian—but there is a large class of disciples who think it a kind of duty, and a just acknowledgment of the fact of human depravity, to be seeing always dark things. They judge evil judgments because they will be more faithful, and will be only doing to others just as they do to themselves. This habit is like a poisonous atmosphere in the house. It kills all springing sentiments of confidence and esteem. That charity which believeth all things, and hopeth all things, appears to be already stifled in it. What shall a child aspire to, when there is no really estimable growth, and good, and beauty, any where?

It is a great vice also, as regards the Christian training of a family, that there is a habit in the parents of receiving nothing by authority, and really disowning authority in all matters of religious. God reigns himself by authority, and because he is God; and parents are to govern by authority, partly, in the same manner. If the parent is a debater with God in every thing, saying always No, to God, till he has gotten his proofs, the spirit will go through the house. The children will demand a reason for every thing required, and will put the parents always on trial, instead of being put under authority themselves. Nothing breaks down faster the religious conscience, or untones more completely the divine affinities of the childish nature, than to have lost the feeling, ceased to hear the ring, of authority. Abraham could believe God's words, and so it was in him to command his children after him.

Anxiousness is another infirmity, or vice of characacter, that has always a noxious effect in the training of Christian families. Where there is but a little faith, there is apt to be great anxiousness. And nothing will so dreadfully torment the life of a child, as to be perpetually teased by the anxious words and looks and interferences of this unhappy superintendence. And if the pretext given is a concern for the child's piety, the effect is only so much more disastrous. What can he think of piety, when it has only worried him at every play and every natural pleasure of his life? Just contrary to this feeble, half-believing, half-Christian vice of anxiety, the parental habit should be one of confidence; gladdened always in the faith that God is the child's covenanted keeper, and will never fail to guard the trust that is faithfully committed to his hands, never allow to grow up in sin what parental fidelity is training, by all reasonable diligence, for a godly life.

This enumeration of the moral and religious vices, that spot the beauty and mar the completeness of character, in one way or another, of almost all merely ordinary Christians, could be indefinitely extended. Nothing, in fact, is farther off, generally, from the truth, than the assumption, by nominally Christian parents, of their sufficiency, or their properly qualified state, as regards the training of their children. They are almost all disqualified, or under-qualified, to such a degree to make their work perilous, and as ought to fill them with real concern for their success. What are we all, in the merely initial state of Christian living, but diseased patients, just entered into hospital? We are not all in the same sort of weakness and defect, but all weak and defective—one-sided, passionate, broken in principle, corrupted by mixed motive, lame in faith. How foolish then is it for us to be assuming that, because we have come to Christ and begun to be disciples, we are ready, of course, for the holy nurture and safe ordering of our families. How foolish, also, to be wondering, as we so often do, that the children of one or another Christian, or reputedly good Christian family, turn out so ill— as if it were some evidence of a singularly perverse and reprobate nature in such children. Little do we know what subtle poisons were hid in what we took to be the good Christian piety of those families. After all, it may have been much less good, or more exceptionably good, than we thought.

It may occur to some of you, as a discouraging disadvantage, that, where one parent is duly qualified for the training of the children in piety, the other is not, but is in fact, a real hindrance to the right and safe proceeding of the endeavor. The parents are never equally well qualified; and one, or the other of them, is likely to be a good deal out of line, in some kind of personal defect, or obliquity of practice. Sometimes one of them will be a purely worldly-minded person, or an unbeliever, or, it may be, even fatally corrupted by vicious habits. There is, accordingly, no hope of concert in the endeavor to train the children up in piety. And this, the other party, who is more commonly the mother, may be tempted in some hour of discouragement to think, amounts to a fatal disqualification, such as quite takes away the rational confidence of success. Let me come to her aid, in the assurance that God connects Himself even the more certainly with one party, if only there is, in that one, a believing and truly faithful spirit, prepared for the work. He pledges himself in formal promise to one party, in all such conditions, declaring that the believing wife sanctifies, takes away the defect of, the unbelieving husband. Let her also consider what is said of young Timothy—how the apostle figures the faith of the good grandmother, and her daughter the good mother, descending on Timothy in the third generation, when his father, all this time, was a Greek, probably an unbeliever and idolater. There was not force enough, you perceive, in all that father's influence to break the descent of the faith of these two godly mothers upon his son.

This, then, is the conclusion to which we are brought; that qualifications are wanted for this work as for almost no other, and that where they are really had, if it be only by one party, they are not likely to fail. But how shall they be obtained? that is the question. Who is subtle enough to go through this hunt of the character, and actually find every loose joint of morality in his practice, every vice of defect, or distemper, in in his Christian life? No one, I answer—that is impossible. No weeding process, carried on by ourselves, ever did or can extirpate our evils. The only true method here is the method of faith; to be more perfectly and wholly trusted to God, more singly, simply Christian. God's touch in us can feel out every thing; every most subtle spot of wrong or weakness he can heal. The reason why we have so many of these spots and disqualifying vices is, that we are only a little Christian. Whereas, if we could be fully entered into Christ's keeping, and have our whole consciousness overspread and clothed by his righteousness, we should live, in every part, and be kept in holy equilibrium above our defects and disorders, all the time. Put ye on the Lord Jesus Christ then as a complete investiture, and there will be no poison flowing down upon your children, from any thing in your life and example. If Christ is made, to those who trust in him, wisdom, righteousness, sanctification, and redemption, what is there that he can not and will not be made? Wonderful is the completeness of any soul that is complete in him. How pure and perfect the morality, how wise the discretion, how gentle and full, and free, the life in which he lives! The house and its discipline become a most joyous element to children, when thus

administered.   Every thing good in it is welcome, even
the restraints and supervisions; for they have a general
air of confidence and hope and gentle feeling, that wins
and not repels.   Even authority itself is welcome, because it is enforced by character, and not by tones of
violence, or dictatorial airs of heat and menace.   Whoever comes thus into God's full love, to be in it and of
it, has a true equipment for the family administration.
If it can be said—Herein is Love, what else can really
be wanting?   This bond of perfectness, brings all
needed qualifications with it, so that when the love or
the faith working by it, really reigns and tempers the
man by its impulse, it can truly be said, as of Abraham—For I know him, that he will command his children and his household after him, and they shall keep
the way of the Lord.

III

PHYSICAL NURTURE, TO BE A MEANS OF GRACE

"Feed me with feed convenient for me, lest I be full and deny thee, and say, who is the Lord?"—*Proverbs*, xxx. 8-9.

A MOST fit subject of prayer! And if the feeding of an adult person, such as Agur, has a connection so intimate with his religious life and character, how much more the feeding and the physical nurture of a child. I use the text, therefore, to introduce, for our present consideration, as a kind of first point, the food or feeding of children, and their physical treatment generally.

It will not be incredible to any thoughtful person, least of all to any genuinely philosophic person, that the treatment and fare of the body has much to do with the quality of the soul, or mind—its affinities, passions, aspirations, tempers; its powers of thought and senti-ment, its imaginations, its moral and religious develop-ment. For the body is not only a house to the mind as other houses are, which we may live in for a time with no perceptible effect on our character, but it is a house in the sense of being the mind's own organ; its external life itself, the medium of all its action, the in-strument of its thought and feeling, the inlet also of all its knowledges and impressions, and the instigator, by a thousand reactions, of all such spiritual riot and corruption as have had their leaven brewed in as many physical abuses and disorders. So intimate is this connection of mind and body, so very close to real oneness are they, that no one can, by any possibility, be a Christian in his mind, and not be in some sense a Christian in his body. If his soul is to be a temple of the Holy Ghost, then his body must be. If his soul is under government, then his body will be. And if his body is not under government, then his soul, by no possibility, can be; save that, in every such case, it will and must be under the government of the body; subject to its power, swayed by all its excesses and distempers.

Hence that most determined, almost proud, resolve of the apostle, when he declares—"I will not be brought under the power of any." Under the body? No! he will scorn that low kind of thraldom. Meats, drinks, appetites—none of these shall have the mastery in him. He will assert the supreme right of the soul or person, above the house it lives in; so God's preeminent right in the soul. He will say to the body— "stay thou down there"—as they that fast do, in fasting; and, what is more profoundly, more scientifically rational than fasting, when it is practiced in the real insight of its reasons? It is the soul rising up, in God's name, to assert herself over the body; over its appetites, passions, tempers, and, if possible, distempers. And how often the poor, coarse, stupid, sensual, fast-bound slaves of the body, calling themselves disciples, need this kind of war, and a regular campaign of it, to get their souls uppermost and trim themselves for the race.

One must be a very inobservant person, not to have noticed, that all his finest and most God-ward aspirations are smothered under any load of excess, or over-indulgence. It is as if the body were calling down all the other powers, even those of poetry, magnanimity, and religion, to help it do the scarcely possible work of digestion. At that point they gather. The sense of beauty is there, and the soul's angel of hope, and the testimony of God's peace, and the music of devotion, and the thrill of sermons, dosing, all together, and sough-ing in dull dreams round the cargo of poppies in the hold of the body. To raise any fresh sentiment is now impossible. Even prayer itself is mired, and can not struggle out. The news of some best friend's death can only be answered by dry interjections, and forced postures of grief, that will not find their meaning till to-morrow.

And much the same thing holds true, only under a different form, when the body is prematurely diseased and broken, by the excesses of self-indulgence. Its distempers will distemper the higher nature; its pains prick through into the sensibilities, even of the spiritual nature. Out of the pits of the body, dark clouds will steam up into the chambers of the soul, and all the devils of dyspepsia will be hovering in them, to scare away its peace, and choke the godlike possibilities, out of which its better motions should be springing.

So important a thing, for the religious life of the soul, is the feeding of the body. Vast multitudes of disciples have no conception of the fact. Living in a swine's body, regularly over-loaded and oppressed every day of their lives, they wonder that so great difficulties and discouragements rise up to hinder the Christian clearness of their soul. Could they but look into Agur's prayer, and take the meaning—feed me with food convenient for me, lest I be full, and deny thee, and say, who is the Lord?—they would find a real gospel in it. And making it truly their own, they would dismiss, at once, whole armies of doubts; their faith would get wings to rise; they would rest their soul in an element of power, and peace, and sweetness, and would run the way of God's commandments with a wonderful clearness and liberty.

I have spoken, thus briefly, to a fact of adult experience, because it is adult conviction which my subject needs to obtain. To simply look on children from without, and tell what effects will be wrought on their religious tempers and habit by their feeding, and the general nurture of their body, will not carry any depth of conviction by itself; for there is no creature of God less adequately understood, or conceived, than a child. And therefore it is that I appeal to parents, in this manner, requiring them to make some observation of themselves; to notice what becomes of them, and their sentiments, and senses of Christ and of God, when they are down under the burdens of an overloaded, or permanently diseased body.

The principle I am here asserting, as regards the religious import of feeding and bodily nurture, in the case of children, is the same on which the child Daniel and his friends acted, in the choice of their very simple and temperate diet. Whether Daniel had been brought up from his infancy in this manner does not appear. He may have been prompted to this choice, by a purely divine impulse. But whether he came into it by one method or the other, makes little difference; for, in either case, the most important matter is to observe the result, and that such kind of feeding was chosen, or instituted, for the sake of the result that would follow, on perfectly natural principles, viz: to give greater clearness to the religious perceptions and sentiments of the soul. The body grew toward perfect health, because it was burdened and distempered by no excesses. And the soul was just as much more open to God and the sense of unseen things, as the body was more serenely and blissfully well, in its physical condition. In this manner the child's nature grew apace, in the molds of a perfectly evened judgment, and was also wonderfully opened to God and all highest discoveries of his will. In a certain sense, he became a great prophet by his physical nurture—"God gave him knowledge, thus, and skill, in all learning and wisdom, and he had understanding in all visions and dreams." His feeding stood with his health, and with all purest affinities and deepest openings toward God.

Let us glance a moment, now, at some of the points

here involved, and distinguish, if we can, the results
that are always depending on the right feeding of
children.

The child is taken, when his training begins, in a
state of naturalness, as respects all the bodily tastes and
tempers, and the endeavor should be to keep him in
that key; to let no stimulation of excess, or delicacy,
disturb the simplicity of nature, and no sensual pleas-
uring, in the name of food, become a want or expectation of his appetite. Any artificial appetite begun, is
the beginning of distemper, disease, and a general dis-
turbance of natural proportion. Intemperance! the
woes of intemperate drink! how dismal the story, when
it is told; how dreadful the picture, when we look
upon it. From what do the father and mother recoil,
with a greater and more total horror of feeling, than
the possibility that their child is to be a drunkard?
Little do they remember that he can be, even before he
has so much as tasted the cup; and that they themselves can make him so, virtually, without meaning it,
even before he has gotten his language! Nine-tenths
of the intemperate drinking begins, not in grief and
destitution, as we so often hear, but in vicious feeding.
Here the scale of order and simplicity is first broken,
and then what shall a distempered or distemperate life
run to, more certainly, than to what is intemperate?
False feeding genders false appetite, and when the soul
is burning, all through, in the fires of false appetite,
what is that but a universal uneasiness? and what will
this uneasiness more naturally do, than betake itself to

the pleasurable excitement of drink? What is wanted is a sensation—the soul is aching for a sensation; for it is one of the miseries of food that the tasting pleasure is soon over and the cloyed body turns away in disgust; one of the excellencies of drink, that the sensation is a long one, and may be easily drawn out so as to cover whole hours of duration. Food, sleep, friends, the self-enjoyment of character—what an excellent and easy substitute it is for them all! Thus, for example, when a very young child, taken by the captivating flavor of some dainty or confectionery, has refused to restrain itself, and has kept on, as by a kind of spell, repeating the sensation again and again, till the organs, dried and cloyed by excess, refuse to give it longer, you will see that a wonderful uneasiness follows, asking what sensation next? and really there is nothing that can fill the vacant space, or quiet the uneasiness. One toy or another will be seized and thrown into the fire. The plays that before satisfied look insipid and do not please. The world goes ill because there is nothing good enough in it, and a general cry finishes the overdone pleasure of the day. And here you have in small, as in a single view, just that misery of distemper and uneasiness which is wrought, by the bad feeding of childhood, and prepares the vice of intemperance, even before it appears.

It is only a larger and more comprehensive mischief of the wrong feeding of children, that it puts them under the body, teaches them to value bodily sensations, makes them sensual every way, and sets them lusting in every kind of excess. The vice of impurity is taught, how commonly, thus, at the mother's table. The finer sentiments and wits of children are smothered also and deadened, by this same animalizing process. They make a dull figure at school. Their feeling is coarse, their conscience weak, their passions low and violent. Their higher affinities, those which ally them to God and character and unseen worlds, appear to be closed up, and the lines of their faces, particularly about the mouth, give a low sensual expression, even when the upper-head is large and full. A certain degree of selfishness is likely to be somehow developed in children, for sin of every kind is selfish, but the lowest, meanest, and most utterly degraded type of selfishness, is the sensual; that which centers in the body, and makes every thing bend to bodily sensation. And yet the early feeding and growth of children tends, how often, to just this and nothing higher. Saying nothing of genius and great action, impossible to be developed in this manner out of the finest possible organization, what hope is there under such abuse of nature, that religion will there begin to loosen her noble aspirations, and claim her sonship with God? What place can the love of God find open, in a soul that is shut up under the bruitishness of sensuality? What sensibility is left for Christ and God, when the body has become the total manhood?

And exactly this it will most certainly be, if first it becomes the total childhood. We have a way of saying, continually, that children are creatures of the

senses, and we please ourselves in making allowances
for them in this manner, and raising expectations of
them that suppose the likelihood of their, by-and-bye,
coming out of their senses, into the higher ranges of
thought and spiritual impulse.   But we do not remember, always, the immense distinction between being in
the senses and being in the sensualities; between going
after the eyes, and going after the stomach; between the
almost divine curiosity of intelligence, exploring all
objects, sounds, and colors, to get in the stock of its
mental furniture, and the totally incurious hankering of
appetite, for some finer, freer indulgence of the animal
sensation.   Little hope is there of a child, who is in the
senses, after this latter fashion.   This he will quite seldom or never outgrow; on the contrary, it will overgrow him, and subjugate all nobler impulse in him, by
a kind of natural law; even as disease propagates more
disease and not health.   In this manner, a child can be
fairly put under the body for life, by the time he is five
years old.   And just this, I verily believe, is often true.
Kindness, it may be, has done it, but it is that kindness
which is better called cruelty.   Coarseness of feeling,
lowness of impulse, gluttony, dissipation, drunkenness,
adultery—all foul passions that kennel in a sensual
soul, it has cherished as a foster-mother; not once imagining the fact, in the indiscreet feeding of the hapless
creature trusted to its care.

This, too, will be rendered yet more probable by
reviewing, briefly, some of the methods by which a

more judicious, and more properly Christian feeding will conduce toward a different and happier result.

First of all, it will not be a permitted practice, to quiet the child in states of irritation, or stop it in crying, or pacify it in fits of ill-nature, by dainties that please the taste. What is this but a schooling and drawing out of sensation, by making it the reward of just that which is most totally opposite to self-government? It must be a very dull child that will not cry and fret a great deal, when it is so pleasantly rewarded. Trained, in this manner, to play ill-nature for sensation's sake, it will go on rapidly, in the course of double attainment, and will be very soon perfected, in the double character of an ill-natured, morbid, sensualist, and a feigning cheat beside. By what method, or means, can the great themes of God and religion get hold of a soul, that has learned to be governed only by rewards of sensation, paid to affectations of grief and deliberate actings of ill-nature?

Simplicity also, as opposed to luxuries, condiments, and confections, is a condition of all right feeding for infancy and childhood, which ought to approve itself to the most ordinary measure of parental discretion. Of course I do not mean to say that the child is never to have his holiday feast—that would be to cut him off from another kind of benefit—I only insist that he is not to have a perpetual holiday, and be stimulated by continual flavors on his organs, till the beautiful simplicity of his appetite is gone and nothing pleases longer, but that which is intense enough to be rather poison than food.   Coffee, for example—what can be worse for a child's body, or his future character, than to be dosed every morning with his cup of coffee?   No matter if he cries for it, all the worse if he does; for it shows that he has been already taught to love it, and is so far taken away, prematurely, from the natural simplicity of his tastes.   And how is the child going to be drawn by the beauty of God, and the sacred pleasures of God's friendship, when thinking always of the dainties he has had, or is again to have, and counting it always the main blessing of existence, to have his body seasoned by the flavors of sensation? Instead of praying, as possibly he may be taught, in words—"Feed me with food convenient for me"—he prays, in fact, from morning to night, with all diseased longings and hankerings, to be fed, in the exact contrary, with what will most increase his already overgrown sensuality.   In a manner faithfully characteristic of his low, prudential morality, Paley advises that all children and young person should live simply, because they are now susceptible enough to relish simple things; in order that, as their tastes grow duller with advancing age, they may allow themselves a freer indulgence in the stimulations of appetite, and may so maintain the feeding pleasures to the last.   Counsel not to be questioned, even if these pleasures were the chief end of life itself.   We are only disappointed and vexed by the lowness of it, when we recall, what is the real and true penalty of youthful indulgence, that it takes away the possible relish of truth, duty, and religion, and makes the soul forever inaccessible to these noblest powers of character and blessedness.

In a wise, physical nurture, it is a matter of great import also to regulate the times of feeding. For this induces the sense of order, which is closely allied to a habit of self-government. If the nursing child is simply stuffed to its last limit, at any and all hours, then it is put in the way, not of intelligent feeding, which is interspaced by rest, but of always being filled to its limit. The feeding must, of course, be as much more frequent in infancy as the demands of a more rapid consumption require, but there should be times, and a degree of order established, as soon as possible; otherwise the stuffing method will go on into childhood, and boyhood, and by that time the bodily habit is in total disorder, carrying the tempers and general character with it. The breakfast before breakfast, and the dinner before dinner, and the casual snatching and feeding at all hours between, bring the child to the table with a scowl upon his face, and a nervous, morbid look of disgust, which declare, as plainly as possible, that there is nothing good enough prepared for him; and, quite as plainly, that he is a poor, misgoverned and spoiled child. He is overtaken by all the woes of sensuality, and yet has gotten almost none of its pleasures; for he is always kept, by his irregular, ungoverned feeding, so close up to the line of possible appetite, that peevishness and ill-nature are the spice of all his sensations, and his body and soul are about equally distempered by the morbid irritations and dyspeptic woes that have come upon them. What a prep-

aration is this for the calm, sweet, thoughtful motives
of religion, and the gentle whispers of God's truth in
the heart!

It should also be understood in the religious training
of children, how great mischiefs are likely to follow,
when much is made of the pleasures of the table. If
the feeding is the great circumstance of the house and
the day, if the discourse turns always on the peculiar
relish of this, or the wonderful delicacy of that, and the
main stress of life in general on the bliss of good living,
it will not much avail, that the parents have a certain
wish to see their children grow up in religion. A
stranger falling into such a family, will be amazed to
find how pervasive and spirit-like this most unetherial,
undiffusive kind of bliss may be. The smack of appetite will seem to be in the atmosphere of the house. It
will be as if the gastric nerve of the family were become the whole brain. A certain coarseness of feeling
and character will appear in every thing. The grain
will be coarse, both of body and soul; and the general
expression of manners, faces, and voices, will be such
as indicates a reduction of grade, in all the finer impulses of society, intelligence, and duty. The family
affections themselves will seem to have fallen back, to
make room for the valued bliss of the appetites. No
matter how much of prayer and regular church-going
there may be in such a family, the child brought up in
it has a most sad fortune to bear, in the savoring habit
to which it trains him. Nor is it only in some high
conditioned family, where wealth is steeping itself in

luxury, that this kind of woe is put upon children. It quite as often begins at the coarse, low table of the sensually minded poor. These are even most likely of all to live, and teach their children to live, for what they may eat. The humble Christian mother, it may be, having no luxuries of dress and show to give her children, makes it a great point to have them enjoy the feeding of their bodies; and so, instead of fining them to a nobler pleasure in the virtues of frugality, order, gentle society, and good action, she graduates them into just that coarsest sensuality which is the bane of all character, for this life and the next.

It is a much greater point, in this connection, than is commonly supposed, that children should be trained to good manners in their eating. Good manners are a kind of self-government which operates continually to keep the body under, and hold the sensualizing tendency of food in check. Animals have no manners, and the higher gift of manners is allowed to man, to keep him from the coarseness and lowness to which his animal nature would otherwise run. In this view, good manners are even a sort of first-stage religion, for the reduction of the body. If the child is practiced carefully, at his food, in deferring to superiors and seniors; in the restraint of haste, or greediness; in the proprieties of positions, and the handsome uses of tools; in the limitation of his feeding by his wants, and a good-natured submission to restriction when restriction is needed for his good; he will not grow sensual in that manner, but his mind will be all the while getting sovereignty over the body. Good breeding and civility are, in this view, indispensable. The Christian training of children, without any care of their manners in these respects, is only the training, in fact, of barbarians and savages, in the houses of such as call themselves Christian people.

There is great importance also, for a similar reason, in the observance of a Christian blessing, or giving of thanks at the table. The mere form, taken only as a constantly recurring acknowledgment of God and the obligations of gratitude, laid on the family by his goodness, is a matter of inestimable value. The bare recollection of a higher nature and the higher meaning of life, coupled uniformly thus with the order of the table, qualifies the lower sensations, and raises them to a kind of spiritual dignity. It is even a pitiful figure, in this view, which the great Franklin makes, when, with so little show of philosophy, saying nothing of Christian reverence, he recites, in a manner of evident pleasure, the wit of his boyhood: asking his father, at the packing of his barrel of meat, why he did not say grace over the whole barrel at once, and save the necessity of so many repetitions? These repetitions are the very things most wanted. They compose the liturgy of the table, and have their value, not in the quantities of meat they season, but in the seasoning of the partakers themselves, by so many reiterations of their, at least, formal homage and gratitude. At the same time there should be much care taken to make these blessings of the table more than a form; to connect a real and felt meaning with them, and make them the expression of a living and true gratitude in all present. Children can be so trained, in this matter, as even to miss the flavor of their meat, when no blessing is upon it. What then can be expected, in a Christian family, when the children are put to their food with no such recognition of God, and have their faces turned downward always upon it, even as if they were animals? Doubtless the blessing may, too often, be a mere form, but it is a form which, apart from any conscious glow of sentiment, no Christian family can afford to lose.

Much also may be done for children, by associating subjects, and sentiments, and plans of practical charity, with the blessings and pleasures of the table. To do this requires no very ingenious methods, or deeply studied plans. It will be done almost, of course, if the parents themselves are, at all, given to such things; for, in such a case, they can hardly fail to speak of the children of the poor, and the bitter pains and pinings of their unsatisfied hunger. If the appetites of children are eager and easily turned to a habit of sensuality, their sympathies also are quick, and their compassions wonderfully tender. Let these last be called into play, and kept in play, as they may be always by a few simple words of charity, and proposed acts of bounty to the children of want, and the former, the appetites, will become incentives even habitually, to what is noblest in feeling and remotest from a properly sensual character. The body itself becomes the interpreter, in such a case, of want, and offers itself dutifully to mercy, to be used as its organ.

Such are a few of the suggestions that require to be noted and observed, in the right feeding of children. Others will occur to you daily, as your work goes on, if only you are really awake to the transcendent importance of the subject. Let it never be assumed, for one moment, that you are now doing nothing and can be doing nothing for your children, because you are only feeding their bodies. A very considerable part of your parental charge lies just here; in giving your children such a nurture in the body, as makes them superior to the body; subordinates the passions, and evens the tempers of the body; prepares them to a state of robust and massive healthiness; gives them clearer heads, and nobler sentiments of truth; preparing them, in that manner, to be good scholars, to have their affectional nature opened wide by a general love, to have their perceptive feeling quickened to all highest forms of beauty and good, and so to have them ready, more and more ready, for a state of eternally unsealed affinity with God. There is not any thing, in the highest ranges of their spiritual and religious nature, that will not be somehow affected, and powerfully too, by the feeding of their bodies. Even their conscience itself, which is God's own organ or throne, so to speak, in their nature—the most self-asserting and, as we should say, most indestructible of all their powers—can be made to ring out clear and true, like a bell in the night, or it can be stifled and choked, so as scarcely to be audible—all by the mere feeding of the body. So there is a feeding that makes a manly life, and a feeding that makes a mean, weak, ignoble life. So there is a feeding which makes room for God, and a feeding that leaves him no vacant space or chamber to fill. The question here is not, exactly, what converting power is exerted or not exerted, what Christian truth impressed or not impressed, but it is what kind of metal, in fact, the future man is to be made of; for all that is entered, thus early, into the feeding habit of the body, is about as really composite and substantial as that which is prepared in the inborn properties of nature itself. This feeding nurture, if we take the real sense of it, is to grow in good or bad affinities and possibilities; to grow a body under the soul, or over it; to form a good or bad staple, in the substance of the man, which is going to remain unchanged, by all his future changes and transformations, about as certainly as his face, or gait, and in much the same degree.

To complete this view of the bodily nurture and keeping, something ought also to be said of personal neatness, and also of dress, in both of which the bodily habit is concerned, though in a more external and less decisive way.

As regards the matter of personal neatness, I will only suggest the very close relationship of association between it, as a habit, and the spiritual habit of the soul in religion. In this holy endeavor of grace, or religion, the soul aspires to be clean. Conscious of great defilement in sin, it hears a call to come and be made white, even as the snow. It begins with the prayer—"Create in me a clean heart, O God," and the longing after purity, and a clean consciousness before Him, draws it on. To be washed, purified, made clean—under these, and such like terms of aspiration, it is exercised, in all the keeping of the life, that it may incur no spot or stain, and be effectually purged from all most subtle defilements. In this view, bodily neatness, or the cleanly keeping of the person, is a kind of outward religion going before, preparing tastes, images, sensibilities, habits that make the soul more akin to religion, readier to feel the obligation, and labor in the purifying endeavor. And, in this view, the mother, the poor Christian mother, who has nothing of this world's good, as we commonly speak, to put upon her children, has yet one of the best goods of all, which she may, without fail, bestow, viz: a cleanly habit. She gives them a great mark of honor, and sets them in a way of great hope and preferment, as regards all highest character, when she trains them to a felt necessity of neatness and order. On the other hand, if she allows them to grow up in a filthy and loose habit, crowding all bounty upon them, and breathing out her soul beside, in prayer and fasting on their account, it will be wonderful if they have much sensibility to the defilements of the soul, or come to God in any determinate longings after purity. Nay, it will be wonderful if the dirt upon their persons and clothing is not found upon their conscience also, and if they do not go on to live the disorder in their souls, which has been the untidy element of their bodies.

There is also this very peculiar excellence in neatness, that it is not ambitious, not for show, but more for
what it is in itself—an honest kind of benefit, or good,
that brings along no bad or false motive with it.
Hence there is no temptation in the practice. Honor
and ornament and grace of poverty, as it often is, it is
only the more truly such, that it simply fulfills and perpetuates a fixed necessity, looking after no reward, save
what it is to itself. Formed to such a habit, and
scarcely conscious of it, the children grow into a kind
of pure simplicity in good, which is itself one of the
finest symbols and surest outward preparations of the
religious life and character.

The subject of dress, taken as related to religious
character in youth, is one of transcendent importance,
but as I am treating mostly of what is to be done for
children, in the few first years of their training, I shall
dismiss the subject with only a few suggestions, such as
my particular purpose appears to require.

There is this very singular and striking contrast between animals and men, that they are born dressed,
and these to be dressed; while yet the fact of a dress
is equally necessary to both. The object of the distinction appears to be, to allow, in the latter case, a
certain liberty of form and appearance, even as there is
given a grand central liberty of life and character
within. It allows us to choose what shall be added to
finish out our form, or appearing; and it is a singular
fact, in this connection, that we always take our dress
to be, in some sense, ourselves; just as if it grew out

of our bodily substance; so that we feel ourselves ordinarily limited and hampered, in behavior and manners, in thought and feeling, and fancy, by the dress we have on. The consciousness of being badly, or half absurdly dressed, makes us awkward. We can not sit down to write in a sordid and tattered dress—thought can not sufficiently respect itself, the feeling nature and the taste and the fancy can not be in trim in such a guise. As a king would not like to appear in the dress of a convict, so they ask a dress that more respects their quality. There is a fearfully powerful reaction, thus, in dress, upon what is inmost and deepest in character. And so much is there in this fact, that every Christian parent should be fully alive to it, even from the first; understanding that the child is going to enlarge his consciousness, so as, in a sense, to take in his dress and be configured to it—inverting the common order of speech on the subject, when we talk of cutting the dress to the child; for it is equally true, in a different sense, that the child will be cut to his dress.

Hence the dreadful mischief done to a child, by what may be called the dolling of it; that is, by dressing, or over-dressing it, just to please, or amuse, or, what is really more true, to tickle a certain weak and foolish pride in the parents. What meantime has become of that most tender and godly concern, which belongs to the Christian charge put upon them, in the gift of this same child? It takes whole months, how often, to get the child's looks and dress into such trim that it can be offered by them for baptism, making the desired impression; in which it turns out that the chief object, to them, of baptism, is the exhibition of the doll they have been dressing; not to get the seal and sacrament of God's mercy upon it, as a creature in the heritage of their own corrupted life.

And then, afterwards, the dressing goes on still, in faithful keeping with its sad beginning. In a few days this same child appears, marching the streets, in the figure of a little gentleman with a cane; or if it be a daughter, hung with necklaces and chains, and set off with as much of finery as can well be supported—visibly conscious, in either case, of the fine show being made; even as the foolish parents, it might fitly despise, were just now admiring their doll at home, and praising to itself the pretty figure it made!

Is this now the dress of a Christian child? is this such a dress as a properly Christian nurture prescribes? What is this child training for, but simply to be a fop, or fashionist, or fool? This taste for show, and finery, and flattery—what is it but the beginning of all irreligion? and what will the after life be, but the continuance of this beginning?

Just contrary to this, whoever will bring up a child for God, must put him, at the very first, into God's modes and measures. The real question of dress, is what shall be put upon this child, to make it feel most like a Christian—what will give him the finest feeling with the least of show and vanity? What will leave him in a state most natural, and simple, and farthest from affectation? What will be most like to the putting on of Christ himself, his righteousness, beauty, truth, meekness, and dignity? Dress your child for Christ, if you will have him a Christian; bring every thing, in the training, even of his body, to this one final aim, and it will be strange, if the Christian body you give him does not contain a Christian soul.

IV

THE TREATMENT THAT DISCOURAGES PIETY

"Fathers provoke not your children to anger, lest they be discouraged."
—*Colossians*, iii. 21.

DISCOURAGED, the apostle means, in good; that is, in worthy purposes and pious endeavors. Nothing will more certainly put a child in a discouraged feeling, than to be angered by a parent's ill-nature and abuse. The anger is, most certainly, far enough from being itself a state of discouragement; but anger is a passion that can not hold long and the after state into which it subsides, in the case of inferiors and dependants, is commonly a giving up to the bad, a passionless and low desperation, that is equivalent to a general surrender of all high aims and aspirations.

In this view, it would not be altogether amiss, and certainly no improper use of the apostle's words, if I were to offer under them a lecture to parents, on the provoking ways of treatment and government. But I have chosen them for a different purpose, and one that is more inclusive, viz: to introduce and give sanction to a discourse on—

The discouragement of piety in children; the ways in which it is discouraged, and the great care necessary to avoid a mistake so injurious.

I speak here, of course, to parents who really desire the spiritual welfare of their children. Nothing is farther off from their design, than to push their children away from Christ into a state of alienated and discouraged feeling. And yet they do it, very often, by faults of management not suspected, and never afterwards discovered; unless, possibly, after the injury is done, when it can no longer be repaired.

It becomes, in this view, a very serious and practically important question, how, or by what methods, Christian parents, unawares to themselves and contrary to their really good intentions, discourage piety in their children? Let us see if we can partially answer the question.

We begin, then, where the apostle begins with his remonstrance. His language is particularly addressed to fathers; for he seems to have in view the case of children, who are in the more advanced stages of childhood, or in what we call the period of youth. And yet the language is equally applicable to the case of mothers and very little children. It might not be wholly amiss for a half-grown lad, or youth, who has violated his father's feelings, by some really base act of crime, or disobedience, to see, by the smoke of his indignant passion, how deeply his right sensibility is revolted. That will never discourage him in any thing good. It might even rouse his moral nature, when nothing less violent would suffice. The father will really discourage good in his son, only when he stings him with a sense of injustice, and keeps him in a wounded feeling, by his own ungoverned, groundless passion. But in the case of the mother, dealing with her very young child, there is no place even for so much as a feeling of impatience. No crisis occurs that she has any right to carry by a storm. And yet there are many mothers who breed a climate of storms for their children to grow up in, even from the first. They make an element of pettishness and passion, and call it Christian nurture to maintain a kind of quarrel with their children, from infancy upward. We do not commonly conceive that the children are discouraged, thus, in the matter of piety; but the real fact is, that their better, higher nature, quite worn down by such treatment, sinks at last into a kind of atrophy, which is the essence of all discouragement. By the time they are passed through this first chapter of torment, their faces even have begun to take on a forlorn expression, as if their well-abused feeling had been quite choked off from every thing hopeful or good. Nothing is more beautiful than the God-ward affinities, and glad impulses to good, in a childish soul; but when it has once been kiln-dried in this hot furnace of motherly or fatherly passion, there is no more any putting forth after the divine. A kind of indifference, or sullen prejudice, sets off the heart from God, and the gentle affinities close up under the stupor of so great early abuse and discouragement.

Children are also discouraged and hardened to good by too much of prohibition. There is a monotony of continuous, ever sounding, prohibition, which is really awful. It does not stop with ten commandments, like the word of Sinai, but it keeps the thunder up, from day to day, saying always thou shalt not do this, nor this, nor this, till, in fact, there is really nothing left to be done. The whole enjoyment, use, benefit, of life is quite used up by the prohibitions. The child lives under a tilt-hammer of commandment, beaten to the ground as fast as he attempts to rise. All command-ments, of course, in such a strain of injunction, come to sound very much alike, and one appears to be about as important as another. And the result is that, as they are all in the same emphasis, and are all equally annoy-ing, the child learns to hate them all alike, and puts them all away. He could not think of heartily accept-ing them *all*, and it would even be a kind of irrever-ence to make a selection. Nothing so fatally worries a child, as this fault of over-commandment. The study should be rather to forbid as few things as possible, and then to soundly enforce what is forbidden. Such kind of prohibitions the child will even like, and will be all the happier, that he has something good to observe. But nothing can be more impotent, in the way of au-thority, than the din of a continual prohibition. Even the commandments of God will, in such a case, be robbed of all just authority, by the custom of a gen-eral weariness and distaste; in which all highest man-dates are leveled to equality with the pettiest and most useless restraints.

Again, it is a great discouragement to piety in chil-dren, when they are governed in a hard, unfeeling, way or in a manner of force and overbearing absolutism.

Any thing which puts the child aloof from the parent, or takes away the confidence of love and sympathy, will as certainly be a wall to shut him away from God. If his Christian father is felt only as a tyrant, he will seem to have a tyrant in God's name to bear; and that will be enough to create a sullen prejudice against all sacred things. Nor is the case at all better when the child is cowed under fear of such a parent, and reduced to a feeling of dread or abject submission. There is a beautiful courage in children as respects approach to God, when God is not presented as a bugbear; and this natural state of courage, is just that which makes the time of childhood so ingenuously open to religion. But if their courage, even toward their father, is already broken down into fear and servile submission, they will only think of God with as much greater fear, and shrink from all the claims of piety with a kind of abject recoil, as from a thing forbidden. No gentleness even of Christ will suffice, in such a case, to win, or reassure the broken courage of the soul. I recall a family in which the father, known as a man of condition and of no little repute for his Christian good works, brought up a large family of boys to be ruled at a distance. He addressed them in a kind of imperious, unfeeling way; not with any violence of manner, but with a stern faced grin that seemed to say, "it is well that you fear me." And fear him they most certainly did—fear was the element in which they grew. And the result was that having no self-respect, and living under a law of mere suppression, they fell into base immoralities from their childhood, and were never afterwards known, even one of them, to have so much as a thought of piety.

Another and even more common way of discouraging children in matters of piety is by an over-exacting manner, or by an extreme difficulty of being pleased. Children love approbation, and are specially disappointed, when they fail of it in their meritorious endeavors. Their chagrin is never more complete, in fact, than when, having set themselves to any purpose of well-doing, they are still repulsed by a manner of fault-finding at the end, and blamed on account of some trivial defect which they did not know, and would really have tried to avoid. Some parents appear to think it a matter of true faithfulness, that they be not too easily pleased, lest their children should take up loose impressions of the strictness of duty. They do not consider how they would fare themselves, if God were to make a point of treating them in the same manner. His manner with them is exactly opposite. He perceives that he will only repel them, by making it a matter of difficulty to please him, and that he could never draw them on, if he did not yield them his smile under great faults and shortcomings, and did not give them the testimony that they please him, when they are a great way off from his own scale of perfection. In all which we may readily see how great discouragement is put upon children, in all their good attempts, when their parents will not allow themselves to be pleased with any thing they do. Possibly they are withheld by scruples of orthodoxy. If so, the mischief is only the greater. What can win a child to the

attempt to please God, when his parents dare not suffer
so much as a thought of the possibility in him, and,
for the same reason, dare not so much as approve him
themselves. Such kind of orthodoxy can not be too
soon forsaken, or too earnestly repented of.

Closely akin to this, is the fault of holding displeasure too long, and yielding it with too great difficulty.
It is right that children, doing wrong, should encounter
some kind of treatment that indicates displeasure. But
the displeasure should not take the manner of a grudge,
and hold on after the wrong is visibly felt and repented of. On the contrary, there should even be a
hastening toward the child, in glad recognitions and
cordial greetings, when the tokens only of relenting
begin to appear; even as the prodigal's father is represented, in the parable, as discovering him, in his return,
when he is yet a great way off, and advancing to meet
and embrace him. By this tender figure God is shown
us, and the holy generosity of his fatherhood is represented. We see that he is only the more ready to be
pleased, because of his magnanimity; holding no re-
sentments, putting off the feeling of offense at the earliest moment, and the cheapest possible rate. Nay, He
will even take our good by anticipation; accepting us
for what we ask, before he can accept us for what we
are. Well is it for those parents who think it incumbent on them, to hold their displeasure till the culprit
is sufficiently scathed by it, if they do not hold it just
a little too long; turning, thus, even his repentance into
a sullen aversion, and setting it in his feeling, that there

is the same heavy tariff of displeasure still to be paid, when he would forsake his sins and turn himself to God. When will it be learned that penance is no fit beginning of piety?

And here let me speak of the very great danger, after a time of discipline, that the parent may hold his displeasure too long; as he certainly will, if there is any ugly feeling, or wicked, natural resentment in him. Thus Jean Paul beautifully says:—" A punishment is scarcely of such importance to a child as the succeeding quarter of an hour, and the transition to forgiveness. After the storm, the seed finds the soil warm and softened; the terror and hatred of the punishment are now past, which before resisted and struggled against the word, and gentle instruction finds its way, and brings healing with it, as honey assuages the sting of bees, and oil the pain of a wound. In this hour we can say much, if we use the utmost gentleness of voice, and by the manifestation of our own pain, soothe that of the child. But every continuance of wintry anger is poisonous. Mothers easily fall into this prolongation of punishment. This continuance of anger; this would-be punishment of pretending a diminution of love, either fails to be comprehended by the child, because he is wholly immersed in the present and so misses its effect, or else he becomes satisfied with a deprivation of the signs of love, and learns to do without it; or else he is embittered by the continuance of punishment for a sin which he has already buried. Through this prolongation of harshness, we lose that beautiful and touching transition into forgiveness, which, by coming slowly and after a long period, only loses its power."*

Hasty and false accusations again are a great discouragement to piety in children. Their good feeling, or intention, appears to be rated low by their parents, when they are put under the ban of dishonor, by false and groundless imputations; and they are very likely, as the next thing, to show that they are no better than they were taken to be. On this account, a wise parent will be religiously careful of all volunteer and random charges of blame, lest he may discourage fatally all pious or ingenuous aspirations by them; for to batter self-respect, or insult the sense of character, thus gratuitously, is the surest way possible to break every natural charm of virtue and religion. The effect is scarcely better where acknowledged faults are exaggerated, and set off in colors of derision. It will do for a parent to be just, severely just; for, by that means, he will best impress the sacred severity of principle. God is just in all his charges and reproofs; but there is no manner of excess or spirit of exaggeration in them. And exactly this it is which makes his kindness so beautiful, so inspiring to our courage, so attractive to our love. But harsh justice, exaggerated justice, is injustice. When a child, therefore, is persecuted by railing words, cauterized by satire, blamed without reason or measure for faults not easily corrected, the severity is really unprincipled as well as unfriendly, and is only the more dreadfully mischievous, that it takes on airs of piety,

---

* Levana iii. § 65.

and bears the Christian name. How can he be drawn
by that which has no grace of allowance, and yields no
sympathy to the struggles of his infirmity? How many
poor children are beaten out of all their natural affinities for good, by just this kind of cruelty! They had
parents who, in fault of the better evidences of love and
patience, thought to make up the deficit in being at
least severe enough to be Christian; which, though it
was an easy grace for them—the only grace at their
command—was, alas! fearfully hard on the subjects.

We bring into view a different class of discouraging
causes, when we speak of that anxiousness, or always
miserable concern, for children, by which some parents
keep them in a continual torment of suppression. We
have really no right to allow a properly anxious feeling
any where. Anxiety is a word of unbelief, or unrea-
soning dread. Full faith in God puts it at rest; any
solid conviction of necessity and right is chloroform to
the pain of it. And we have the less right to be
anxious, that it is a feeling which destroys the comfort
of others whenever and wheresoever it appears. Only
to be in a room with an anxious person, though a stranger, is enough to make one positively unhappy; for the
manner, the nervous unsteadiness, and worry, and shift,
are so irresistibly expressive, that no effort of silence, or
suppression, is able to conceal the torment. To go a
journey thus with an anxious person, is about the worst
kind of pilgrimage. What then is the woe put upon
a hapless little one or child, who is shut up day by day
and year by year, to the always fearing look and depre-

cating whine, the questioning, protesting, super-caution-
ary keeping of a nervously anxious mother. If the
child catches the infection himself, he will never come
to any thing; never dare any great purpose that belongs to a man, or a Christian. And if he does not
catch it, which is more probable, then he will pitch himself into a campaign of will and passion with all that
kind of control, a good deal less rational, probably,
than the control itself. Simply to enter the house will
raise a breeze in his feeling, and he will be worried and
fretted, till he has somehow made his escape. Nothing
is more opposite to the hopeful and free spirit of childhood, and nothing will so dreadfully overcast the sky
of childhood, as the sad kind of weather it is always
making. It worries the child in every putting forth
and play, lest he should somehow be hurt; takes him
away, or would, from every contact with the great
world's occasions, that would give fit schooling to his
manhood. And then, since the child will most certainly learn, at last, how little reason there was in the
eternal distress of so many fears and imaginations
of harm, he is sure to be issued finally, in a feeling
of confirmed disrespect, which is the end of all good
influence or advice. ·And then it will be so much the
worse, if the anxiety whose bagpipe melody has been
the torment of his early days, has shown itself in the
same unregulated way in matters of religion. Nothing will set a child farther off from religion, or make
him more utterly incapable of sympathy with it, than
to have had it put upon him in a whining and misgiv-

ing way, in all his moods and occasions. No! there must be a certain courage in maternity and the religion of it. The child must be wisely trusted to danger, and shown how to conquer it. A pleasure must be taken in giving him a certain range of adventure; and he must see that his courage and capacity are confided in. And then it must be seen, in the same way, that his truth, fidelity, piety, are as much expected as his manhood. In a certain good sense, the mother may be anxious for him, burdened in her prayers in his behalf, but she must take on hope and confidence nevertheless, and show that courage in him, as regards all good endeavor, is met and supported by courage in herself.

Again, it will be found that piety is very commonly discouraged in children, by giving them tests of character that are inappropriate to their age. There is an immense cruelty put upon children here, by parents who have really no design but simply to be faithful. Their child, for example, loses his temper in some matter in which he is crossed; and the conclusion is forthwith sprung upon him that he has a bad heart, and is certainly no Christian child. Whereupon he ceases to pray; or, if he is put to it as a form, does it with an averted and reluctant feeling, as if the wrong were conclusive against his prayers. It is only necessary to ask how the father, how the mother would themselves fare, tested by the same rule? If irritation, passion, any loss of temper, is conclusive against the little being who has scarcely began to be practiced in self-government, how is it with them who ought by this time to be immovably fixed in their serenity? So if the child has played, or shown some eagerness for play on Sunday, has not the father, or the mother, who indeed has outgrown all such care for play, been delving still, even in the church worship itself, and at the table of communion, in schemes, and projects, and works, that thrust out, for the time, even these most sacred things from any due place in their attention. If sometimes a mere child is carried away by exuberant life and playfulness, is that worse than to be cankered by the love of gain, or by the severe and sober sins of a grasping, eager, worldly manhood? The sins of children are ingenuous and open, and on just that account are to be less severely judged. The sins of manhood are sins of gravity, prudence, self-seeking, always contriving to wear some plausible aspect of sobriety and dignity; but they are not any the more consistent with piety on that account. We do not judge that any one is of course without piety, or is no Christian, because he has faults, or failings, or even because he is overtaken by sins; why then should a child be condemned, as having no just evidence of piety, just because he is only a little less under the power of evil than his Christian father and mother? God, I am certain, judges children's faults in no such manner, and therefore it is never to be assumed by us that they are without piety, because they falter in some things. If they only falter, seeming still to love what is good, and struggle ingenuously after it, there is just as good reason to hope that their hearts have been touched by the Spirit of God, as there is that the hearts of older persons have been, when they are groping always in the seventh chapter of the Romans, having a mind to serve God, but always failing in the service. The child must be judged or tested in the same general way as the adult. If he is wholly perverse, has no spirit of duty, turns away from all religious things, it will not discourage any thing good in him to tell him that he is without piety; but if he loves religious things, wants to be in them, tries after a good and obedient life, he is to be shown how tenderly God regards him, how ready he is to forgive him; and when he stumbles or falls, how kindly he will raise him up, how graciously help him to stand. Nor does it make any difference that no time is remembered, when he seemed to be brought unto God, by a great change of experience, such as adult persons are often the subjects of. He ought not to be the subject of any such change; and if he is properly trained, will not be. As regards the testing of his condition or character, nothing at all depends on that. It will even be a good sign for him that he has always seemed to love Christ; and it will be no proper evidence to the contrary, that he sometimes falters. Children are very ingenuous, and they may even show some disinclination, for a time, to all religious duties, without creating any such evidence. Adults often suffer such disinclination, when they do not allow it to appear. The sum of all I would say here is, let children be judged as children, and let them not be cruelly discouraged in all thoughts of love to

God, because they falter, as older people do; only in a different manner.

I must also speak of another and more general mode of discouragement, in what may be called the holding back, or holding aloof system, by which children are denied an early recognition of their membership in the church, and an admission to the Lord's table. I have spoken of this membership already, in another place, and shall also speak, hereafter, of the supper in its more positive uses. What I now refer to, more especially, is the negatively bad or discouraging effect thrown upon their piety, by these methods of detention, or exclusion. The child giving evidence, however beautiful, of his piety, is still kept back from the fellowship and table of Christ, for the simple defect of years. As if years were one of the Scripture evidences of grace. Sometimes the difficulty is that he can speak of no experience, or change, such as we call conversion; and sometimes, if he can, that he is yet too young to be confided in. And so it turns out, after all that is said of the membership initiated in baptism, that nothing is practically made of it, or allowed to be made of it. The membership it creates is only a disjunctive conjunction; words for a show, answered by no conditions or consequences of fact. The poor child still is virtually counted or assumed to be an alien, required to be converted in just the same fashion as all heathens are, and to show the fact by the same kind of evidences. The little, saintly daughter, for example, of a venerable Presbyterian minister, aching for a place at the Lord's table, goes to her father, after being several times post-poned by him and by the session, asking—"father, when shall I be old enough to be a Christian?" He and his session, alas! did not believe that of such is the kingdom of heaven. Had the dear child gone to Jesus, she would most certainly have gotten a different answer. True, the religious experience of children is of course small—only not as small, or unreliable, by any means, as the experience commonly is of an adult convert only a few weeks old. Besides, what is the use of a fold, if the lambs are to be kept outside till it is seen whether they can stand the weather?

The chilling, desolating effect of this very unnatural and cruel practice, will be understood without diffi-culty. No plan could be devised for the discourage-ment of piety in children, that would be more certain of its object. They are only mocked and tantalized by their baptism itself. They are thrust away and kept aloof from the communion of Christ, for reasons that make it impossible for them to be reliably Christian. And so their courage is broken down, and all their religious longings are crippled, just when they most want grace and sympathy to draw them on.

The remedy is plain. In the first place, there ought to be some exercise or service in every church, to which the baptized children may be called, in common with the adult members, there to be recognized in a begun relationship. They should be formally addressed and prayed with. But the chief exercise, in which they can as heartily partake as any, should be the singing

of simple hymns to Christ, such as are used by the Moravian brethren for this purpose.   In this manner, too,
they will quite as much edify, as be edified, by the
adult brethren.   Their childish sympathies will, in this
manner, be laid hold of at the earliest moment.   They
will perceive that so much, at least, of worship and
religion is open to them as to others, and will begin to
feel themselves at home among the brethren.

In the next place, there should be some arrangement,
in which it is understood that children, piously disposed, though not confirmed or accepted formally as
members on their own account, may be allowed, either
on consultation with the pastor or without, to come to
the Lord's table for the time, on the score of their
initial membership in baptism, and their hopefully gracious character.   In this manner, some confidence will
be shown that they are going to claim their place, in
full church relations, as soon as they are better matured
in character and evidences; and this kind of confidence
will have great power with them, to encourage and support their struggles, and help them forward into an
established Christian life.

And then, once more, no child should ever be kept
back from a complete and formal, or formally professed,
membership in the body of Christ, simply because of
his age.   Some children will give more reliable evidence of Christian character at seven years of age than
others at fourteen.   Were every thing as it should be,
and as the most genuine ideas of baptism and Christian
nurture suppose, nearly all the subjects would be found

in the church, as brethren accepted, by the time they are twelve years old, and the greater part of them before they are ten years old.

While the church coöperates, in this manner, cherishing the baptized children as her own, it is understood, of course, that parents are to be engaged in putting forward their children and preparing them to bear the Christian profession. They are not to assume that the matter of true prudence here is all on one side, the side of detention; as if there were nothing to be sure of but that their children do not get on too fast. If that were all, it were the easiest thing in the world to settle every question, by the argument of delay; which negative grace, alas! is about the only kind of function some parents are equal to. No, this grip of detention is not any so easy and safe kind of duty. It may put the child by his time for life. It may fatally discourage all his beginnings of godliness, and may so far choke his growth in good that he will never be recovered.

The matters which I have gathered up in this discourse, it is not to be denied, my brethren, make a melancholy picture. When we discover in how many ways even Christian parents themselves discourage the piety of their children, it ceases to be any wonder that they so often turn out badly, and come to a sad figure in their life. There are very few children brought up in Christian families, who do not, at some time, show a particular openness and tenderness to the calls of religion. These flowering times of piety, ought to be all setting times of fruit, and I verily believe that they would be, if the flowers were not broken off by some rough handling, or discouraging treatment. And it should scarcely be any wonder that so many children of Christian parents come forward into life, in a dulled, uncaring mood; as if their conscience were under some paralysis, or as if they had somehow fallen out of all sense and sentiment of religion. The reason is, how often, that all their religious affinities have been battered by parental discouragement. They think of religion, if they think of it at all, only as a kind of forbidden fruit; and since it has never been for them, why should it ever be?

Here, too, is the solution of, alas! how many cases, where Christian parents speak, with great sadness, of a time when this or that child, now utterly submerged under the world, or the world's vices, was greatly exercised in matters of religion, fond of prayer, wanting even to be admitted to Christ's table. How many children have been discouraged, kept back, with just the same effect! Treated as if their piety was impossible, how could it become a fact? O, if they had been wisely and skillfully encouraged, assisted, led along, how different probably the state and character in which they would now be found!

A heavy shade is here thrown, too, upon all those sorrowful regrets in which Christian parents bewail what they call the mystery of their lot, in having children grown up to a prayerless and godless maturity. Alas! it is too easy, in most cases, to account for this mystery. When we see in how many ways children may be thrown off from the courses of holy obedience, or discouraged in them, we have a strong ground of presumption that the mystery deplored by their parents is not as deep as they suppose. For myself, when I look over this field of misuse, misconception, misdirection, seeing in how many and subtle ways children are turned off from Christ, when they might be and ought to be drawn to his fold, it is no longer a wonder that they go astray; it would only be a greater wonder if they met the call of Christ more faithfully, and stood in a character more answerable to the privilege he gives them.

V

FAMILY GOVERNMENT

"One that ruleth well his own house, having his children in subjection with all gravity."—1 *Timothy*, iii. 4.

To BE a Christian bishop, whether in a clergy of one order or of three, is to be set in a high office, demanding high qualifications. What may be taken as qualifications, the apostle is here specifying; and among the rest, he names the character evinced by maintaining a good and sound government in the house. "For if a man know not how to rule his own house, how shall he take care of the church of God?" A very singular test, in one view, for a Christian bishop; one that passes by the matter of learning and eloquence, and church reputation, laying hold, instead, of a gift in which some very ordinary men, and not a few ordinary women, excel. And with good reason; for, in fact, how very much alike, in the elements of merit and success, are all that purchase to themselves a good degree, in whatever rank, or sphere—alike in fidelity, order, patience, steadiness, attention, application to the charge that is given them. Nay, when the apostle drops in thoughtfully what he takes to be the same thing in effect, as ruling one's house well, viz: "the having his children in subjection with all gravity," the words themselves, appear to have a sound of character and office in them, as if spoken of a bishop with his flock. And what indeed is the house but a little primary bishopric under the father, taking oversight thereof?

Family Government, then, is the subject here suggested for discussion. And we naturally endeavor—

I. *To ascertain what is the true conception of family government.*

Of course it is to be government; about that there ought to be no hesitation. It is not to be a mere nursing, or dressing, or provisioning agency; not to be an exhorting, advising, consulting relationship; not to be a lavishing of devotion, or parental self-sacrifice; but the radical constitutive idea, that in which it becomes family government, is that it governs, uses authority, maintains law and rules, by a binding and loosing power, over the moral nature of the child. Parents, it would sometimes appear, fall into a practical ambiguity here—as if the governing power were a kind of severity, or harsh assumption; not perceiving that, by common consent, we speak of an ungoverned family as the synonym of a disorderly, wretched, and dishonored, if not ruined, family. There is no greater cruelty, in fact, than this same false tenderness, which is the bane of so many families. There is a kind of cruelty indeed, which is exactly opposite, and misses the idea of government on the other side, viz: that brutish manner of despotic will and violence, which makes no appeal to the moral nature at all, driving straight by, upon the fears, in a battery of force. And yet, whether even this be really more cruel in its effects, than the false tenderness just named, is a fair subject of doubt. The true idea, that which makes the domestic order and state so beneficent, is that it is to be a state of government; a state where love has authority, and presides in the beneficent order of law.

But when we have reached this point, that family government is to govern, we shall find that multitudes of parents who assume the Christian name, have yet no practical sense of the intensely religious character of the house, or the domestic and family state. They go into their office loosely, and without any conception, for the most part, of what their authority means. This, I will now undertake to show, drawing out especially the points in which they most commonly seem to fall below the real sense of their office, in the opinions they hold concerning it.

First of all, their family government is never conceived, in its true nature, except when it is regarded as a vice-gerent authority, set up by God, and ruling in his place. Instead of creating us outright, God has seen fit to give us existence under laws of reproduction; having it for his object, in the family order and relationship, to set us forth, under a kind of experience in the small, and in terms of sense, that faithfully typifies our wider relationship to Him, the eternal Father and invisible Ruler of the worlds. We are infants too, men and women in the small, that we may be as flexible in our will as possible. Our parents, if they are godly themselves, as by the supposition they will be, are to personate God, in the double sense of bearing his natural and moral image before us, ever close at hand; and also in the right of authority with which they are clothed. And, that they may have us at the greatest advantage, it is given them to clothe us, and feed us, and bathe us, day and night, in the unsparing and lavish attentions of their love; enjoying our enjoyments, and even their own sacrifices for us. First, the mother has us, at her bosom, as a kind of nursing Providence. Perused by touch and by the eyes, her soul of maternity, watching for that look and bending ever to it, raises the initial sense of a divine something in the world; and when she begins to speak her soft imperative, putting a little decision into the tones of her love, she makes the first and gentlest possible beginning of authority. And then the stiffer tension of the masculine word, connected with the wider, rougher providence of a father's masculine force, follows in a stouter mode of authority, and the moral nature of the child, configured thereto, answers faithfully in a rapidly developed sense of obligation. The parents are to fill, in this manner, an office strictly religious; personating God in the child's feeling and conscience, and bending it, thus, to what, without any misnomer, we call a filial piety. So that when the unseen Father and Lord is Himself discovered, there is to be a piety made ready for him; a kind of house-religion, that may widen out into the measures of God's ideal majesty and empire. Hence the injunction, "Children obey your parents in the Lord." They could not make a beginning with

ideas of God, or with God as an unseen Spirit; therefore they had parents given them in the Lord—the
Lord to be in them, there to personate and finite himself, and gather to such human motherhood and fatherhood, a piety transferable to Himself, as the knowledge
of his nobler, unseen Fatherhood arrives.

Again, it is another point, very commonly over-
looked, or forgotten, that parental government is genuine, only as it bears rule for the same ends that God
Himself pursues, in the religious order of the world.
True family government will be just as religious as His,
neither more nor less. It will have exactly the same ends
and no other. Just here, accordingly, is the main root of
mischief and failure in the government of Christian families. The parents are not Christian enough to think of
bearing rule for strictly Christian ends. They drop into
a careless, irresponsible way, and rule for any thing that
happens to chime with their own feeling or convenience. They want their children to shine, or be honorable, or rich, or brave, or fashionable; so to serve themselves in them, or their pride, or their mere natural
fondness. They bring in, thus, bad motives to corrupt
all government, and even to corrupt themselves. If
they have some care of piety in their government, it is
a kind of amphibious care, sometimes in one element
and sometimes in another. They are never truly and
heartily in God's ends. And the result is that what
they do in the name of religion, or to inculcate religion,
shows their want of appetite, and has really no effect
but to make both God's authority and theirs irksome.

Nothing answers the true purpose here, but to bring in all the noblest ideas of truth, and forgiveness and self-sacrifice, and assert a pitch of virtue in the house high enough to be inspiring. The government will then have a genuine authority and power, because the rule of God is in it. As it rules for God, and with God, God will be in it; otherwise it is mortal self-assertion only.

Closely related is the conviction to be firmly held, that family discipline, rightly administered, is to secure, and may secure, a style of obedience in the child that amounts to a real piety. If we speak of conversion, family government should be a converting ordinance, as truly as preaching. For observe and make due account of this single fact, that when a child is brought to do any one thing from a truly right motive, and in a genuinely right spirit, there is implied in that kind of obedience, the acceptance of all best and holiest principle. I do not mean, of course, that children are to be made Christians by the rod, or by any summary process of requirement. There is no such short method of compulsory piety here, as some are reported to have held, or put in exercise. But it is not absurd to expect and aim to realize in the family, a genuine spirit of obedience; obedience, that is, from the principle that God enthrones, and which underlies all piety—just what the apostle means, if I understand him rightly, by having children "in subjection with all gravity." In the phrase "all gravity," he is looking at a kind of obedience that touches the deepest notes of principle and character. Contrary to this, there is an obedience without principle, which is obedience with all levity; that which is paid to mere will and force; that which is another name for fear; that which is bought by promises and paid by indulgences; that which makes a time-server, or a coward, or a lying pretender, as the case may be, and not a Christian. This latter—that which makes a Christian—is the aim of all true government, and should never be out of sight for an hour. Let the child be brought to do right because it is right, and not because it is unsafe, or appears badly, to do wrong. In every case of discipline for ill-nature, wrong, willfulness, disobedience, be it understood, that the real point is carried never till the child is gentled into love and duty; sorry, in all heartiness, for the past, with a glad mind set to the choice of doing right and pleasing God. How often is it true that in the successful carrying of such a point, (which can not be carried, save by great resources of love and gospel life in the parents,) the fact of a converted will is gained. And one must be a dull observer of children and their after life, who has not many times suspected that just the ones who are said to be converted afterwards, and suppose themselves to be, had their wills, not seldom bowed to this in their childhood, under the government of the house.

Having so far indicated what is the true idea of family government as a Divine institution, let us next inquire —

II. *By what methods it will best fulfill its gracious and beneficent purposes ?*

It is hardly necessary to say that the vice-gerent office to be maintained, and the gracious ends to be secured, make it indispensable that parents should themselves be living in the Spirit, and be so tempered by their faithful walk, as to have the Christly character on them. Nothing but this will so lift their aims, gentle their passions, steady their measures and proceedings, as to give them that personal authority which is requisite. For this authority of which I speak supposes much—so much of grace and piety, that God is expressed in the life; so much as to even it in all principle, fasten it in all moderation of truth and justice, gladden it in heaven's liberty and peace, and, above all, clear it of sanctimony; for if any thing will drive a poor child mad with disgust of religion, it is to be tormented day and night with the drawlings and mock solemnities of a merely sanctimonious piety. Children love the realities, and are worried by all shams of character. If then parents can not be deep enough in religion to live it naturally, and have it as an element of gladness, clear of all sanctimony, it is doubtful whether they might not better be even farther off from the semblance of it than they pretend to be. Of this one thing they may be sure, that they get no addition of personal authority by any thing put on; or by any prescribed longitudes of expression. The most profoundly real thing in the world is this matter of personal authority. Jesus had it as no other ever had, because he had most of reality and divine truth in his character; we shall have the same only as we have the same steady affinities in us, and the same Spirit without measure upon us.

There is also another precondition of authority in parents closely related to this; I mean that they be so far entered into the Christian order of marriage, as to fulfill gracefully what belongs to the relation in which they are set, and show them to the children as doing fit honor to each other. By a defect just here, all authority in the house is blasted. Thus Dr. Tiersch, in his excellent little treatise on the Christian Family Life, says:—" A wife can not weaken the authority of the father without undermining her own, for her authority rests upon his, and if that of the mother is subordinated to that of the father, yet it is but one authority, which can not be weakened in either of the two who bear it, without injury to both. The mother, therefore, must consider it a matter of family decorum which is not to be broken, never even in little matters to contradict the father in the presence of the children, except with the reservation of a modest admission of his right of decision, and that in cases which admit of no delay. But just as much is it the duty of the husband to leave the authority of his wife unassailed in the presence of other members of the household; and when he is obliged to overrule her objections, to do it in a tender and kindly form. If he turns to her with roughness and harshness from jealousy of his place of rule, it is not only the heart of his wife which is estranged from him, with the children too intervenes a weakening of the moral power, under which they should feel themselves placed. If in their presence their mother is blamed as foolish or obstinate, and so lowered to the place of a child or a maid-servant, that sanctity immediately vanishes, which, in the eyes of the children, surrounds the heads of both father and mother in common."*

Again it is of the highest importance in family government, that parents understand how early it begins—how easily, in fact, the great question of rule and obedience may be settled, or well-nigh settled, before the time of verbal order and commandment arrives. Thus there is what may be fitly called a Christian handling for the infant state, that makes a most solid beginning of government. It is the even handling of repose and gentle affection, which lays a child down to its sleep so firmly, that it goes to sleep as in duty bound; which teaches it to feed when food is wanted, not when it can be somehow made uneasy, or the mother is uneasy for it; which refuses to wear out the night in laborious caresses and coaxings, that only reward the cries they endeavor to compose; which places the child so firmly, makes so little of the protests of caprice in it, wears a look so gentle and loving, and goes on with such evenness of system, that the child feels itself to be, all the while, in another will, and that a good will; consenting thus by habit and quietly to be lapped in authority, just as it consents to breathe in the lap of nature and her atmospheric laws. And so it becomes a thoroughly

* Page 99.

governed creature, under the mere handling of its in-fantile age. Neither should it seem that this is, in any sense, an exaggeration. For though the government we speak of here is silent, and utters for the time no law, there still is law enough revealed to feeling in the mere motions and modes of the house. Who is ignorant that by jerks of passion, flashes of irritation, unsteady changes of caprice and nervousness, fits of self-indulgence, disgusts with self and life that are half the time allowed to include the child, songs and caresses both of day and night, that are volunteered as much to compose the mother's or the nurse's impa-tience as the child's—who is ignorant that an infant, handled in this manner, may be kept in a continual fret of torment and ill-nature. Meantime there is, just op-posite, what a beautiful power of order, and quiet, and happy rule, when the motions and modes of the hand-ling are such as token peace, repose, firmness, system, confidence, and a steady all-encompassing love. Here is law, felt, we may even say, in every touch, entered into every sensational experience, confided in, submit-ted to, with all gravity. So that when the time of words arrives, the child is already under government, and the question of obedience and order is already half settled.

We come now to the age of language, or the age when words begin to be used to express requirement and authority. Indeed this will be done, assisted by tones and signs of manner, even before the child itself is able to speak.

And here it is to be noted that much depends upon the tone of command, or the kinds of emphasis employed. It is a great mistake to suppose that what will make a child stare, or tremble, impresses more authority. The violent emphasis, the hard, stormy voice, the menacing air, only weakens authority; it commands a good thing as if it were only a bad, and fit to be no way impressed, save by some stress of assumption. Let the command be always given quietly, as if it had some right in itself, and could utter itself to the conscience by some emphasis of its own. Is it not well understood that a bawling and violent teamster has no real government of his team? Is it not practically seen that a skillful commander of one of those huge floating cities, moved by steam on our American waters, manages and works every motion by the waving of a hand, or by signs that pass in silence; issuing no order at all, save in the gentlest undertone of voice? So when there is, or is to be, a real order and law in the house, it will come of no hard and boisterous, or fretful and termagant way of commandment. Gentleness will speak the word of firmness, and firmness will be clothed in the airs of true gentleness.

Nor let any one think that such kind of authority is going to be disrespected, or disregarded, because it moves no fright or fear in the subjects. That will depend on the fidelity of the parent to what he has commanded. How many do we see, who fairly rave in authority, and keep the tempest up from morning to night, who never stop to see whether any thing they forbid or command is, in fact, observed. Indeed they really forget what they have commanded. Their mandates follow so thickly as to crowd one another, and even to successively thrust one another out of remembrance. And the result is that, by this cannonading of pop-guns, the successive pellets of commandment are in turn all blown away. If any thing is fit to be forbidden, or commanded, it is fit to be watched and held in faithful account. On this it is that the real emphasis of authority depends, not on the wind-stress of the utterance. Let there be only such and so many things commanded, as can be faithfully attended to— these in a gentle and firm voice, as if their title to obedience lay in their own merit—and then let the child be held to a perfectly inevitable and faithful account; and, by that time, it will be seen that order and law have a stress of their own, and a power to rule in their own divine right. The beauty of a well-governed family will be seen, in this manner, to be a kind of silent, natural-looking power; as if it were a matter only of growth, and could never have been otherwise.

At first, or in the earlier periods of childhood, authority should rest upon its own right, and expect to be obeyed just because it speaks. It should stake itself on no assigned reasons, and have nothing to do with reasons, unless it be after the fact; when, by showing what has been depending, in a manner unseen to the child, it can add a presumption of reason to all future commands. It is even a good thing to the moral and religious nature of a child, to have its obedience required, and to be accustomed to obedience, on the ground of simple authority; to learn homage and trust, as all subject natures must, and so to accept the rule of God's majesty, when the reasons of God are inscrutable. There is little prospect that any child will be a Christian, or any thing but a skeptic, or a godless worldling, who has not had his religious nature unfolded by an early subjection to authority, speaking in its own right.

Nay, I will go farther; there is a certain use in having a child, in the first stages of government, feel the pressure of **law** as a restriction. For, as the law of God is a schoolmaster to bring us to Christ, so there is a like relation between law and liberty in the training of the house. It is by a certain friction, if I may so speak, on the moral nature, a certain pressure of control, not always welcome, that the sense of law gets hold of us. Observances that we do not like, prepare us to a kind of obedience, further on, that is free—that welcomes the same command because it is good, the same authority because it is wholesome and right. And so it comes to pass that a son, grown almost to manhood, will gladly serve the house, and yield to his parents a kind of homage that even anticipates their wishes, just because he has learned to be in subjection, with all gravity, under restrictions that were once a sore limit on his patience.

At the same time it should never be forgotten, in this due assertion of authority and restrictive law, that there is a great difference between the imperative and

the dictatorial; between the exact and the exacting. I
have spoken already of the common fault of commanding overmuch, and forgetting or omitting to enforce
what is commanded; there is another kind of fault
which commands overmuch, and rigidly exacts what is
commanded; laying on commands, as it seems to the
child, just because it can, or is willing to gall his peace
by exacting something that shall cut away even the
semblance of liberty. No parent has a right to put
oppression on a child, in the name of authority. And
if he uses authority in that way, to annoy the child's
peace, and even to forbid his possession of himself, he
should not complain, if the impatience he creates grows
into a bitter animosity, and finally a stiff rebellion.
Nothing should ever be commanded except what is
needed and required by the most positive reasons,
whether those reasons are made known or not.

Another qualification here to be observed, belongs
to what may be called the emancipation of the child.
A wise parent understands that his government is to
be crowned by an act of emancipation; and it is a
great problem, to accomplish that emancipation gracefully. Pure authority, up to the last limit of minority,
then a total, instantaneous self-possession, makes an
awkward transition. A young eagle kept in the nest
and brooded over till his beak and talons are full-
grown, then pitched out of it and required to take care
of himself, will most certainly be dashed upon the
ground. The emancipating process, in order to be well
finished, should begin early, and should pass imper-

ceptibly, even as age increases imperceptibly. Thus the child, after being ruled for a time, by pure authority, should begin, as the understanding is developed, to have some of the reasons given why it is required to abstain, or do, or practice, in this or that way instead of some other. The tastes of the child, too, should begin to be a little consulted, in respect to his school, his studies, his future engagements in life. When he is old enough to go on errands, and to labor in various employments for the benefit of the family, he should be let into the condition of the family far enough to be identified with it, and have the family cause, and property, and hope, for his own. Built into the family fortunes and sympathies, in this manner, he will begin, at a very early day, to command himself for it, and so will get ready to command himself for himself, in a way that will be just as if the parental authority were still running on, after it has quite run by.

Is it necessary to add that a parent who governs at the point of authority will not, of course, allow himself to be known only as a bundle of commandments? In order to have authority, he must have life, sympathy, feeling unbent in play. He must connect a gospel with his law, and so instead of being a law over the house, he must undertake to be a law written in the heart; winning love as commanding out of love, consummating obedience, by the glad and joyous element in which he bathes the playful homage and trust of his children.

As to the motives addressed by family government,

in a way of maintaining or securing obedience, they
need to be of two kinds; such as belong to a character
in principle, and such as belong to a character that is
equivocal in it, or fallen below it. The first kind
should never be left out of sight. They are such as
these: doing right because it is right; loving God because he loves the right; God's approbation; the approbation of a good conscience; the sense of honor
with himself, as opposed to the meanness of lying and
deceit. These are, by distinction, the religious motives;
and where these are completely ignored, all others are
radically faulty, of course. But there is, beside, a very
great and hurtful mistake that is commonly made in
choosing, from among the lower and second-class motives, those which are really most questionable, and
most likely to be followed by sinister effects. Here
again we are to follow God, who undertakes to dislodge
us, in the plane below principle, or keep us from set-
tling into it, by raking it, every way, in a cannonade
of penalty and fear. No, say the plausible sophisters
of our day, in what they take to be its better wisdom,
fear is a mean and servile motive; we will not make
cowards of our children. They do not observe the
very considerable distinction between terror and fear;
that terror lays hold of passion, fear of intelligence;
that one dispossesses the soul, the other nerves it to a
wise and rational prudence; that one scatters all distinctions of principle, and the other turns the soul
thoughtfully towards principle. Missing this distinction, they make their appeal sometimes to the sense of

honor before men, frequently to the sense of appearance, or to what will be the appearance of the family, not less frequently to the desire of success in life; praising the shows of bravery and spirit, deifying, so to speak, human conventionalities and laws of fashion. They do not see the total want of dignity in these appeals; how they all put shams and shows, and falsities, in the place of solid realities; how they sort with all lying semblances of virtue, run the soul into all most cowardly fictions of time-serving, pretense, hypocrisy, sycophancy, and make even hollowness itself the principal substance of life. Therefore it is that God appeals to fear, backs authority and law by penalties that waken fear; because this one prudential motive has a place by itself, in not being positive or acquisitive, in any sense, but only negative; and so far has the semblance of unselfishness. It makes no one selfish to fear, though fear, as a motive, is not up to the level of principle loved for its own sake. The wise parent, therefore, will not be wiser than God; and wheresoever fear is needed, he will speak to fear, and make as little as possible of appearance, popularity, and opinion, understanding that, if he is to have his children in subjection with all gravity, they must be brought into God's principle, by a motive that is unambitious, unworldly and real, and turns the soul away by no computations of pride and airy pretense.

There is, then, to be such a thing as penalty, or punishment, in the government of the house. And here again is a place where large consideration is requisite.

First of all, it should be threatened as seldom as possible, and next as seldom executed as possible. It is a most wretched and coarse barbarity that turns the house into a penitentiary, or house of correction. Where the management is right in other respects, punishment will be very seldom needed. And those parents who make it a point of fidelity, that they keep the flail of chastisement always a going, have a better title to the bastinado themselves than to any Christian congratulations. The punishments dispensed should never be such as have a character of ignominy; and therefore, except in cases of really ignominious wickedness, it would be better to avoid, as far as may be, the infliction of pain upon the person. For the same reason the discipline should, if possible, be entirely private; a matter between the parent and child. Thus it is well said by Dr. Tiersch, "If ever a severe punishment is necessary, it must be carried out so as to spare the child's self-respect; not in the presence of his brothers and sisters, nor of the servants. For a wholesome terror to the others, it is enough if they perceive, at a distance, something of that which happens. And if only the smallest triumph over his misfortune, the least degree of mockery arise, bitterness and a loss of self-respect are the consequences to the child."*

Punishments should be severe enough to serve their purpose; and gentle enough to show, if possible, a tenderness that is averse from the infliction. There is no abuse more shocking, than when they are administered

---

* Page 153.

by sheer impatience, or in a fit of passion. Nor is the case at all softened, when they are administered without feeling, in a manner of uncaring hardness. Whenever the sad necessity arrives, there should be time enough taken, after the wrong or detection, to produce a calm and thoughtful revision; and a just concern for the wrong, as evinced by the parent, should be wakened, if possible, in the child. I would not be understood, however, in advising this more tardy and delicate way of proceeding, to justify no exceptions. There are cases, now and then, in the outrageous and shocking misconduct of some boy, where an explosion is wanted; where the father represents God best, by some terrible outburst of indignant violated feeling, and becomes an instant avenger, without any counsel or preparation whatever. Nothing else expresses fitly what is due to such kind of conduct. And there is many a grown up man, who will remember such an hour of discipline, as the time when the ploughshare of God's truth went into his soul like redemption itself. That was the shock that woke him up to the staunch realities of principle; and he will recollect that father, as God's minister, typified to all dearest, holiest, reverence, by the pungent indignations of that time.

There is great importance in the closing of a penal discipline. Thus it should be a law never to cease from the discipline begun, whatever it be, till the child is seen to be in a feeling that justifies the discipline. He is never to be let go, or sent away, sulking, in a look of willfulness unsubdued. Indeed, he should even be required always to put on a pleasant, tender look, such as clears all clouds and shows a beginning of fair weather. No reproof, or discipline, is rightly administered till this point is reached. Nothing short of this changed look gives any hope of a changed will. On the other hand, when the face of disobedience brightens out into this loving and dutiful expression, it not only shows that the malice of wrong is gone by, but, possibly, that there is entered into the heart some real beginning of right, some spirit of really Christian obedience. Many a child is bowed to holy principle itself, at the happy and successful close of what, to human eyes, is only a chapter of discipline.

In order to realize this Christian issue of discipline, it is sometimes recommended that the child should be first prayed with, and made conscious, in that manner, of his own wrong, as before God, and of the truly religious intentions by which the parent is actuated. No rule of this kind can be safely given; for there is great danger that the child will begin to associate prayer and religion with his pains of discipline; than which nothing could be more hurtful. It would be far better, in most cases, if the prayer were to follow, coming in to express and gladden his already glad repentances.

There are many things remaining still to be said, in order to a complete view of the subject; but there are two simple cautions that must not be omitted, and with these I close—

1. Observe that great care is needed in the processes

of detection, or the police of discovery. The child must not be allowed to go on breaking through the orders imposed, or into the ways of vice, not detected. This will make his life a practice in art and hypocrisy; and what is worse, will make him also confident of success in the same. Nothing will corrupt his moral nature more rapidly. There must be a very close and careful watch on the part of fathers and mothers, to let no deviation of childhood pass their discovery. And then, again, the greatest care and address will be needed, to keep their circumspection from taking on the look of a deliberate espionage, than which nothing will more certainly alienate the confidence and love needful to their just authority. Nothing wounds a child more fatally, than to see he is not trusted. Under such an impression, he will soon become as unworthy of trust as he has been taken to be. On the other hand, he will naturally want to be worthy of the trust he receives. For the same reason, he should never be set upon by volunteer charges, or accusations which have no other merit than to be the ground of a cross-questioning process. It is a harsh experiment that insults a child, in order to find out whether he is innocent or guilty. Besides, if he is guilty, there is no small risk of drawing him on to asseverations of innocence, that will fatally break down his truthfulness. Neither will it answer, in the case of little children, to make them reporters of their own wrongs, by allowing the understanding that they shall so obtain pardon. For then they are only trained to a manner of sycophancy that mocks all government. What then shall be done? First of all, make much of the fact, that when a child is doing any secret wrong, he grows shy, ceases to be confiding and demonstrative, even as Adam, when he hid himself among the trees. Then let the watch grow close—watch his companions, the way he goes, the way he returns, his times, what he says, and what he particularly avoids speaking of at all; speak of his shyness, and observe the reasons he assigns, question his reasons. It will be difficult for any young child to escape this kind of search. Indeed, this kind of search will almost never be needed if children are inspected carefully enough, at a very early period, when, as yet, they are simple, and the art of wrong has not begun to be learned. Accustomed then to the feeling that art hides nothing, they will never try to hide any thing by it afterwards.

2. Have it as a caution that, in holding a magisterial relation, asserting and maintaining law, discovering and redressing wrong, you are never, as parents, to lose out the parental; never to check the demonstrations of your love; never to cease from the intercourse of play. If you assert the law, as you must, then you must have your gospel to go with it; your pardons judiciously dispensed, your Christian sympathies flowing out in modes of Christian concern, your whole administration gentled by tenderness. Above all, see that your patience is not easily broken, or exhausted. If your authority is not established in a day, you have small reason, in that fact, to be fretted, or discouraged,

and the less reason if you are and are seen to be, to believe that it ever can be established. There will sometimes be a child, or children, given, that have a more restive and less easily reducible nature than others, and partly because they have more to reduce. Time with such is commonly a great element, and as time is needed for them, patience will be needed in you. Let them have a little more experience of themselves, and of what a good and wise regulation means; let their rational nature be farther unfolded and come to your aid, and they will be gradually taking sides with your authority. The other and more tractable children, winning on their respect, will also assist in the taming of their repugnances. Meantime God, who perhaps gave you this trial to complete your patience, and purify all graces in you, will be raising you to a higher pitch of character and authority, which no most wayward child can well resist. And so it will be your satisfaction to see, in due time, that your reward is coming; that your children are growing into all truth and order together; melting into all confidence and good understanding with authority itself. Your triumph will now be sealed. You will have your house in subjection with all gravity; a little bishopric, as the apostle would say, gathered in heaven's truth and unity, obedient Christian, filial, and free.

VI

PLAYS AND PASTIMES, HOLIDAYS AND SUNDAYS

"And the streets of the city shall be full of boys and girls playing in the streets thereof."—*Zechariah*, viii. 5.

HAPPY days are these that figure in the prophet's vision. The people of the city are accustomed to scenes that are widely different, and give a peculiar zest to his picture. In the times of pestilence, in the horrors of the siege, in the sweeping out of captivity, what silence of desolation have they seen—the silence of ghastly death, the silence of gaunt famine, the silence of emptiness and depopulated life. It shall no more be so; the city shall be God's mountain, sheltered under his care, exempt from all the past desolations of pestilence and war—peaceful, populous, secure, and strong. All which is shown by two simple touches that make out the complete picture—"There shall yet old men and old women dwell in the streets of Jerusalem, and every man with his staff in his hand for very age. And the streets of the city shall be full of boys and girls, playing in the streets thereof."

We can see, too, for ourselves that the prophet's feeling goes into his picture; and that he has a natural delight in it himself. He sees the venerable crones gathering at the corners, and blesses himself in the sight; hears the ring of happy voices in the streets and market-places, and plays his feeling in, with the playing boys and girls of the Lord's glad mountain. Inspiration has not taken the nature out of him, but has only made him love the innocent glee of childhood the more.

I draw it, accordingly, from this beautiful touch of the prophet's picture, *that religion loves too much the plays and pleasures of childhood, to limit or suppress them by any kind of needless austerity.*

Having set the young of all the animal races a playing, and made their beginning an age of frisking life and joyous gambol, it would be singular if God had made the young of humanity an exception; or if, having put the same sportive instinct in their make, he should restrict them always to a carefully practical and sober mood. What indeed does he permit us to see, in the universal mirth-time which is given to be the beginning of every creature's life, that he has, Himself, a certain pleasure in their exuberant life, and regards their gambols with a fatherly satisfaction? What, too, shall we judge, but that as all instincts are inserted for that to which they tend, so this instinct of play in children is itself an appointment of play?

Besides, there is a very sublime reason for the play-state of childhood which respects the moral and religious well-being of manhood, and makes it important that we should have our first chapter of life in this key. Play is the symbol and interpreter of liberty, that is, Christian liberty; and no one could ever sufficiently conceive the state of free impulse and the joy there is in it, save by means of this unconstrained, always pleasurable activity, that we call the play of children. Play wants no motive but play; and so true goodness, when it is ripe in the soul and is become a complete inspiration there, will ask no motive but to be good. Therefore God has purposely set the beginning of the natural life in a mood that foreshadows the last and highest chapter of immortal character. Just as he has made hunger in the body to represent hunger in the soul, thirst in the body to represent thirst ln the soul, what is sweet, bitter, sour in the taste to represent what is sweet, bitter, sour in the soul's feeling, lameness to represent the hobbling of false principle, the fierce combustion of heat to represent the rage of angry passion, all things natural to represent all things spiritual, so he prepares, at the very beginning of our life, in the free self-impulsion of play, that which is to foreshadow the glorious liberty of the soul's ripe order and attainment in good. One is the paradise of nature behind us, the other the paradise of grace before us; and the recollection of one images to us, and stimulates us in, the pursuit of the other.

Holding this conception of the uses, and the very great importance of play, as a natural interpreter of what is highest and last in the grand problem of our life itself, we are led, on sober and even religious conviction, to hold in high estimation the age of play. As play is the forerunner of religion, so religion is to be the friend of play; to love its free motion, its happy scenes, its voices of glee, and never, by any needless austerities of control, seek to hamper and shorten its pleasures. Any sort of piety or supposed piety that is jealous of the plays and bounding activities of childish life, is a character of hardness and severity that has, so far at least, but a very questionable agreement with God's more genial and fatherly feeling. One of the first duties of a genuinely Christian parent is, to show a generous sympathy with the plays of his children; providing playthings and means of play, giving them playtimes, inviting suitable companions for them, and requiring them to have it as one of their pleasures, to keep such companions entertained in their plays, instead of playing always for their own mere self-pleasing. Sometimes, too, the parent, having a hearty interest in the plays of his children, will drop out for the time the sense of his years, and go into the frolic of their mood with them. They will enjoy no other play-time so much as that, and it will have the effect to make the authority so far unbent, just as much stronger and more welcome, as it has brought itself closer to them, and given them a more complete show of sympathy.

On the same principle, it has an excellent effect to make much of the birthdays of children, because it shows them, little and dependent as they are, to be held in so much greater estimation in the house. When they have each their own day, when that day is so remembered and observed as to indicate a real and felt interest in it by all, then the home in which they are so cherished is proportionally endeared to feeling, and what has magnified them they are ready to magnify.

On the same principle, too, public days and festivals, those of the school, those of the state, and those of religion, are to be looked upon with favor, as times in which they are to be gladdened by the shows, and plays, and simple pleasures appropriate to the occasions; care being only taken to put them in no connection with vice, or any possible excess. Let them see what is to be seen, enjoy what is to be enjoyed, and shun with just so much greater sensibility whatever is loose, or wild, or wicked.

Religious festivals have a peculiar value to children; such I mean as the festivals of Thanksgiving and Christmas—one a festival of thanks for the benefits of Providence, the other for the benefits of that supernatural providence which has given the world a Saviour and a salvation. Both are religious, and, in that fact, have their value; for nothing will go farther to remove the annoyance of a continual, unsparing, dry restraint upon the soul of childhood, and produce a feeling, as respects religion, of its really genial character, than to have it bring its festive and joyously commemorative days. One of the great difficulties in a properly religious nurture is, that religion has to open its approaches to the soul, and make its beginnings in the shape of law; to say God requires of you this, forbids you in that, makes it your life to be set in all ways of obedience. It takes on thus a guise of constraint, and so far wears a repulsive look; but if it can show how genial it is, how truly it loves even childish enjoyment, by gild-ing for it days of joy and festive celebrations, then the severities of law and responsible obedience take on themselves a look of benignity, and it begins to be felt that God commands us, not to cripple us, but to keep us safe and lead us into good. Such days, it is true, may be greatly abused by what is really unchristian; what is sensual and low, and very close to vice it-self; and it is much to be regretted that the Christmas festival, otherwise so beautiful and appropriate, taken as a Christian commemoration of the greatest fact of the world's history, has been so commonly associated with traditional looseness and excess. The friends of such a day can not do it any so great honor, as to clear it en-tirely of the excess and profane jollity by which it was made to commemorate any thing and every thing but Christ, that, setting it in character as a genuine religious festivity, they may give it to all friends of Christ as a day of universal observance.

Happily there is now such an abundance of games and plays prepared for the entertainment of children, that there is no need of allowing them in any that stand associated with vice. Those plays are generally to be most favored that are to be had only in the open air, and in forms of exercise that give sprightliness and robustness to the body. At the same time, there needs to be a preparation of devices for the entertainment of children indoors in the evening; for the prophet did not give it as a picture of the happy days of Jerusalem, that the streets of the city should be full of boys and girls playing there in the evening, or into the night, away from their parents and the supervision of their home. There is any thing signified in that but happiness and public well-being. Christian fathers and mothers will never suffer their children to be out in the public streets in the evening, unless they are themselves too loose and self-indulgent to assume that care of the conduct and the hours of their children, which is imposed upon them by their parental responsibilities. In country places, far removed from all the haunts of vice, and in neighborhoods where there are no vicious children, it might work no injury if boys were allowed to be out, now and then, in their coasting or skating parties in the evening. But the better rule in large towns, the absolute rule, having no exceptions as regards very young children, will be that they are never to be out or away from home in the evening. Meantime, it will be the duty of the parents, and a kind of study especially of the mother, to find methods of making the house no mere prison, but a place of attraction, and of always cheerful and pleasant society. She will provide books that will feed their intelligence and exercise their tastes, pictures, games, diversions, plays; set them to inventing such themselves, teaching them how to carry on their little society, in the playful turns of good nature and fun, by which they stimulate and quicken each other; drilling them in music, and setting them forward in it by such beginnings that they will shortly be found exercising and training each other; shedding over all the play, infusing into all the glee, a certain sober and thoughtful look of character and principle, so that no overgrown appetite for sport may render violent pleasures necessary, but that small, and gentle, and easy, and almost sober pleasures, may suffice; becoming, at last, even most satisfactory. Here is the field of the mother's greatest art, viz: in the finding how to make a happy and good evening for her children. Here it is that the lax, faithless, worthless mother most entirely fails; here the good and wise mother wins her best successes.

Meantime some care must be exercised, that the religious life itself be never set in an attitude of repugnance to the plays of childhood. There must be no attempt to raise a conscience against play. Any such religion will certainly go to the wall; any such conscience will be certainly trampled, and things innocent will be done as if they were crimes; done with a guilty feeling; done with as bad effects every way, on the character, as if they were really the worst things. Nothing is more cruel than to throw a child into the attitude of conflict with God and his conscience, by raising a false conscience against that which both God and nature approve. It is nothing less than making a gratuitous loss of religion, required by no terms of reason, justified by no principle, even of Christian sacrifice itself.

Suppose, for example, that a child has begun to show many pleasant evidences of love to God and all good things, but that he is eager still in play, or sometimes gets quite wild in the excitement of it. If, at such a time, it is sprung upon him, as a conclusion, that he does not truly love God, because he is so much taken by the excitements of play, he will thus be discouraged without reason, in all his confidences of piety, and it will be strange, if by-and-bye he does not begin to show a settled aversion to religious things. How can he do less, when he is compelled to see it, as in conflict with all the most innocent and most truly natural instincts of his age? Or, to make the case more plain, drawing the question to a closer point, suppose the child, having so many evidences of piety in his dispositions, to be found at some kind of play in the family prayers, or that he rushes out from such prayers, in a manner that indicates eagerness and an emancipated feeling, or that he sometimes shows uneasiness in the hours of public worship on Sunday, or gives manifest tokens, in the morning, of a desire to escape from it, is it then to be set down, in your parental remonstrances with him, that he has, of course, no love to God, or the things of religion? By no means. How often does the adult Christian feel even a disinclination to such things; how often hurry away from his formal prayer, that he may get into his shop, or his field, or into some negotiation that has haunted his sleep in the night; how often sit through sermons with his mind on the game of politics, on the investment made or to be made; on his journey, or his mortgage, or the rivals he has in his trade? Is it worse for a child to be after his plays, with only the same kind of eagerness? Doubtless all such engrossments of the soul, whether of one kind or the other, are to be taken as bad signs, and, as far as they go, to be allowed their due weight. But which is worse and more fatal, the child's undue possession by the spirit of play, or the man's by the spirit of gain—the honest, artless, letting forth of nature by one, or the deliberate, studied, scheming of the other—it is not difficult, I think, to guess. No matter if the latter is more sober and thoughtful in the mood, observing a better show of gravity. For just that reason he is only to be judged the more harshly. If then we can bear with adult Christians, who are much in the world, and, forgetting themselves often, fall into moods of real disinclination to their duty, are we to set it down as some total evidence against the piety of a child, that, by mere exuberance of life, he is occasionally hurried away from sacred things, into matters of play? Nothing is more unjust. Why should we require it of a child to be perfect, when we do not require it of a man? And if we tolerate inconstancy of feeling or impulse in one, why not a much less worldly and deliberate inconstancy in the other?

Thus far we speak for the side of play, showing how far off it is from the purpose of religion to take away, or suppress, the innocent plays of childhood; how ready it is, on the other hand, to foster them and give them sympathy. But it is not the whole of life, even to a child, to be indulged in play. There is such a thing as order, no less than such a thing as liberty; and the process of adjustment between these two contending powers, begins at a very early date. Under the law of the house, of the school, and of God, the mere play impulse begins very soon to be tempered and moderated by duty, and the problem is to make divine order itself, at last, a state of liberty analogous to the state of play, as already suggested. But the law that is to fashion such order will be first felt as a restriction; then, when it becomes the spirit of the life, the order itself will be liberty. There is no such thing, therefore, as a possibility to childhood of unrestricted play. Restriction must be encountered as often as the order of the house demands it, then as often as the school demands it, then as often as the duties of religion demand it. Though such restrictions are never to be looked upon as hostile to the child's play, but only as terms that are really necessary for his training into the organic relations under which he is born, best for his character, and even best for the enjoyments of his play itself. Otherwise he would either become sated by it in a short time, or his appetite for it would become so egregiously overgrown, that no possible devices or means could be invented to keep pace with it. Besides, a child, thus put to nothing but mere play, would very soon grow into such lightness and dissipation of feeling, as to be mentally addled, and would so be wholly incapacitated for any of the more sober and manly offices of life.

Here, then, begins a process of training into moral order, which, without wishing to be any restriction upon play, is yet of necessity such a restriction. The child is required to conform his conduct, including his

plays, to the peace of the house, to the conditions of
sick persons in it, to the hours and times and general
comfort of other inmates older than himself. Errands
are put upon him that require him to forego his pleasures. When he is old enough, he is set to works of
industry, it may be, that he may contribute something
to the general benefit. By all which restrictions of play,
he is only prepared to enjoy his pastimes and plays the
more. The restrictions he will doubtless feel, at the
time, and may be somewhat restive under them; but
when he is thoroughly brought into the order of the
house, and is set in the habit of serving it, as an interest of his own, then he will obey, contrive, and work,
and even drudge himself to serve it, constrained by no
motive but the service itself.

In the same manner it will be laid upon him to be at
his place in the school, to be punctual to his times, to
miss no lesson, to hold his mind to his studies by close,
unfaltering application, even though it cost him a loss
of just that liberty in play that he would most like,
and take it as the very bliss of his good fortune to have.
Restricted thus by the order of the school, he will only
enjoy his play-times the more, and finally will come to
the enjoyment of study itself for its own sake.

And so it will be in religion. There must, of course,
be in it, what may be called restrictions upon children.
All law is felt as restriction at the first, but it will not be
that God makes war on their innocent plays; they only
need as much, to be established in right conduct, well-
doing, and piety, as to have their indulgence in such

pleasures. If God will take them away from all mis-
rule and wretchedness, and will bring them into all best
conditions of blessedness and peace, and even of liberty
itself, he must put them under his commandments, train
them into his divine will, and settle them in his own
perfect order; and if he is obliged, in such a design, to
infringe here and there upon their plays, it is not because he likes the infringement, but only that he seeks
the higher bliss of character for them. Thus when a
little child is required to say his prayers and retire at
the proper time for sleep, there is nothing to complain
of in that kind of constraint, even though he wants to
continue his play; for the thing required is plainly for
his good—this for the double reason that it trains him
toward obedience to God, and a life in heaven's order,
and because it even gives him a better appetite, and a
fuller fund of vigor for, his play itself. And so it is
universally; no constraint is to be blamed as infringement on his happiness, or a harsh severity against his
pleasures, when, in fact, all highest happiness and
widest range of liberty depend on the requirement
imposed.

The suggestions and distinctions thus far advanced,
have, it will now be seen, another kind of use and importance, when taken as preparatives for the settlement
of a great practical question, viz: how to use the Christian Sabbath, or Sunday, so as to best honor the day
in its true import, and best secure the ends of Christian
nurture. The question is one that relates to a whole

seventh part of the child's time, and to just that part which is most peculiarly religious in the form, and most likely to assist the implanting and due fostering of religious impressions. So much indeed is there in this matter of a right use of Sundays, that the success of family nurture will be more exactly represented and measured by that use, than by any thing else. Sunday is preëminently the child's day for the soul, and the defective or bad use of it is never going to be compensated, by any wisest, best use of the other six days of the week. Indeed there is so much depending on this day, as regards human society, and the growth, and purity, and power of religion, that where it is lost in the training of families, no other kind of advantage—no liturgical drill, or eloquent preaching, or faithful and clear doctrine—can possibly make up the loss.

The main question, here, is how much, or little, of restriction is to be laid upon children in the due observance of the day? And the tendency is, it will be observed, to one or the other of two opposite extremes—that of undue severity, or that of unchristian looseness—and this, for two distinct sets of reasons. Sometimes for the reason of self-indulgence, or indolence in the parents; and sometimes for the reason of insufficient views of the day, as it stands in the Scripture, or in the judgments to be held of its uses. Thus it will be noted—

1. That, where parents are too indolent for any kind of painstaking in their families, they will contrive to ease the burdens of their duty by one or the other of

two distinct methods. They will either take up the notion that it is best and most soundly orthodox, to make a very stiff practice for their children; in which case they will perhaps require them to sit down within doors a good part of the day, learning catechism or scripture, stilling the house in that manner so as to allow them to sleep; or else they will take up the notion that, in modern times, we are to be more liberal, of course, being more intelligent; in which case they will get their children off to the Sunday-school, (with a lesson, or without,) or if they better like it, send them into the streets, or the fields. Here is the first great obstacle to be encountered, in securing a right and useful Sunday in families, viz: that invincible self-indulgence in parents, which is the bane of all true care and responsibility; the poison, too, of all honest judgment in finding what the way of duty is. They have frequently no such earnest and prayerful desire of the religious benefit of their children, as fastens their own attention, or presses them into a study of plans and expedients for creating a religious interest in their minds. And then a double mischief follows, viz: that they grow rusty themselves in their religious character, and having no good conscience, subside into a state of silence and acknowledged incapacity; and next, that, having become mere drones of respectful nothingness in the positive duties of religion, they stand as actual impediments in the way of all genuine religious impressions in their families. The man who can make sacrifices and take pains for his children at home will grow, and be a useful Christian every where; and the man who can not, will be a dead weight every where. Here is the secret of a great part of that drying up of character which we so often deplore; and the secret also of that strangely irreligious temper, that hatred and contempt of all religion, that so often excites our wonder in the children of nominally Christian families. Let no parent hope to have God's blessing on the Sundays of his house, or indeed on any thing else that concerns the religious welfare of his children, unless he is willing to take pains, make sacrifices, burn as a light of holy example, for them and before them. Pass then,

2. To the inquiry what is the true conception of our Lord's day, or Sunday? What, according to the Scripture, and to all sound judgment of the day, as related to the Christian training of families, and to the general welfare of society, is the mode and amount of restriction imposed by it? I think it will be found, in giving a right answer to this question, that the true use of the day lies between two errors, or extremes, that stand over against each other; one that makes a virtually Jewish day of it, and an opposite that, with undue haste, quite sweeps it away. Neither is the mode of scripture, and the two are about equally weak, as regards their philosophic grounds and reasons.

According to the Scripture, God ordained a religious day, called a Sabbath, at the very morning of the creation. This was the day that Moses found already existing and only re-enacted in the ten tables of the moral law, as he did the statutes against lying and murder.

The Sabbath stands, therefore, on precisely the same ground, scripturally, as the others; on the same too morally, save that the precise natural and social reasons for it, equally clear to God, are not so to us; and that, so far, it has the character to us of a simply divine institute, while the other nine statutes of the decalogue have the nature of acknowledged principles, grounded in their perceptible moral reasons. Could we also grasp, as God does, the precise natural reasons for observing just one day in seven as holy time, tracing perfectly the vast religious, and social, and moral, and physical effects involved, it would have no more the look of an institute, and would become a principle of natural obligation, like the others that stand with it.

In this view, it can not be repealed any more than the statute against theft, or false witness. It is not a Jewish day, in any proper sense of the term, but a day of humanity, a world's-creation day; type also and ground of the new-creation day of the Lord. Moses went on, it is true, after the delivery of the decalogue, and ordained laws civil, and police regulations, by which the Sabbath was to be observed and enforced, and it was these that gave a Jewish character to their Sabbath. And, so far, no farther, it was that the Sabbath was repealed, in becoming a Lord's day. When Paul complains to the Colossians, that they "observe new moons and Sabbaths," and boldly rebukes the Galatians, that they "turn again to the beggarly elements desiring to be in bondage," and "observe days, and months, and times, and years," he does not mean to call the seventh

day of the decalogue beggarly elements, any more than
he does the command to have but one God, or not to steal
or kill. The beggarly elements are the political additions, those rigors of observance that were added by the
political statutes and the religious drill of the ritual;
designed, as it was, for a slavish people, low in their
perceptions, and unable to know religion at all, save in
the practice of austerities under it. Restriction was to
them, at their low point, about the only religious conception they were equal to, and their whole ritual economy had a great part of its merit, in the stringent close-
ness of it, and the perpetual girding of their practice
under its hard austerities. So far the whole economy
was to be displaced, and the civil-law Sabbath was to
go down with it. But the more ancient Sabbath be-
longed to the covenant of promise itself, and had the
same kind of freedom and genial life in it that per-
tained, in Paul's view, to the whole Abrahamic order in
religion. We can see too, for ourselves, that, so far as
it is affirmed in the moral code of the decalogue, in distinction from the civil law, it has a character of extreme
beauty and benignity. What can be a more genial token for God, than that he appoints such an institute of
universal rest from labor? And what could evidence
a more beautiful mercy than that God should take the
part, in this manner, of all labor, even that of servants
and slaves, and indeed of the laboring beasts, the oxen
and the asses, asserting his protection over them (beautiful lesson of mercy to animals!) even against the selfishness of their owners, and allowing them to have a

respite to their otherwise endless toils. There is, in fact, no restrictive word in the commandment, save what may be felt of restriction in the injunction to "keep the day holy," and even that is interpreted, to a great degree, by the simple requirement of a cessation from labor; though it is, doubtless, to be understood that the day is duly hallowed, only by a careful devotion of it to the uses of religion. Is there any thing harsh or unduly restrictive in such a day? Does Christianity itself find any thing to accuse, or any want of benignity in it?

There is, then, no pretext of authority in the Scripture for making the Lord's day, or Sunday, a Jewish day to children. And those parents who make it a point of fidelity to lay it on their children, according to the strict police regulations of the Jewish code, would be much more orthodox, if they went farther back, and took up conceptions of the day some thousands of years older. When they assume that every thing which can be called play in a very young child is wrong, or an offense against religion, they try, in fact, to make Galatians of their children; incurring a much harsher, Christian rebuke, than if they only turned to the beggarly elements themselves, and laid their own souls under the bondage. What can a poor child do, that is cut off thus, for a whole twenty-four hours, from any right to vent his exuberant feeling—impounded, strictly, in the house and shut up to catechism; or taken to church, there to fold his hands and sit out the long solemnities of the worship, and what to him is the mysterious lingo of preaching; then taken home again to struggle with the pent up fires, waiting in dreary and forlorn vacancy, till what are called the mercies of the day are over? What conception does he get of religion, by such kind of treatment, but that it comes to the world as foe to every bright thing in it; a burden, a weariness, a tariff, on the other six days of life?

But there comes in, here, a grand scripture reason for some sort of restriction, viz: that restriction is the necessary first stage of spiritual training every where. Instead of rushing into the conclusion, therefore, as many parents do, that all religious observances which create a feeling of restraint, or become at all irksome to chidren, are of course hurtful, and raise a prejudice in their minds against religion, the Scripture boldly asserts the fact that all law begins to be felt as a bondage. Law and gospel have a natural relationship, and they are bound together every where, by a firm interior necessity. It is so in the family, in the school, and in religion. The law state is always felt to be a bondage, and the restriction is irksome. By-and-bye, the goodness of the law, and of them by whom it is administered, is fully discovered, and the obedience that began as restriction merges in liberty. The parents are obeyed with such care, as anticipates even their wishes; the lesson, that was a task, is succeeded by that free application which sacrifices even health and life to the eagerness of study; and so the law of God, that was originally felt only in the friction, rubbed in by that friction, is finally melted into the heart by the cross of Jesus, and becomes the soul's liberty itself. It is no fault then of a Sunday that it is felt, in some proper degree, as a restriction; or even that the day is sometimes a little irksome to the extreme restiveness of children. All restraint, whether in the family or the school, is likely to be somewhat irksome at the first. The untamed will, the wild impulse of nature, always begins to feel even principle itself in that way of collision with it. Nor is it any fault of the Sunday observance, that it has, to us, the character of an institute. If it were a mere law of natural morality, we might observe it without any thought of God's will; but if we receive it as an institute, we acknowledge God's will in it; and nothing has a more wholesome effect on just this account, than the being trained to an habitual surrender to what God has confessedly enjoined or instituted by his will. It is the acknowledging of his pure authority, and is all the more beneficial, when the authority is felt in a somewhat restrictive way. The transition too is easy from this to a belief in the supernatural facts of Christianity. The conscience and life is already configured to such faith; for whatever is accepted as an institution of God, is accepted as the supernatural injunction of his will.

The flash judgments, therefore, of many, in respect to the observance of Sunday, are not to be hastily accepted. We are not to read the prophet, as if promising that the streets of the city shall be full of boys and girls, on the Lord's holy day, playing in the streets thereof; or as if that kind of license were necessary to clear the irksomeness of an oppressive observance; or as if the power of religion were to be increased by removing every thing in it, which disturbs the natural impatience of restraint. Some child that was, for example, now grown up to be a man—a profligate it may be, a sworn infidel, a hater of·all religion—laughs at the pious Sundays that his godly mother made him keep, and testifies to the bitter annoyance he suffered under the irksome and superstitious restrictions thus imposed on his childish liberty. Whereupon some liberalist or hasty and superficial disciple, immediately infers that all Sunday restrictions are injurious, and only raise a hostile feeling in the child toward all religion. Whereas it may be, in the example cited, for such are not very infrequent, that the child was never accustomed to restriction at any other time as he ought to have been, or that his mother was too self-indulgent to exert herself in any such way for his religious entertainment, as to respite and soften the strictness of the Sunday observance. Perhaps the requirement was really too restrictive, or perhaps it was so little and so unevenly restrictive, as to make it only the more annoying. Be it as it may, in this or any particular example, a true Sunday observance needs to be restrictive in a certain degree, and needs to be felt in that way, in order to its real benefit. What is wanted is to have God's will felt in it, and then to have it reverently and willingly accepted. A Sunday turned into a holiday, to avoid the supposed evil of restrictiveness, would be destitute or religious value for just that reason.

The true principle of Sunday observance, then, appears to be this: that the child is to feel the day as a restriction, and is to have so much done to excite interest, and mitigate the severities of restriction, that he will also feel the true benignity of God in the day, and learn to have it as one of his enjoyments. When the child is very young, or just passing out of infancy, it will be enough that, with some simple teaching about God and his day, a part of his more noisy playthings are taken away; or, what is better than this, that he have a distinct Sunday set of playthings; such as may represent points of religious history, or associate religious ideas, abundance of which can be selected from any variety store without difficulty; then, as the child advances in age, so as to take the full meaning of language, or so as to be able to read, the playthings of the hands and eyes will be substituted by the playthings of the mind; which also will be such as connect some kind of religious interest—books and pictures relating to scripture subjects, a practice in the learning and beginning to sing Christian hymns, conversations about God and Christ, such as bring out the beauty of God's feeling and character, and present Him, not so much as a frightful, but more as a friendly and attractive being; for the child who is only scared by God's terrors and severities, will very soon lose out all proportional conceptions of him, and will want to hear of him no more. Even the Sunday itself that only brings him to mind will, for just that reason, become a burden. The endeavor should be to excite a welcome interest in the day and the subjects it recalls.

And the devices that may be used are endless. The natural history of Palestine, the rivers, lakes, mountains, every city, every plain, will be easily associated in the child's memory, with the events and characters, and religious transactions of the sacred history; so with lessons of duty and sentiments of piety. For such uses, an embossed map of the Holy Land would be invaluable in a family of young children. Here are marked the sites of towns and cities, and the face of the ground is given on which they stood, or stand. Here was the locality of a battle, on this mountain or slope, or in this plain, or by this river. Here dwelt some patriarch, or prophet, or ministering woman. Looking over these ranges of mountain, through these valleys, and across these lakes and plains, questions of locality, geography, prospect, transaction, miracle, travel, can be raised with endless variety, such as will sharpen the intellectual curiosity, and the sense of religion together. The whole country may be daguerreotyped in this manner on the child's mind, and a tenfold interest excited in every event, whether of the Old or New Testament history.

The day itself also will be raising fruitful topics of inquiry. The topics of public preaching, especially those which relate to Christ—Christ the child, Christ the friend, brother, bread, way, reconciling grace—will raise interesting questions in the child's mind, and he will be delighted if the parent can make out a good and lively child's version of them.

Hearing much too of the church, and the communion

of saints in its order and ordinances, he will want to know more exactly what the church is, what it is for, and who are in it. And when he is rightly informed concerning it, as being God's holy family, or school, in which all the members are disciples or learners together, and how Christ himself dwells in it, unseen, as the teacher and head, preserving its order from age to age, and dispensing gifts of life and salvation to them that are folded with him in it, how tenderly will it move his feeling, and with what gladness, to hear that he also is a member, whom Christ has accepted beforehand, to grow up as a disciple in it. His feeling will thus begin at once to take sides with it, as with his family itself, and he will be drawn along into the spirit and cause of it, just as he is into the cause of his family.

Perhaps too he will have witnessed the sacraments, the holy supper, and baptism as administered to infants, and he will be asking, probably, for some explanation of these. And nothing can have a more benign effect on a child's religious feeling than to be trained to a genuine faith in sacraments. But, in order to this, they must be sacraments; that is, observances appointed by God, as the occasions of a special faith in the special visitations and powers he engages to bestow on the receivers.

We have become even a little jealous of sacraments. Our recoil from the extravagances of priestly magic has been carried too far. We keep them on foot, but we can scarcely be said to have faith in them, or to use them. The very attitude of mind they require is what

we want—want in the family, want in the church.
They set us before God in just the way to receive Him
best. He knew exactly what we wanted, and therefore gave them to communicate his own divine power
in them. Suppose that Carthage, in giving to her sons
an oath (*sacramentum*) of eternal hostility to Rome, had
been able to pledge a war-grace also, going into battle
with them to make them strong before their enemy
and always victorious, how eagerly would they have
taken hold of it, in the terrible encounters of the field!

The supper then is to be a sacrament and no merely
monumental affair, as if it were a coming to the tomb
of Jesus to read his inscription; but it is to be an occasion where he is to be discerned, manifested as discerned, in his most real, only real, presence; dispensing himself and his reconciling peace to the soul. Explained thus to the child, in a manner adapted to his
understanding, it is also to be added—" this is for you,
and Christ is waiting to receive you and bless you in it,
whenever you can ask it truly believing that he will,
according to the faith to which you were pledged in
your baptism." I see no objection whatever to his being
taken to the supper casually, whenever his childish piety
really and seriously desires it; unless some opposing
scruples in the church, or the minister, should make it
unadvisible. Christ, I am sure, would say—" Suffer
the child and forbid him not."

The sacrament of baptism, which he will often see
dispensed to infants—and they ought always to be presented in a public way, or in the open church, for that

purpose—can be handled, in these Sunday conversations, with still greater effect. This preëminently is the
child's sacrament; signifying no regenerative work
done upon the child, (*opus operatum,*) but the promise
of an always cherishing, cleansing, sealing mercy, in
which he is to be grown, as one that is born in due
time; and which he is always to believe in, and be
taking hold of, in all his childish struggles with evil.
And he is to have it, not as a sacrament dispensed once
for all and ended, but as a perpetual baptism, always
distilling upon him, pledged to go with him, overliving
his many faults and falls, and operating restoratively
when it can not progressively, assisting repentances
when it can not growths in good. He is thus to be
always putting on Christ, as being baptized into Christ,
and to live in the washing of regeneration and the
renewing of the Holy Ghost, shed on us abundantly
through Jesus Christ our Saviour. Sentiments of pro-
foundest reverence for his baptism are to be always
cherished in him. He is to have it as the one pure
thing that has touched, and always touches him. Family government, the family prayers, the saintly mother's
kiss, every thing earthly, has the touch and stain of
evil; but the sacrament of God's pure Spirit has not.
All purest sympathy of God is here with him. He is
God's child, and is to be God's man. Using thus his
baptism, growing up into his baptism, obligation will
be serious, but never oppressive; for he breathes for-
giving help, and has it for his element.

Now all these subjects of the Sunday conversation—

the church, the supper and baptism—being institutes
of God, like the day itself, chime with the day, and go
to keep alive the same institutional faith, thus to keep
alive the faith of a supernatural religion and make it
habitual. Nature being all, there is no Sunday, no
church, no sacraments. All God's institutes are set
up on the world by His immediate authority, never
grown out of nature and her causes. And it is just
here that the childish affinities are most readily taken
hold of by religion. Children want the supernatural;
and the Lord's day, used in this manner, or enlivened
by this kind of teaching, will prepare an ingrown habit
of faith, and will never annoy them, or worry them, by
its reasonable restrictions. They will "count the Sabbath a delight, and the holy of the Lord honorable,"
and will have beside, all the blessings of the prophet
that follow. Under such a practice, religion, or faith,
will be woven into the whole texture of the family life,
and the house will become a truly Christian home.
Nothing will be remembered so fondly, or steal upon
the soul with such a gladsome, yet sacred, feeling afterward, as the recollection of these dear Sundays, when
God's light shone so brightly into the house, and made
a holiday for childhood so nearly divine.

VII

THE CHRISTIAN TEACHING OF CHILDREN

But continue thou in the things which thou hast learned and hast been assured of, knowing of whom thou hast learned them.—2 Timothy, iii. 14.

THIS exhortation of the apostle to his young friend Timothy, is the more remarkable that it relates to his training in the Old Testament scriptures, which were the only sacred writings known at the time of his childhood—"And that, from a child, thou hast known the Holy Scriptures, which are able to make thee wise unto salvation, through faith which is in Christ Jesus." His father was a Greek, (Acts xvi. 1,) and probably an unbeliever; but his mother was a woman of such piety, that she omitted nothing in the training of her son, and the apostle speaks of her, in the same epistle, even as having let down upon him a kind of piety by entail. But her faithful lessons—these are what he is now calling to mind; and it is affecting to notice that he not only charges it on him to remember what he has learned from the Scriptures, because they are God's word, but also to value the same things the more, "knowing of whom he has learned them;" that is, from his gracious and faithful mother. Under cover of this beautiful example, as it appears in all the parties concerned, the young minister and disciple, the godly mother and her instructions, the apostle and his congratulations, you will perceive that I am going to speak of—

The Christian teaching of children.

And I can not do better than to notice, in the beginning, three points which stand upon the face of the apostle's exhortation.

1. The very great importance of this teaching, when rightly dispensed. It is not indeed the first duty of the parent, for other duties go before, as we have already seen, preceding even the use of language. Neither is it, as a great many parents appear to assume, a matter in which their religious duties to their children are principally summed up. It is not every thing to teach, or verbally instruct their children, least of all to indoctrinate them in the formulas and theoretic principles of the faith. But how very great importance must there be in the teaching, when an apostle, setting his young friend in charge as a preacher of the gospel, bids him continue still in the teachings of his godly mother, and even to remember them for her sake. The New Testament preacher is exhorted still to be an Old Testament son, and is sent forth, in the power of the ancient Scripture, even after Christ has come. And just so it will ever be true of the ripest and tallest of God's saints, who were trained by His truth in their childhood, that however deep in their intelligence or high in spiritual attainments they have grown to be, the motherly and fatherly word is working in them still; and is, in fact, the core of all spiritual understanding in their character.

2. It is to be noted that the teaching of Timothy's mother was scriptural—" And that, from a child, thou hast known the Holy Scriptures." They had, as far as we have been able to learn, no catechisms in that day. The ten commandments and certain selected Psalms, were probably the scriptures in which they were most exercised, and which probably Timothy had " learned," in the sense of having them stored in his memory. And there is this very great advantage in the scriptural teaching, or training, that it fills the mind with the word and light of the Spirit, and not with any mere wisdoms of opinion. And there is the less reason, now, for going out of the divine word to get lessons for the teaching of children, that our scripture roll is enlarged by the addition of the words and history of Christ himself. In a right use of the Scripture, thus amplified by the gospel, there is no end to the subjects of interest that may be raised. The words are simple, the facts are vital, the varieties of locality, dialogue, incident, character, and topic, endless.

I do not undertake to say that nothing shall be taught which is not in the words of the Scripture. But it must be obvious that very small children are more likely to be worried and drummed into apathy by dogmatic catechisms, than to get any profit from them. If exercised in them at all, it should be at a later period, when their intelligence is considerably advanced; that they may, at least, get some shadow of meaning in them, to repay the labor of committing them to memory. It is generally supposed, in the arguments urged for a training in catechism, that the real advantage to be gained is the fastening or anchoring of the child in some fixed faith. But the deplorable fact is, that what is called a fastening is really the shutting in, or encasing of the soul, in that particular shell of opinion—the training of the child to be a sectarian *before* he is a Christian. His anchorage in some Christian belief, which is certainly desirable, would be accomplished much more effectually, if he were trained, for example, to recite the Apostle's or the Nicene creed. Here he does not merely memorize, but he assents; and, what is more, does it by an act of practical homage, or worship—a confession. And then what he assents to is no matter of opinion, or speculative theology, but a recitation of the supernatural facts of the gospel, taken simply as facts. For these facts are intelligible even to a very young child, and will be recited always with the greater interest, that the recitation is itself a religious act, or confession.

I am principally concerned here with the case of very young children, not with such as are farther advanced in age, or intelligence; and there is no room for doubt, in their case, whatever may be decided in respect to others, that the teaching of Timothy's mother, the scripture teaching, is to be preferred. The memorizing of the ten commandments and the Lord's prayer, followed by the Apostle's creed and the simplest Christian hymns, connected with scripture readings, conversations, and discussions, will compose a body of teaching specially adapted to a child, and most likely to make him wise unto salvation.

3. It is to be noted that the most genuine teaching, or only genuine teaching, will be that which interprets the truth to the child's feeling by living example, and makes him love the truth afterwards for the teacher's sake. It is a great thing for a child, in all the after life, to "know of whom" he learned these things, and to see a godly father, or a faithful mother, in them. No truth is really taught by words, or interpreted by intellectual and logical methods; truth must be lived into meaning, before it can be truly known. Examples are the only sufficient commentaries; living epistles the only fit expounders of written epistles. When the truly Christian father and mother teach as being taught of God, when their prayers go into their lives and their lives into their doctrine, when their goodness melts into the memory and heaven, too, breathes into the associated thoughts and sentiments to make a kind of blessed memory for all they teach, then we see the beautiful office they are in, fulfilled. In this manner, Timothy was supposed to have a complete set of recollections from his mother woven into his very feeling of the truth itself. It was more true because it had been taught him by her. There was even a sense of her loving personality in it, by which it always had been, and was always to be, endeared. On the other hand, it will always be found that every kind of teaching in religion, which adds no personal interest, or attraction to the truth, sheds no light upon it from a good and beautiful life, is nearly or quite worthless. And here is the privilege of a genuinely Christian father

and mother in their teaching, that they pass into the
the heart's feeling of their child, side by side with God's
truth, to be forever identified with it, and to be, themselves, lived on and over with it, in the dear eternity it
gives him.

But these are general considerations, which it is sufficient to have suggested without further dwelling upon
them. There are yet a great many subordinate and
particular points, of a more promiscuous character, to
which also I must call your attention. And I deem it
here a matter of consequence to make out, first of all, a
somewhat extended roll of things, which are *not* to be
taught; for so many things are taught which are not
true for any body, and so many which are only theologically true for minds in full maturity—to all others
meaningless and repulsive—that many a child is fatally
stumbled in religion, just because of his teaching.

First of all, then, children are not to be taught that
they were regenerated in their baptism. That will only
convert the rite into a superstition, and put the child in
a totally false position, where he will rest his Christian
title on a mere outward transaction already past, and
what is even worse, on a function of priestly magic.
Furthermore, if the child should turn out, when he is
fully grown, to be a totally reckless and profane person,
having no pretense, or even semblance of religious
character, it will now be discovered to him that his regeneration meant nothing, had no practical effect or
value, and since there is no second baptismal regenera-

tion, it will only be left him to have neither any care for the old, or hope of a new that is better. Indeed he must now be saved, for aught that appears, without re-generation; which makes a very awkward kind of gos-pel. If the child could be taught that his baptism *signifies* regeneration; supposing a pledge on God's part of the necessary grace, and so the fact presumptive, that the faith and careful training of his parents shall be so far issued in a gracious character, that his very first putting forth of good endeavor, (having been divinely prepared,) shall be crowned with Christian evidence, it would be well. But no young child can grasp such a conception evenly enough to hold it. The most that can be said to him, therefore, of his baptism, is that God gave it to his parents and to himself, as a pledge of the Holy Spirit, and all needed help, that he may grow up into good, as a regenerated man.

As little are young children to be taught that they are of course unregenerated. This, with many, is even a fixed point of orthodoxy, and of course they have no doubt of it. They put their children on the precise footing of heathens, and take it for granted that they are to be converted in the same manner. But they ought not to be in the same condition as heathens. Brought up in their society, under their example, bap-tized into their faith and upon the ground of it, and bosomed in their prayers, there aught to be seeds of gracious character already planted in them; so that no conversion is necessary, but only the development of a new life already begun. Why should the parents cast away their privilege, and count their child an alien still from God's mercies?

Again, you are not to teach your children that they need, of course, to be regenerated, because they fail in obedience, show bad tempers, and display manifold other faults. Have you no faults yourselves? Do you then spring it as a conclusion against yourselves, that you are unregenerate persons, or do you take hold of God's help, with new earnestness and confidence, that you may get strength to overcome your faults and be clear of them? Shortcomings, faults, casual disinclinations of feeling, are bad signs, such as ought to waken distrust, but they are not, of course, conclusive evidences.

As little are you to teach them that they are certainly unregenerate, or without piety, because they are light in many of their demonstrations, full of play, abounding in frolicsome gayeties. Which is worse and farthest from God, these innocent exuberances of life, or the covetous, overcaring, overworking, enviously plotting, sobriety of their parents?

Again you are never to teach your very young children that they are too young to be good, or to be really Christian. Never allow them to see that you expect them to be pious only at some future day, when they are older. What you despair of, or assume to be no possibility for them, they certainly will not attempt, and the discouragement of good, thus thrown upon them, may be even fatal to their future character. Draw them rather into your own exercises, taking always for granted, that they will be with you. Promise them a common part with you in God's friendship, and as your love to God makes you good to them, careful of them, tender toward them, show them how it will make them good to one another and to you, and all good and happy together.

Again, do not teach them that they can never pray, or do any thing acceptable to God, till *after* they are converted or regenerated. This, with many, is a great point of orthodoxy, and I would not speak of it with severity, because it is a very natural mistake; and yet it is one of the most hurtful delusions, short of real infidelity, that can be put into language. It is not only not true for children, but it is not true for any body, and is, in fact, a kind of barricade before the heavenly gate for every body, still outside. It is very true that no one can pray, or do any thing acceptably, to God, as being and remaining unconverted, unregenerated; but that is a very different thing from showing that no one can pray, or do any thing acceptably till *after* they are converted, or regenerated. The difference is just as wide as between all good possibility and none whatever. God is ready to hear every child's prayer, every man's prayer, calls him to come and be heard for all he wants, only let him pray as coming to be converted, or born of the Spirit, *in* his prayer. If the prayers of the wicked are an abomination, as they certainly are, let them come to cease being wicked, and be made right with God. Can not a wicked man become right, and at what time and where, better than when God is hearing and helping his prayer? His very prayer will be a praying out of wickedness into right. But when he can not think, work, pray; can not do any thing acceptably, till after he is born of the Spirit, that word *after* fences him back, shuts him up in his sin, there to bide his time. What multitudes of children have been shut away from the kingdom of God, by this one misconception of piously intended orthodoxy.

The mistake of teaching is scarcely less fatal, when the child is put to the doing of good works, and the making up of a character in the self-regulating way. That kind of duty is so legal and painful, and the poor child will be so often floored by his failures in it, that he will not continue long. A kind of despair will come upon him in a short time, and religion itself will take on a hard impossible look, that is even repulsive. Nothing will draw the child onward in ways of piety, but the sense of forgivenesses, helps, felt sympathies of grace and love. Salvation by faith, is the only kind of religion that a child can support. If there is no ladder to heaven but a ladder of will-works and observances, he will not be climbing it long. Where Luther fell off and lay groaning, infant steps will not persist.

It is a great mistake, too, and a great Christian wrong, under salvation by faith, to be always showing children what a hard, dry service the Christian life must be. A great many parents do this unthinkingly, because it is just so to them. Where there is a real living faith, and children believe most easily, cheerfulness, brightness, liberty, joy, are the element of life itself. But if the parent is down in the lowest grades of possible devotion, worried and not blessed by his piety, galled and not comforted; if the children hear him mourning always in his prayer, and confessing shortcomings and defeats and poverty enough to ungospel all the gospel promises, it should not be wonderful that they are not particularly drawn to that kind of piety.

These, now, are some of the things which are not to be taught, but carefully avoided in the training of children. There are a great many other things which are not to be taught, for the reason that they can not be sufficiently apprehended, and will only confound the understanding instead of giving it light. These are to be taught, not formally or theologically, but implicitly, in a kind of child's version, which the confessions commonly do not give. Thus depravity in Adam, the fall of the race, the atonement by Christ in any view that makes it a ground of forgiveness, regeneration itself as a metaphysically defined change in character— none of these can be taught as a doctrine for young children. And yet they can all be taught implicitly. Thus we may represent to children that we are all sinners, and that God is displeased with us whenever we do or think what is wrong; that we want a better and a clean heart, so that we shall love to do what is right, and that Christ came down into the world to give it to us; that when we feel sorry for wrong he loves to forgive us, and that when we feel weak and are much tempted he will help us, hearing our prayer, and coming to us by his Spirit, to give us strength. Meantime we must not omit teaching that Jesus had a most dear love to children, took them in his arms, blessed them, loved them even the more tenderly because of the bad world into which they are come; and that breathing his own love into them, he was able to say that of such is the kingdom of heaven. Proceeding in this manner, let the call be to the child to become good, and to be always trusting Christ to make him so, and he will get the force, implicitly, of a whole gospel, in this very simple and summary version.

While the whole teaching centers at this point, the mind of the child will not be wearied, of course, by a continual reiteration of the same very simple matter, but it will be led about, into free ranges and excursions, among the facts and very dramatic incidents of the Scripture history. Little debates will be raised about duties in common matters; characters will be held up for approbation, or to be condemned. The matters of creation, from the sky downward, will come into notice, and be used to show God's wisdom and greatness. And so there will be a rotary movement of inquiry and teaching, all round the great central point of being good, and the readiness of Christ to help us in it.

Due care will be taken also not to thrust religious subjects on the child, when he is excited by other things, in a manner to make it unwelcome. His times of thought and appetite must be watched. Play with

him when he wants to play, teach him when he wants
to be taught. Untimely intrusions of religion will
only make it odious—the child can not be crammed
with doctrine.

Children often break upon their parents with very
tough questions, and questions that wear a considerable looking towards infidelity. It requires, in fact, but
a simple child to ask questions that no philosopher can
answer. Parents are not to be hurried or flurried in
such cases, and make up extempore answers that are
only meant to confuse the child, and consciously have
no real verity. It is equally bad, if the child is scolded
for his freedom ; for what respect can he have for the
truth, when he may not so much as question where it
is ? Still worse, if the child's question is taken for an
evidence of his superlative smartness, and repeated
with evident pride in his hearing. In all such cases, a
quiet answer should be given to the child's question
where it can easily be done, and where it can not, some
delay should be taken ; wherein it will be confessed
that not even his parents know every thing. Or, sometimes, if the question is one that plainly can not be
answered by any body, occasion should be taken to
show the child how little we know, and how many
things God knows which are too deep for us—how reverently, therefore, we are to submit our mind to his, and
let him teach us when he will, what is true. It is a very
great thing for a child, to have had the busy infidel lurk-
ing in his questions, early instructed in regard to the
necessary limits of knowledge, and accustomed to a

simple faith in God's requirement, where his knowledge fails.

Observe also, at just this point, the immense advantage that a Christian parent has in Jesus Christ, as regards the religious teaching of his children. I speak here of the fact that all truth finds in him the concrete form. Truth is not less really incarnate in him, than God. Indeed he testifies, himself, that he is the truth. And he is so, not merely in the sense that he parabolizes the truth, and gets it thus into human conditions or analogies, but that his own person also and life are the eternal form of truth; that he lives it, acts it forth, groans it in his Gethsemane, sheds it from his veins in the bleeding of his cross. You may take your children along therefore, through his childhood, into his ministries of healing, on to his death-scene itself, and it will be as if you led them through a gallery, where all divinest, most life-giving truth is pictured. No abstractions will be wanted, no difficult reaches of comprehension required; you have nothing to do but to show them Jesus as he is, and the Great Teaching will be in them—all that is needed as the vital bread of their intelligence, and heart, and character. The blessed child's doctrine of the world is Christ. Have it then as your privilege to be always unfolding your child's understanding, and spiritual nature, by that which will be life and healing to both; even Jesus Christ, the Word of the Father's glory. Converse much of him and about him, make him familiar, and it will be strange if you do not find that both your

conversation and theirs is in heaven, where he sitteth
at the right hand of God.

And of this you will be the more certain if you
teach Christ not by words only, but by so living as to
make your own life the interpreter of his. There is
no feebler and more unpractical conception, than that
children are faithfully taught, when they are abundantly lectured. If you will put in Christ, you must
put him on. There is no such gospel for them, as that
which flavors your own conduct, and fills your personal
atmosphere with the Christly aroma.

At the same time it should be the constant endeavor
with children, to make the subject of religion an open
subject, and keep it so, never to be otherwise. Nothing
is wider of dignity, or more mischievous in its effects,
than the remarkable shyness of religious conversation
in most Christian families. It argues either some great
neglect of the parents, in which they have let the subject fall out of range as a subject not to be named, or
else it shows that, in trying to make it an open subject,
so much of cant or untimely exhortation has been
mixed with it, as to make it unwelcome. Rightly conceived, there is no subject of so great interest and such
inexhaustible freshness, as that which pertains to the
soul and the future life. Good conversation, too, upon
it, in the house, is better than sermons. Why then
should a Christian family, where every other subject
is welcome, taboo this, requiring it to pass in silence,
as if it were in fact the forbidden fruit of their intelligence?

But I must speak, in closing, of what appears to be a somewhat general misconception, as respects the *aim* of Christian teaching in the case of very young children. According to the view I am here maintaining, it is not their conversion, in the sense commonly given to that term. That is a notion which belongs to the scheme that makes nothing of baptism and the organic unity of the house; that looks upon the children as being heathens, or aliens, requiring, of course, to be converted. But according to the scheme here presented, they are not heathens, or aliens; but they are in and of the household of faith, and their growing up is to be in the same. Parents therefore, in the religious teaching of their children, are not to have it as a point of fidelity to press them into some crisis of high experience, called conversion. Their teaching is to be that which feeds a growth, not that which stirs a revolution. It is to be nurture, presuming on a grace already and always given, and, for just that reason, jealously careful to raise no thought of some high climax to be passed. For precisely here is the special advantage of a true sacramental nurture in the promise, that it does not put the child on passing a crisis, where he is thrown out of balance not unlikely, and becomes artificially conscious of himself, but it leaves him to be always increasing his faith, and reaching forward, in the simplest and most dutiful manner, to become what God is helping him to be. On this point Dr. Tiersch says, with very great insight, both of the gospel and of children—

"It is certainly not difficult to bring a child into a condition of emotion and anxiety, by representations of natural corruption, of the judgment, and of the influence of the enemy; and to fill him with doubts of his own salvation, thereby moving him to any thing that may be desired. It is possible that by these means, deep experiences of the communion of the soul have been brought to light. But these are consequences that should rather be objects of our fear than of our rejoicing. For here comes in the worst of all dangers, the early wasting of such impressions and experiences, and a creeping in of untruth, whilst the power vanishes and the forms of speech remain. For both the most delicate and the most solemn experiences become, after this method, objects of continual reflection and conversation, under which, at last, solemn earnestness, as well as all delicacy, is destroyed, and there remains either a continual self-deception, with the semblance of the reality of godliness, or a gnawing consciousness of an increasing untruthfulness, and of an inner unfruitfulness beneath a mass of phrases."*

It is a delicate matter for children to navigate in this rough sea of conversional tossings, where the stormy wind lifteth up the waves, and they go up to the heaven, and go down again to the depth, and their soul is melted because of trouble. There is, for the little ones, a more quiet way of induction. Show them how to be good, and then, when they fail, how God will help them if they ask him and trust in him for help.

---

* Christian Family, p. 133.

In this manner they will be passing little conversion-like crises all the time. Rejoice with them and for them as they do, only do not put them on the consciousness, in themselves, of what you seem to see. Let them be accustomed to it as a fact of experience that they are happy when they are right, and are right when God helps them to be, and that he always helps them to be when they put their trust in him. The Spirit of God is nowhere so dovelike as he is in his gentle visitations and hoverings of mercy over little children.

What is wanted is, to train them by a corresponding gentleness, and keep them in the molds of the Spirit. No spiritual tornado is wanted that will finish up the parental duties in a day; but there is to be a most tender and wise attention, watching always for them, and, at every turn or stage of advance, contributing what is wanted; enjoying their bright and happy times of goodness and peace with them, helping their weak times, drawing them out of their discouragements, and smoothing away their moods of recoil and bitterness; contriving always to supply the kind of power that is wanted, at the time when it is wanted. Very young children religiously educated, it will be remembered by almost every grown up person, have many times of great religious tenderness, when they are drawn apart in thoughtfulness and prayer. The effort should be to make these little, silent pentecosts and gentle openings God-ward sealing-times of the Spirit, and have the family always in such keeping, as to be a congenial element for such times; and to suffer no possible hindrance, or opposing

influence, even should they come and go unobserved.
Under such kind of keeping and teaching, God, who is
faithful to all his opportunities, as men are not, will be
putting his laws into the mind and writing them in the
heart, and the prophet's idea will be fulfilled to the letter; it will not be necessary to go calling the children
to Christ, and saying, know the Lord; for they will
know him, every one, the least as the greatest, and the
greatest as the least, each by a knowledge proper to
his age.

VIII

FAMILY PRAYERS

"And it shall come to pass in that day, I will hear, saith the Lord, I will hear the heavens, and they shall hear the earth, and the earth shall hear the corn, and the wine, and the oil, and they shall hear Jezreel."— *Hosea* ii. 21-2.

By this very elaborate and poetically ingenious figure, the prophet appears to be giving a contrived representation of the fact, that when God brings in the promised day of his universal reign in the earth, there will be a grand convergency of causes to prepare it, and, like so many concurrent prayers, to make common suit for it before Him. Thus he figures the world as being the beautiful valley called Jezreel, which is the garden, so to speak, of the land. And it is to be as when the people of Jezreel get their harvest, by having every thing in a train of concurrent agency to prepare it— they make petition by their careful tillage to the corn, the grapes, and olives, that they will grow apace; these, in turn, make suit to the earth to give them nutriment; this again hears them, and lifts its petition to the heavens, asking rain and dew; whereupon, last of all, the heavens hand up the prayers to God, to furnish them water, and let them shed it down; which petition he graciously hears, and the harvest follows. So he conceives it will be, as the harvest of the world approaches. It will be as if all things were put striving together, and a prayer were going up for it through all the concurrent circles of Providence. God's counsel and kingdom are constructing always a perfect harmony, by their convergence on his perfect end. Then, as the perfect end is neared, and the harmony with it grows more complete, it will be as if more things were concurring in it and asking for it, and prayer, falling in as a cause among causes, will have them all praying with it, or handing up its request. In which we may see what holds good of all prayer, and how or by what law it prevails. In one view, the whole future is prayed in by the whole present, being such a future as the whole present demands. The more things, therefore, prayer can get into harmony with itself in its request, the more likely it is to prevail; and the more alone it is, and the more things it has opposite to it, in the field of causes, the less likely it is to prevail—even as Adam had less hope of success in praying for Cain, that the blood of Abel was crying to God against him from the ground.

All prayer being under this general condition, family prayer will be of course; and of this I now propose to speak. I choose to handle the subject in this form, in the conviction that the prayers of families are so often defeated by the want of any such concert in the aims, plans, tempers, works, and aspirations of the house, as are necessary to a common suit before God; in other words, because the prayers, commonly so called, are defeated by the suit of so many causes contrary to them.

We sometimes use the terms *family worship* and *family prayers*, without any reference at all to their spiritual acceptance with God, or to any gifts and benefits to be bestowed, in the way of answer to such prayers. We speak of the worship, or the prayers, as a kind of morning observance ; a religious formality that is to have its value, under the laws of drill and habitual repetition ; good therefore, in that sense, to be kept a going, and not expected to be good on the high ground of faith and living intercourse with God. That it is to be the opening of heaven and the keeping of it open to the family, under the conditions of prevailing prayer, is either not commonly supposed, or not made a point of practical endeavor. The benefits thought of are to be such as will come of mere observance itself, and the religious reverence impressed by it.

Now that some such kind of benefit may be expected to follow, I am not about to question. Any such external observance, kept up in the family, must probably beget a deeper sense of religion, and prepare all the members to a readier admission of the great principles of faith, and spiritual devotion to God. And in that view, the observance of family worship is a matter of such consequence in a family, that the parent, who confessedly is not a Christian person, ought still to feel it incumbent on him to maintain that observance. And if such were the persons with whom I am dealing in this discussion, I should urge it upon them, as a matter indispensable, and never to be omitted. But my subject is different. I am addressing Christian parents, on the subject of the Christian training of their children; showing it to be the same thing as a training into Christ, and how that training will secure the real initiation of their children into a state of genuine discipleship. Having this aim therefore, I shall drop out of notice family worship as observance, and speak of it only as the open state of prayer and communion with God in the house. For, as the greater includes the less, we need not be careful about the less; but only about the greater. And I shall speak, in the conviction that a great and principal reason why the family religion of those who are really Christian believers, carries no saving benefit with it, is that they are content with the less when they ought to claim the greater; maintaining the family prayers, in the way of observance only, and not as an appeal of faith to God. They imagine some impossibility perhaps of maintaining the family religion on so high a key. It will not only be a wearisome and over-exhaustive painstaking for themselves, but they sometimes imagine that the children, too, will be finally drugged by such over-dosing, in the spiritual intensities of religion, and be only the more repelled from it.

But they greatly mistake, in this kind of judgment, by mistaking first, in their conception of what is necessary to the prevalent effect of the family prayers, and the always open state of the house towards God. No rhapsodies are wanted, or flights of feeling, or heavings of passional intercession, as many are wont to assume, but simply that there should be a sober, calculated harmony between all the plans and appointments of life, and the prayers or petitions made. The great difficulty in faith, after all, is to be faithful. God is not carried by shrieks of emotion, but by the honestly meant and soberly contrived ordering of things, to make them work in with, and, if possible, work out the prayers. In this view, let me call your attention—

I. To the manner in which prayers, of all kinds, get their answer from God. Two things are wanted, as conditions previous to the favoring answer. First, that the matter requested should agree with God's beneficent aims, or the ends of good to which his plans are built. Secondly, that the prayer should agree with as many other prayers, and as many other circles of causes as possible; for God is working always toward the largest harmony, and will not favor, therefore, the prayers of words, when every thing else in the life is demanding something else, but will rather have respect to what has the widest reach of things and persons making suit with it. It is at this latter point that prayers most commonly fail, viz: that they are solitary and contrary, having nothing put in agreement with them; as if some one person should be praying for fair weather when every body else wants rain, and the gaping earth, and thirsty animals, and withering trees, are all asking for it together. Or a man, we may conceive, prays for holiness, getting off his knees to go and defraud his neighbor; or that he may be prospered in some plan that requires industry, and, by indolence and inattention, leaves all the causes of nature making suit against him.

God is for some largest harmony in the hearing of pray-ers, as in every thing else. All the prayers that he will hear too must, in some sense, be from Himself, which is the same as to say that they must chime with His ends, and the working of his plans generally.

See how it is, for example, in the great realm of nature. The first thing here to be discovered is that every thing requires every thing; or, if we take the figure of prayer, that all events make suit for all. Omit any one, and there would be a shock of discord felt in the whole frame-work. As regards the interior principle of causes, we know nothing; we only see them all playing into all, and all demanding all, and then, all together, making suit for a certain general future, somehow accordant with them and their harmonies. Thus it will be seen to hold, even scientifically, in the grand astronomic sys-tem of worlds, that all the innumerable parts have a perfect concurrence, demanding exactly every thing that comes to pass, in the motions, changes of position, perturbations of parts, and processions of the whole. The principle, every thing for every thing and all to-gether one, is so exact, that every atom and tiniest insect feels the touch, in fact, of every heaviest, high-est, and remotest orb, and every such orb a respective-ness of action reaching downward, after every such minim of matter and life.

Such is nature, and it would be exactly so, were it not for sin, in the supernatural order, viz: in the wants, and works, and prayers, and heavenly gifts of God's spiritual empire. Sin harmonizes with nothing.

It is a principle of general discord with all God's purposes, plans, and creations; refusing to be included in
any terms of intellectual unity and order. But God is
none the less intent on harmony here, that the constitu-
ent harmony of his realm is broken. All that He is
doing as a world's Redeemer, is to gather together in
one, all the loosened elements of discord, and settle the
world again, in everlasting concord and unity. And
toward this final issue he puts all things working together as for the same good issue.

Thus it will be found that the Bible history shows
a grand convergency of all the matters included in it,
and that a mysterious concert weaves all its facts together, and keeps them working toward the same
result. The ritual of Moses, and the forty years' march,
and all the captivities and dispersions of the people, and
the dispersions of the Greek and Roman languages, and
all the philosophic exhaustions, and all the crumblings
of the false religions, and all the great wars of the Romans, and all the fortunes of empire determined by
those wars, and then the universal pacification of the
world—by all these vast concurrences the world is made
ready, and set waiting for Christ to be born. The stu-
dents of history, looking over this field, are astonished
by the vastness of the preparation, and it is to them, as
if they heard all these world-wide powers voiced in
prayer together for the coming of Jesus. Just here,
then was the time for him to come. And thus, in fact,
he came, in the exact fullness of time, when the largest
harmony was asking for l. n.

In the same way, it will be seen, descending to a
lower field, that every conversion to God takes place
when some largest harmony demands it. Not always,
or commonly, when some friend, or wife, or good mother,
prays it, wholly alone, but when others join them, or
when, at least, there is a large concurrence of providences and causes, making the same suit, and joining
in the general conspiracy of reasons. And so much is
there in this, that the subject himself will almost always
feel a conviction of some wonderful conjunction of
means, and conditions, and prayers, just then brought
together, to accomplish the otherwise difficult or impossible result.

Other illustrations, without limit, could be cited from
the processes of God's spiritual administration; for it is
always working toward the largest harmony. But we
come directly to the matter of prayer itself. And here
we meet the promise, first of all, that—"if we ask any
thing according to his will he heareth us;" for the design is here to draw the petitioner into the most intimate acquaintance, and bring him into the most exact
conformity with, God's purposes and ends. And probably the whole economy of prayer, or giving gifts to
prayer, which might as well be given otherwise without prayer, is to affect this radical agreement of the
petitioners with God. Next we have that peculiar
phrasing of the doctrine of prayer, by Christ, when he
says—"If two of you shall agree, on earth, as touching
any thing, that they shall ask, it shall be done for
them;" where the intent of the doctrine is to bring the

petitioners into the largest possible circle of harmony among themselves. Hence the promise too—"Ye shall seek me and find me, if ye search for me with all your heart;" where the purpose is to bring each individual into the largest harmony with himself, and not leave half his dispositions, or aspirations, or lustings, praying virtually against his prayers. Hence, again the command—"Watch and pray lest ye enter into temptations;" where the endeavor is to set the voluntary powers chiming with the prayers, and working toward a grand petitional harmony with them. By the whole economy of prayer, then, God is working toward the largest, most inclusive harmony, and prayer is to be successful, just according to the amount of concurrency there is in it. First, there is to be the completest possible concurrency with God; then a concurrency of one or two hundred, or, if so it may be, two hundred millions of petitioners in a common suit; and then all these are to be total in the suit, bringing all their lustings, affections, works, plans, properties, and self-sacrifices, into the petition; whereupon the prayer will grow strong, just in proportion to the amount of agreement, or concurrence there is in it.

Under this great law, therefore, prayer, as a matter of fact, has been getting and will always be getting more strength by the larger harmonies it embodies. Noah prayed alone for his very ungodly times, and could not be heard—the blood of Abel was crying to God for justice over against him, and so were all the crimes of violence and murder in his own most bloody and cruel age. Abraham prayed for Sodom, but there were no fifty, forty, thirty, twenty, ten, or, as far as we know, more than one righteous man to pray with him; and therefore he fails, obtaining only the safety of that Godly brother's family. Afterwards Daniel, in a matter of great peril, was able, going to his house to pray, to set his three friends praying with him, and he found the light on which even his life depended. Still farther on, Esther set all her countrymen in the city praying and fasting with her, and obtained, in that manner, the deliverance of her whole people, and their promotion to honor in the kingdom. And so, again, the more wonderful scene of power which inaugurates the church, on the day of Pentecost, is distinguished by this principal, all-determining fact, that the disciples are all with one accord in one place, praying for the heavenly gift.

Not to extend these illustrations farther, we may safely put it down as a conclusion, that prayer wants the largest possible harmony praying with it; or what is the same, as many reasons, and causes, and wants, and conditions, and persons, as possible, chiming in the suit of it; so that God may answer it for harmony's sake, and not against harmony. It may seem that I have led you a long way to reach this conclusion, especially when my subject is family prayer. But we shall now be able—

II. To dispatch that particular subject as much more briefly; and besides, I have been able to hit upon no other method, which promised to unfold the real conditions of family prayer, and show the reasons of utter failure and abortiveness in it so distinctly and impressively.

The great infirmity of family prayers, or of what is sometimes called family religion, is that it stands alone in the house, and has nothing put in agreement with it. Whereas, if it is to have any honest reality, as many things as possible should be soberly and deliberately put in agreement with it; for indeed it is a first point of religion itself, that by its very nature, it rules presidingly over every thing desired, done, thought, planned for, and prayed for, in the life. It is never to finish itself up by words, or word-supplications, or even by sacraments; but the whole custom of life and character must be in it and of it, by a total consent of the man. And more depends on this, a hundred times, than upon any occasional fervors, or passional flights, or agonizings. The grand defect will, in almost all cases, be, in what is more deliberate, viz: in the want of any downright, honest, casting of the family in the type of religion, as if that were truly accepted as the first thing.

See just what is wanted, by what is so very commonly not found. First of all, the mere observance kind of piety, that which prays in the family to keep up a reverent show, or acknowledgment of religion, is not enough. It leaves every thing else in the life to be an open space for covetousness, and all the gay lustings of worldly vanity. It even leaves out prayer; for the saying prayers is, in no sense, really the same thing as to pray. Contrary to this, there should be some real prayer, prayer for the meaning's sake, and not for the shell of religious decency in which the semblance may be kept. This latter kind looks, indeed, for no return of blessing from God, but only for a certain religious effect accomplished by the drill of repetitional observance. There is also another kind of drill sometimes attempted in the prayers of families, which is much worse, viz: when the prayer is made, every morning, to hit this or that child in some matter of disobedience, or some mere peccadillo into which he has fallen. Nothing can be more irreverent to God than to make the hour of prayer a time of prison-discipline for the subjects of it, and nothing could more certainly set them in a fixed aversion to religion and to every thing sacred. This kind of prayer prays, in fact, for exasperation's sake, and the effect will correspond.

In the next place, what is prayed for in the house by the father, is, how commonly, not prayed for by the mother in her family tastes and tempers, and is even prayed against, in fact, by all the instigations of appearance, and pride, and show, which are raised by her motherly studies and cares. And this, too, not seldom, when her prayers themselves are burdened with much feeling, and bear the appearances of much earnest longing for the piety of her children. Her prayers sound well in the wording, and she verily thinks that she means what she asks for; but the notions of standing she is putting in the head of her son, or the dress she is just now getting up for her daughter, pray, a hundred fold harder than her prayers, only just the other way; calling in results of feeling and character that are selfish, worldly, earthly in the last degree.

It is a matter of the greatest importance, too, as regards the successful training of children, that they should be inducted into ways and habits of prayer themselves, as very frequently they are not. Sometimes even Christian mothers, who pray much for their children, never lead them into the practice of prayer for themselves. They are kept from so doing, by the supposed orthodox belief, first, that their children are of course in the gall of bitterness, and secondly, that such can offer no prayer, which is not an abomination to the Lord; in both which conclusions they are, in fact, neither orthodox nor Christian, and what to the children, at least, is even worse than that, consent to let them grow up in no personal habit of religion. How then can they be reached by the prayers of the house, when they are deliberately put outside of the possibility, even of beginning to pray for themselves? Sometimes they are taught to pray only in the sense of saying prayers, or repeating some little formula appropriate to their age. And there is nothing ill in this, if they only do it occasionally. But the much better method, in general, is for the mother to word a simple prayer for them herself, and let them follow after in the repetition of it, sentence by sentence. The prayer in this case, will have respect to the particular matters of the day; what has been seen, felt, enjoyed, wanted, suffered, and needs to be forgiven. Very soon the child himself, practiced in this way, will begin to drop in a sentence, here or there, that comes directly out of his feeling, and it will not be long before he will be able to word a whole prayer for himself, and will so be led along into the habit of praying with his mother, and be grown, so to speak, into the ruling desires and prayers of the house. In this method, regularly pursued, the child may be trained to a perfectly open state in the matter of prayer; so that when the father is absent, or is taken away by death, he will be ready, at a very early period on his way to manhood, to take his father's place. There will be nothing ghostly, or sanctimoniously separated from the common going on of life, in the way of prayer thus maintained. Having it for the element of childhood, and being grown into the practice of it, the very geniality, and sweetness, and good cheer of home, will seem to be lapped in it, and it will be so far natural, that, if it were taken away, the course of life itself would seem to be even painfully unnatural. A house without a roof, would scarcely be a more indifferent home than a family state unsheltered by God's friendship, and the sense of being always rested in his Providential care and guidance. No sweetness of life is so indispensable to a family, brought up thus, in the open state with God, as to have all the cares, affections, partings, sicknesses, afflictions, prosperities, marriages, deaths, and all kinds of works, habitually blessed, by the sense of God appealed to, and consciously witnessing in them.

But this again, depends on yet another fact, where commonly the defect is manifold greater than it is in the

points already referred to. It is not only necessary to
the genuine state of family religion, or the open state of
godly living in the house, that the prayers should be
prayers and not observances, and that both the parents
should be truly in them together, and the children carefully bred into them also as the common joy of their
home ; but it is necessary also that the practical ends,
tastes, plans, aspirations, and works of the house, should
all come into the same circle of concert, and join their
petition to reinforce the suit of the prayers. And here,
as I have already intimated, is the great cause of failure
in family religion. It is not difficult to get a Christian
father into such a strain of desire for his children, that
he will faithfully maintain the prayers of the house, and
press himself at times into great fervors in his suit for
them. These fervors will, too often, be kindled, in fact,
by the conviction of really great derelictions of duty,
such as come between the family and all God's blessings
upon them. No, the difficult thing here is, not to get
even the fervors of prayer, but to get the life itself and
its works into that honest and deliberate agreement
with the prayers, that will give them a genuine power
and meaning, without any such flights and passional
vehemences. The difficulty is that almost nothing, in
the arrangements, tempers, and practical ends of the
house, agrees with the prayers. The father prays in
the morning that his children may grow up in the
Lord, and calls it even the principal good of their life,
that they are to be Christians, living to God and for the
world to come. Then he goes out into the field, or the

shop, or the house of trade, and delving there, all day, in his gains, keeps praying from morning to night, without knowing it, that his family may be rich.　His plans and works, faithfully seconded by an affectionate wife, pull exactly contrary to the pull of his prayers, and to all their common teaching in religion.　Their tempers are worldly, and make a worldly atmosphere in the house.　Pride, the ambition of show and social standing, envy to what is above, jealousy of what is below, follies of dress and fashion, and the more foolish elation felt when a son is praised, or a daughter admired in the matter of personal appearance, or what is no better, a manifest preparing and foretasting of this folly, when the son, or daughter, is so young as to be only the more certainly poisoned by the infection of it—O these unspoken, damning prayers! how many are they, and how totally do they fill up the days!　The mornings open with a reverent, fervent-sounding prayer of words, and then the days come after piling up petitions of ends, aims, tempers, passions, and works, that ask for any thing and every thing, but what accords with the genuine rule of religion.　The prayer of the morning is that the son, the daughter, all the sons, all the daughters, may be Christian; and then the prayers that follow are for any thing but that, or any thing, in fact, most contrary to that.　Is it any wonder, when we consider this common disagreement between the prayers, even the fervent prayers of the family, and all the other concerns, enjoyments, and ends of the common life beside, that so many fine shows of family piety are

yet followed, by so much of godless and even reprobate character, in the children!

Here then, my brethren, is the great lesson of family
religion; it is that religion, being the supreme end and
law of life, is to have every thing put in the largest
possible harmony with it. And this is to be done by
no superlative fervors, or heats of piety and prayer,
but by the sober, honest, practical arrangement of life
and its plans. Thus, if your children are to grow up
into Christ, that is to be made their prayer, and the
prayer of both the parents, and the prayer of all the
buildings, migrations, plans, toils, trades, and pleasures
of the house. All these are to pray, in sober earnest,
that the children, as the practically best thing possible,
and most to be desired, may be Christian in their life.
There is no difficulty in forming a whole family to God,
when there is grace enough in the parents to make
that really the object, and set every thing in the largest
harmony with it. The only difficulty is in doing it,
when the prayers and the family religion are one side
of every thing else, in a department by themselves, and
the whole body of life's practical works and ends is
operating directly against the result desired and prayed
for. Prayer, in a certain proper view of it, is only one
of the great causes of the world, and all the causes,
natural as well as supernatural, are, in a certain broad
sense, prayers. What is wanted, therefore, is to put all
the causes, all the prayers, into a common strain of endeavor, reaching after a common good, in God and his
friendship. The religious affinities of the house then

take the mold of the prayers, and become a kind of prayer themselves. The children grow into faith, as it were, by a process of natural induction—only it will be intensely supernatural, because their faith is both quickened and grown in the atmosphere of God's own Spirit, always filling the house. He molds the prayers to agreement with God's will, and the prayers of each to the prayers of all, and the works and plans and tastes of all to the prayers; and then, as a consequence, which is also an answer, fills the house with his ingrown sanctifying power, and seals the members with his seal of life.

Let us stop here now, in our closing, and contemplate the dignity and power of a genuine family religion, thus maintained. Consistency and solid reality, we have seen, are its great distinction—the whole ordering of the house is worshipful, and faithfully chimes with the prayers. The very table is sanctified with, as well as by, the blessing invoked upon it; so that when the house are feeding animal enjoyments, and, so far, saying that they are animals, they do not become such. Their sensuality is kept under by a divine spirituality above it. It is not so much their bodies as their souls that are fed. By their holy charities and prayers, the family property is also sanctified, and all the industries by which it is obtained. The training of the house does not end in money, the conversation is not about money, the plans are not plans turning on the supreme good of money, the only losses dreaded or shunned are not losses of money. Their thoughts and affections therefore, mellowed by the family piety, do not clink in their souls, as we sometimes almost hear them with a hard-money sound. For the love of God penetrates and savors, all through, even the works of thrift and all the ennobled virtues of a genuine economy. The mental life also is raised by the family religion, for they live thoughtfully, as in contact with God, and all the highest themes of existence. Events, providences, nay even things themselves, take on senses related to intel- ligence, feeling, and the uses of faith. And so their very talent grows into volume, because it is never im- prisoned, or stunted by the external measures of things; but is led forth, always, into what things signify, as related to the broader affinities and the half-poetic life of religion. They are refined, in this manner, without any ambition to copy the mannerisms of refinement; refined by the fining of their intelligence and feeling. They are not emasculated by their culture, but grow manlier in it; because of the good and great thoughts, and high subjects, into which they are trained by the sober, honest piety of their practice.

The family is thus exalted, every way, by the family religion; because there is such reality and all-diffusive harmony in the scope of it. In the prayers of the day it recalls, in one way or another and with filial reverence, the ancestors that have gone before, and looks hopefully on to the great reunion of the future. Its births are so many arrivals, or presentations, at the gate of eternity; its baptisms and baptismal namings are titles recorded in

the family register of God; its deaths are only the mi·
grations of so many into life, to be followed by the mi-
gration of all; and the sense of a good future, to be
their common heritage, imparts a trustful, quietly cheerful air to their waiting. For that bright gathering of
the house, after the storms are over, gilds their adversi-
ties and sicknesses, and kindles a beautiful expectancy
in their prayers—keeps them looking up and away, without any instigations of asceticism, or false antipathy to
the world. The godly father dwells in such a house,
even as the apostle pictures Abraham, dwelling in tab-
ernacles with Isaac and Jacob, heirs with him of the
same promise viz: that of a city that hath foundations.
Heirs with him—not heirs of his fee-simple, not legatees
in his will, waiting patiently or impatiently for him to
die, but heirs with him of a great angelic future that
rests in character and fruits of well doing, in which
they bless, and by mankind as well as God, are blessed.

What scene of family dignity is more to be admired?
The highest splendors of wealth and show, have but a
feeble glow-worm look in the comparison—a pale, faint
glimmer of light, a phosphorescent halo, enveloping
what is only a worm. Even the poor laboring man,
thanking God, at his table, for the food he earned by
the toil of yesterday, singing still, each morning, in his
family hymn, of the glorious rest at hand, moving on
thitherward with his children, by single day's journeys
of prayer and praise, teaching them, even as the eagles
do their young, to spread their wings with him and
rise—this man, I say, is the prince of God in his house,

and the poor garb, in which he kneels, outshines the robes of palaces.

The beauty of such family scenes has not escaped the notice of poetry itself, or even of mere worldly observation. But we must not, for a moment, forget that the charm of all such family pictures depends on that sound reality of worship, which puts every thing in the house in keeping with the prayers, and carries back the meaning of the prayers into every thing in the house. A flourish of prayer in the morning, followed by all flourishings of vanity and prosperous selfishness, for the rest of the day, will not answer. We look in upon the Christian family, where every thing is on a footing of religion, and we see them around their own quiet hearth and table, away from the great public world and its strifes, with a priest of their own to lead them. They are knit together in ties of love that make them one; even as they are fed and clothed out of the same fund, interested in the same possessions, partakers in the same successes and losses, suffering together in the same sorrows, animated each by hopes that respect the future benefit of all. Into such a circle and scene it is that religion comes, each day, to obtain a grace of well-doing for the day. And it comes not by itself, as in the public assembly, not in a manner that is one side of life and its common affairs. There is no pretense, no show, no toilet practice going before, no reference of thought to fashion, or dress, or appearance. It leads in the day, as the dawn leads in the morning. It blends a heavenly gratitude with the joys of the table; it breathes a cheerful sense of God into all the works and tempers of the house; it softens the pillow for rest when the day is done. And so the religion of the house is life itself, the life of life; and having always been observed, it becomes an integral part even of existence, leaving no feeling that, in a proper family it could ever have been otherwise. A family state, maintained without a fire, would not seem to be more impossible or colder. Home and religion are kindred words; names both of love and reverence; home, because it is the seat of religion; religion, because it is the sacred element of home.

This training, in short, of a genuine, practically all-embracing, all-imbuing family religion, makes the families so many little churches, only they are as much better, in many points, as they are more private, closer to the life of infancy, and more completely blended with the common affairs of life. Here it is that chastity, modesty, temperance, industry, truth—all the virtues that give beauty, and worth, and majesty, to character, get their root. Here it is, above all, that they who are born into life, are led up, in their gracious training, to knit the green tendrils of existence to God. And so, in all the future scenes of duty, and wrong, and grief through which they are to pass, it will be found that they were furnished here, with supplies of grace, and armed with shields of confidence from God, to meet every encounter, bear every burden, and maintain every kind of well doing, till the victory of life is won.

Holding, now, this conviction, as Christian parents, of the importance of a true family religion, allow your-

selves never to forget the condition which alone makes
it of so great value, viz: that it has such scope as to
include and harmonize all the ways, and works, and
cares of the house. See that you plan to be, in your
undertakings, just what you pray to be in your prayers.
Set the general concert of your affairs in God's own
order, to accomplish only what is agreeable to his will,
so to be always praying with you, and the prophet's
rich valley, teeming with all fruits of abundance and
luxury, will but feebly represent the unfailing, never
blighted, always fruitful, piety of your children.